T0247661

"Tom McMillan's *Our Flag Was Still There* is a masterful recounting of one of the most iconic events in American history. Based on extensive research, McMillan offers up an abundance of fascinating detail that will surprise even those who thought they knew all about the story, including me!"

—**Ronald D. Utt**, author of *Ships of Oak, Guns of Iron: The War of 1812 and the Forging of the American Navy*

"In great depth and detail, McMillan tells the story of the 'Star-Spangled Banner' from its first stitches to the present time — a wonderful variety of angles emerge based on his careful reading of copious documents. A rich contribution to our understanding, both of the flag and the song."

—**David Hildebrand**, Ph.D, Director *Emeritus*, the Colonial Music Institute

OUR FLAG WAS STILL THERE

★ ★ ★ ★ ★

THE STAR SPANGLED BANNER THAT
SURVIVED THE BRITISH AND 200 YEARS—AND
THE ARMISTEAD FAMILY WHO SAVED IT

★ ★ ★ ★ ★

A KNOX PRESS BOOK
An Imprint of Permuted Press
ISBN: 978-1-63758-733-1
ISBN (eBook): 978-1-63758-734-8

Our Flag Was Still There:
The Star Spangled Banner that Survived the British and 200 Years—
And the Armistead Family Who Saved It
© 2023 by Tom McMillan
All Rights Reserved

Cover Design by Conroy Accord

Interior Design by Yoni Limor

Permuted Press, LLC
New York • Nashville
permutedpress.com

Published in the United States of America
1 2 3 4 5 6 7 8 9 10

On the cover: The iconic Star-Spangled Banner from Fort McHenry was photographed for the first time in 1873, almost sixty years after the battle, thanks to the foresight of Commodore George Preble who hung it from a building at the Boston Naval Yard. *(Courtesy of American Antiquarian Society, George Preble Papers)*

To Harry Armistead, George Armistead, and Christopher Hughes Morton, direct descendants of the hero of Fort McHenry; to Scott Sheads, legendary historian and park ranger at Fort McHenry; and to Jennifer Jones, curator at the Smithsonian's National Museum of American History, for all that you do to keep the story of The Star-Spangled Banner alive.

TABLE OF CONTENTS

CHAPTER ONE
An American Icon

This is the story behind the story of the most famous flag in U.S. history.

It is on display today at the Smithsonian Institution, a tattered, two-hundred-year-old wisp of its former self, laid gently at a ten-degree angle in an environmentally-controlled chamber with barely enough light to see the imperfections. Visitors peer through the glass in awestruck silence.

Surprisingly massive at thirty by thirty-four feet, but still eight feet shorter than its original width, perforated with holes and barely-visible stitches from two centuries ago, breathtakingly thin, it is what remains of the iconic Star-Spangled Banner that flew over Fort McHenry in Baltimore on September 14, 1814, after Major George Armistead and his exhausted, rain-soaked troops withstood a twenty-five-hour bombardment by the British Navy.[1]

Watching closely that morning was a thirty-five-year-old lawyer and amateur songwriter named Francis Scott Key, whose presence on the deck of a nearby ship was a quirk of fate.[2] Detained by the British during the battle, waiting anxiously for dawn to break as gunfire petered out, Key scribbled frenetic notes, wondering if a U.S. flag still flew over the fort. The end of his song's first verse—completed two days later—was even punctuated with a question mark:

> *O say does that star spangled banner yet wave,*
> *O'er the land of the free and the home of the brave?*

By the time he got around to his notes for a second verse, Key had his answer. Straining through his spyglass from several miles away, he could make out the stars and stripes of the United States, hanging defiantly from the flagpole. The fort and the city had been saved, and perhaps the young country with them. His heart filled with patriotic joy as he applied an exclamation point.

'Tis the star-spangled banner—O long may it wave,
O'er the land of the free and the home of the brave![3]

Key's lyrics, written to the music of "To Anacreon in Heaven" —a tune he knew well—would not become the official national anthem until 1931, but they did more than just give the big flag its nickname; they captured the essence of a defining moment in the country's history.[4] It is easy to forget that the Battle of Baltimore took place only thirty-eight years after the Declaration of Independence. A defeat by the British at Fort McHenry in September 1814 could have altered the "course of human events" in ways we can't imagine. Moreover, although the American flag had been displayed with pride since its creation in 1777, it was still not viewed as a symbol that tied the former colonies together.[5] Key's song, written with the rare perspective of an eyewitness to the battle, gave it that special stature.

"What Key really started," said the Smithsonian's Jeffrey Brodie, "was the transformation of the flag from a military utilitarian symbol to something that embodied new definitions of American identities and ideals."[6]

The idea for such a massive version of the flag had come one year earlier from Major Armistead himself. He wanted a banner at Fort McHenry so large that the British would "have no trouble seeing it from a distance," but he had no idea he was setting in motion a series of events that would lead to the national anthem, the national motto ("In God We Trust," which is lifted from Key's fourth verse) and two centuries' worth of celebration and controversy.[7] The momentous task of making the flag went to a Baltimore seamstress named Mary Young Pickersgill, whose mother had sewn banners for George Washington and the Continental Army during the Revolutionary War.[8] Mary's gigantic masterpiece of fifteen white stars on a blue background, and fifteen red-and-white stripes—the official design of the time—was completed in August 1813 and flew over the fort for a full year before the famous British attack.

And yet it is only because of the diligence of the Armistead family that the old flag exists today. Early details of the chain of custody are murky, but the most likely scenario is that George Armistead took it home as a souvenir sometime after the battle, in a clear violation of U.S. Army regulations. Over the next ninety years, it remained in the private possession of the Armistead family in Baltimore and New York City, passed down to George's wife, Louisa; to his daughter, Georgiana Armistead Appleton; and to his grandson, Ebenezer "Eben" Appleton—each of them caring for the aging relic while mostly keeping it out of public view. Not until Eben grew weary of the pressures of preservation did he give it to the Smithsonian in the early 1900s, ensuring that it would always be "still there."⁹

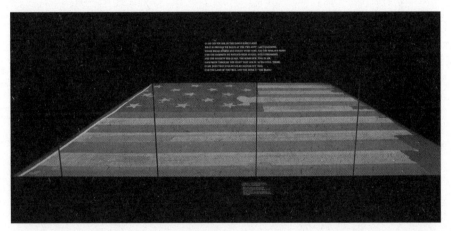

The Star-Spangled Banner from Fort McHenry in 1814 as it is displayed today at the Smithsonian's National Museum of American History. *(Division of Political and Military History, National Museum of American History, Smithsonian Institution)*

"That's the really remarkable part of the story," said Brent D. Glass, director of the National Museum of American History during the flag restoration process in the early 2000s. "Whenever I had a chance to lead foreign dignitaries on a tour of the museum, they were amazed that we had the foresight to save this historic symbol from the 1800s. Sometimes it takes that kind of perspective—the view of someone from a different country—to confirm how important it was to do this. And it all started with private citizens, with the Armistead family, long before it ever came to the Smithsonian." ¹⁰

The improbable story of the flag's survival gives it a hallowed status among American icons, but legends of national history are rarely pristine, and no element of life in the early republic was untainted by slavery. There is no record that George Armistead held slaves, but he came from a long line of slave-holding ancestors in Virginia, and his daughter, Georgiana, was listed as having three Black "servants" in the 1860 Baltimore census.[11] Key certainly owned slaves, an especially shameful critique for one who wrote so glowingly of the "land of the free." Multiple descendants of the Armistead and Key families then fought for the Confederacy in the Civil War, including Brigadier General Lewis Armistead, George's nephew, who led a Rebel brigade in Pickett's Charge at Gettysburg.[12]

But the Fort McHenry flag survived the civic upheaval of the 1800s, enduring a violent tug-of-war over the future of the country and appearing only occasionally at public events before finding a home at the Smithsonian in 1907. Frayed and damaged as it was, battered by time and elements that made it too weak ever to be flown again from a pole, it withstood a series of massive repairs over the next century and never fell apart. A curator of the modern-day exhibit said it best in 2014 when she called the old flag "a metaphor" for the United States: "It's tattered, it's torn, but it still survives, and the message is really the survival of both the country and the flag."[13] Now, more than two hundred years after the perilous fight in Baltimore harbor, the resilience of the original Star-Spangled Banner is reflective of the complex and still-evolving nation it represents.

Though barely remembered today, George Armistead was one of America's foremost heroes in the inaptly named "War of 1812." (It merely *started* that year and did not end until 1815.) He rose to national prominence in May 1813, when he led an artillery attack against the British on the Canadian border and was selected to present captured battle flags to President James Madison in Washington, D.C. So impressed were Madison and U.S. military leaders that Armistead's next assignment was command of the strategically significant Fort McHenry at nearby Baltimore harbor. There, in addition to shoring up eroded fortifications and enticing new recruits to defend against a possible invasion, he ordered a U.S. flag so enormous that the British would be able to see it from miles away.[14]

George had long believed in the power of large flags. The scion of a legendary military family from Virginia, and an army veteran of fourteen years at the time of his appointment, he saw them as serving a dual purpose in battlefield settings: signs of defiance to taunt the enemy and hallmarks of pride to bolster inexperienced troops. The new flag he ordered for Fort McHenry measured thirty feet by forty-two feet, far larger than the standard size of a garrison flag today (twenty by thirty-eight) and yet still not as massive as the epic banner he commissioned for his post at Fort Niagara back in 1802 (thirty-six by forty-eight).[15] But Armistead pronounced himself pleased with the result. Officers on any British ship probing the waters near Baltimore would have no problem seeing it "from a distance."

The thirty-three-year-old commander was well-acquainted with Baltimore and its bustling international harbor by the time he took over the fort's operation on June 27, 1813. He had served there in various roles from 1809–1812 and set down roots by marrying a local lady, Louisa Hughes, daughter of a prominent Baltimore merchant.[16] Duty called him away to distant posts at Bedloe's Island, New York and Fort Niagara during the first twelve months of the war, but his heroic performance against Fort George in Canada (where his "judicious arrangements and skillful execution" helped in "demolishing the enemy's fort and batteries")[17] and a sudden dearth of leadership at Fort McHenry, brought him home to his wife and baby daughter. One of Armistead's first tasks after taking command was to attract new recruits to the vulnerable garrison. He promptly placed an ad in the *Federal Gazette & Baltimore Daily Advertiser*, offering a bounty of "FORTY DOLLARS, and One Hundred and Sixty Acres of Land" to "Reputable Young Men" who took up the cause.[18]

Improved fortifications and increased manpower became even more crucial the following summer, when England's military juggernaut sought to end the war by ransacking towns along the Chesapeake Bay and burning the nation's capital. After brushing aside poorly led American militia at Bladensburg, Maryland on August 24, 1814, British troops roared unopposed into Washington, D.C. that night and set fire to the White House and U.S. Capitol building. Only quick action by Madison's wife, Dolley, and others saved a small cadre of national treasures for posterity, including the official presidential portrait of George Washington.[19] Humiliated Americans expected the worst and feared the next target would be Baltimore.

Scrambling to prepare for an almost-certain attack, Armistead took no chances with the safety of his family, especially Louisa, who was nine months pregnant with their second child. Long before anyone would understand the irony of his decision, he arranged to send her sixty miles away to a small Pennsylvania farming town named Gettysburg. British commanders delayed their next move, however, deliberately debating tactics and options, and the expectant father came to regret the self-imposed separation, fearing he had acted in haste under duress. "I wish to God you had not been compeld to leave Baltimore but you now must be contented as it is impossible from your present condition to attempt a return," Armistead wrote to Louisa in Gettysburg on September 10. "[S]hould they depart from the Bay I will be with you immediately, so be not alarm'd if I pop in on you."[20]

As an aside, he added, "I dremp last night that you presented me with a fine son. God grant it [may] be so and all well."[21]

History would show that he had *not* acted in haste (and that Louisa was still within days of delivering their second child, a daughter). The British briefly pondered a trip up the coast to Rhode Island to escape the deadly Chesapeake "sickly season" but soon reversed course and turned their attention to a plan to annihilate Baltimore.[22] Recently arrived British army veterans, fresh from victory over Napoleon in Europe, would land at North Point ten miles away and unleash their fury on the militia's outer defenses, grinding toward the city center. The Royal Navy, meanwhile, fortified by five of its deadly bomb ships, would hammer away at Fort McHenry until the garrison capitulated and Armistead raised a new flag—a white one—for surrender.[23]

By late afternoon on Monday, September 12, the British had moved so much naval firepower within sight of the harbor that Armistead dashed off a frantic note to the overall commander of Baltimore's defenses: "I have not a doubt but that an assault will be made this night upon the fort."[24]

He miscalculated, but only by a matter of hours. The naval attack opened at 6:30 a.m. on Tuesday, September 13, when the bomb ship *Volcano* lobbed the first of its fearsome two-hundred-pound shells to gauge the distance.[25] The bombardment pounded Fort McHenry virtually nonstop for twenty-five hours. When British ships at one point ventured to within less than two miles of the fort to take even more precise aim, a U.S. soldier remembered that "Major Armistead mounted the parapet and ordered a battery of 24 pounders to be opened upon them…and then the whole Fort let drive at them."[26] But American guns here had a maximum range of a mile and a half, and the British quickly moved back to a frustratingly safer distance. "This to me was a most distressing circumstance," Armistead wrote, "as it left Us exposed to a constant and tremendous Shower of Shells." He noted with pride, however, that "not a Man Shrunk from the conflict."[27]

Portrait of George Armistead from 1816, two years after the battle at Fort McHenry. Armistead descendants recently donated it to the Smithsonian. *(Courtesy of Harry, Liz and George Armistead)*

Beyond the bravery of Armistead and his garrison, the singular advantage for U.S. troops was that much of the battle took place in a torrential downpour. The soggy conditions combined with a stout defensive stance from militia posted on nearby Hampstead Hill to blunt the British infantry assault. Meanwhile, a relentless fusillade of more than fifteen hundred bombs and seven hundred rockets were launched at the fort to no avail. When the "dawn's early light" finally broke through the morning haze on Wednesday, September 14, with Armistead still holding on courageously, British Vice Admiral Alexander Cochrane determined that the grand British mission to capture Baltimore had failed. Shortly after 7 a.m., the harbor fell eerily quiet.[28]

Out on the water just a few miles from the fort, an intrigued American observer struggled to make out the unidentifiable banner hanging wet and limp over the ramparts. Whose flag was it? Key had left Baltimore by boat a few days earlier, on a mercy mission to obtain the release of an elderly American prisoner, but British officers prevented him from returning once an attack plan was fully developed. The uncertainty of the outcome now gnawed at Key in the early morning silence. "As they had no communication with any of the enemy's ships," one of his friends wrote later, "they did not know whether the fort had surrendered or the attack upon it been abandoned." Finally, however, as the mist began to clear, and daylight and visibility increased somewhat, an elated Key made out the familiar pattern of a U.S. flag.[29]

It is *probable* that Key first caught a glimpse of the smaller "storm flag" (seventeen by twenty-five), which would have flown over Fort McHenry during inclement conditions the previous afternoon and night.[30] But the more dramatic moment came at about 9 a.m. that morning, when, as the final British ships weighed anchor to pull away, Major Armistead's magnificent garrison flag was raised over Baltimore's harbor. "At this time our morning gun was fired, the flag hoisted, "Yankee Doodle" played, and we all appeared in full view of a formidable and mortified enemy," one of Armistead's soldiers wrote.[31] The sullen British had a strikingly similar view. "As the last vessel spread her canvas to the wind," a midshipman recalled, "the Americans hoisted a most superb and splendid ensign on their battery..."[32]

Key, a descendant of John Key, poet laureate to England's King Henry IV in the fifteenth century, jotted more notes to capture the buoyant mood.[33] He had been ardently opposed to war with England from the start but briefly volunteered his services to a local militia unit when enemy troops threatened the D.C. region. Now, his view of the conflict had changed completely. "(In) that hour of deliverance and joyful triumph, my heart spoke," Key explained years later. "Does not such a country, and such defenders of their country, deserve a song?"[34]

O say can you see by the dawn's early light,
What so proudly we hailed at the twilight's last gleaming

An amateur wordsmith at best, Key could not have imagined he was drafting the first stanza of what would become, in 117 years, the U.S. national anthem. That was never his goal. He did not even think to give his new song a snappy title. Originally printed on handbills three days later as "The Defence of Fort M'Henry," the lyrics were first published on September 20 by the *Baltimore Patriot* and greeted with widespread acclaim in the city. It was not until late October, however, when a clever Baltimore theatre promoter advertised "a much admired NEW SONG, written by a gentleman of Maryland, in commemoration of the GALLANT DEFENCE OF FORT M'HENRY, called THE STAR-SPANGLED BANNER" that an audience first heard the now-familiar title performed in a formal setting.[35]

The immediate aftermath of the signature U.S. victory of the War of 1812 was not as gratifying for Major Armistead. His relief at defeating the British and saving the fort was decidedly short-lived. Burdened by the stress of command, lack of sleep, and an almost constant exposure to rain and wind while under incessant attack for more than twenty-four hours, he "was taken violently ill with a chill and fever" and fell into a "high state of delirium" on the night of September 15.[36] His wife gave birth to a daughter that same night in Gettysburg, but word would not reach the new father in Baltimore for several days. Armistead could not even complete his official report to Secretary of War James Monroe until September 24, apologizing for the delay because of a "severe indisposition, the effect of great fatigue and exposure."[37]

By that time, still less than two weeks after the battle, he had been promoted from major to brevet lieutenant colonel by President Madison for his gallant service in defense of Fort McHenry. Armistead shared the news in a quick note to Louisa in Gettysburg, describing the "very handsome compliment" from the commander in chief and adding a brief message of hope for their future together:

> So you see, my Dear Wife, all is well, at least your husband has got a name and standing that nothing but divine providence could have given him, and I pray to our Hevenly Father that we may long live to injoy.[38]

Lieutenant Colonel George Armistead died four years later in 1818 at the age of thirty-eight, while he was still in command at Fort McHenry. His wife believed he never fully recovered from the affliction that felled him after the battle, probably a fatal heart condition.[39] Unlike other young heroes of the War of 1812—Winfield Scott and Zachary Taylor among them—George did not live long enough to attain greater military glory in the Mexican War or campaign for national political office, and so his memory faded over time. Beyond a statue that overlooks the harbor he defended at Fort McHenry, the greatest tribute to his legacy is the big flag itself—the original "Star-Spangled Banner" that flew on September 14, 1814—which he kept and took home for safekeeping, never imagining its impact on American history more than two hundred years later.[40]

The story of its jagged journey to reach the Smithsonian, and his family's role in making it happen, has rarely been told in detail.

CHAPTER TWO
Family of Fighters

The first member of the Armistead family to set foot in the New World from England was William in 1635. A deep legacy of military service was already in his blood.[41]

William Armistead was a native of Kirk Deighton, Yorkshire and could trace the roots of his ancestral coat of arms to service in the Crusades under King Richard I. There also were extended family links to warriors of the powerful German state of Hesse-Darmstadt.[42] Arriving in Virginia less than thirty years after the first permanent English settlement in Jamestown, William and his wife, Anne, parlayed an original land grant of 450 acres from the royal governor into expansive holdings across several Virginia counties, including Caroline and Gloucester. Over the next two hundred-plus years, their remarkable family tree produced a military dynasty of generals, colonels, majors, captains, lieutenants, sergeants, privates, and local militia commanders who fought in all the country's wars—not to mention attorneys, political leaders, college executives, and at least three presidents of the United States (William Henry Harrison, Benjamin Harrison, and John Tyler).[43]

William's son, John, known as "The Councillor," was a prototype for the breed. He became sheriff of Gloucester County in 1675 and lieutenant colonel of the local horse militia five years later, the precursor, as such, of future Armistead cavaliers.[44] Similar stories of military pedigree and civic service were common among relatives of the pre-Revolutionary era, and various Armistead men are identi-fied in family genealogies and other documents as "Colonel," almost always denoting a command role in the local militia.

But it was not until the late 1700s, following U.S. independence, and in the sixth generation since William's arrival, that the family of Colonel John Bowles Armistead took military service to a new and more profound level. With skeptical European powers probing America's strength and doubting its long-term viability as a sover-eign country, the time had come to consider a full-time professional army for national defense. It was during this period that five of John's six sons answered the call to be soldiers.

Four of them—Lewis, Addison, Walker, and George—would go on to serve as U.S. Army officers in the War of 1812.

Sometime before 1860, John Bowles Armistead "received by his father's will all of his land in Prince William County and much stock in Culpeper and Caroline."[45] He became a contemporary of General George Washington in America's nascent military class and commanded a militia unit in Caroline County during the raucous revolutionary summer of 1775. It was only when the two friends sparred over land and finances in the post-war era that their once-close relationship fell apart. Writing a pointed letter from Mount Vernon in December 1786, Washington admonished Colonel Armistead that "many months have elapsed since I informed you in explicit terms of my want of the money which is due to me from the Estate of your deceased father." The future president also threatened to take the case to court but eventually backed off and dropped the proceedings.[46]

Given the relatively small population of Caroline County, it was no surprise that Armistead met and married into another well-to-do military family with links to Washington and the independence movement. His wife, Lucinda "Lucy" Baylor, was the granddaughter of Colonel John Baylor III, who served under Washington in the French and Indian War, and the niece of Colonel George Baylor, one of Washington's aides during the Revolution.[47] The elder Baylor was also one of the most accomplished breeders of racehorses in colonial America, dubbing his sprawling plantation "Newmarket" after the English racetrack of the same name. His legendary stallion, Fearnought, purchased in England in 1764, was regularly bred with mares belonging to the biggest names of Virginia gentry, including Washington and Thomas Jefferson.[48]

John Bowles Armistead married Lucy Baylor in a grand ceremony at Newmarket in 1764. Their first son, also named John, was born into relative luxury a year later and set out to write his own chapter in the family's military history. He followed tradition by joining a local militia unit in his early twenties, although his first formal service did not come until 1794, during the "Whiskey Rebellion," an insurrection by western Pennsylvania farmers to protest a newly-levied tax on distilled spirits. Armistead served as aide-to-camp to General Dan Morgan, one of the heroes of the Revolution, and under the overall command of "Light-Horse Harry" Harry Lee, the sitting governor of Virginia (and future father of Robert E. Lee). The action of their makeshift army was quick and decisive, and an "exultant" Washington declared a day of thanksgiving in early 1795 for the "reasonable control which has been given to a spirit of disorder in the suppression of the late insurrection." [49]

The next chance for military honor came in the late 1790s during the undeclared "Quasi War" with France. Though it was strictly a naval contest sparked by French harassment of merchant ships in the West Indies, President John Adams raised a provisional army in 1798 to protect against the possibility of foreign invasion. John Armistead answered the call along with two of his younger brothers—Addison, then in his mid-twenties, and George, still a teenager at eighteen. All three received officers' commissions in January 1799.[50]

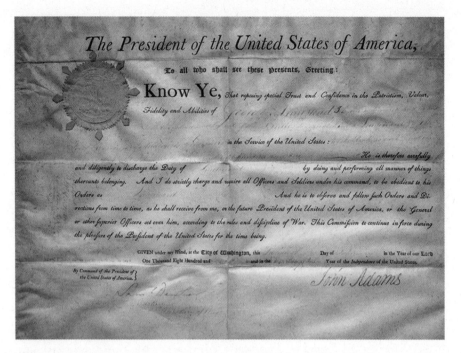

George Armistead's U.S. Army commission, signed by President John Adams *(Courtesy of Harry, Liz and George Armistead)*

These were the very early days of a formalized military, but the Armistead name (pronounced ARM-sted at the time, or by one account, UM-sted) already was becoming well known to U.S. commanders.[51]

Given his experience and family connections, John sought a significant command role in the new military force. A document titled "Candidates for Army Appointments from Virginia, November 1798" noted that he had been an aide to General Morgan on the recent "expedition" and would "not accept an appointment inferior to a Majority in Infantry or Captcy in Cavalry." He was described as "actively and respectably connected," and a "Friend to the measures of government," and General Washington himself wrote that John had "respectable character," which probably was the deciding factor. His captaincy of a U.S. cavalry unit was confirmed on January 8, 1799.[52]

Youngsters Addison and George were thrust into leadership roles of their own when Congress adopted legislation to expand the army, calling for twelve new regiments of infantry. Addison was commissioned as a first lieutenant in the Seventh Infantry on January 10 and the teenaged George became an ensign in the same regiment four days later. George was soon reclassified into a low-level command role with a commission signed by President Adams that remained for years in the family archives: "Reposing special Trust and Confidence in the Patriotism of George Armistead, I have nominated and by and with the advice and consent of the Senate do appoint him a second lieutenant." He was elevated to first lieutenant early in 1800.[53]

But the Provisional Army never fought a battle, because France never invaded the United States, and it was disbanded after hostilities between the countries ended and a peace was reached in mid-1800. John Armistead received an honorable discharge and returned to the local militia, his career having peaked with the Whiskey Rebellion. He never again served in a full-time capacity with the U.S. military.[54] The same could not be said, however, for four of his ambitious siblings, whose career goals were just coming into focus as America looked toward the nineteenth century.

Addison Bowles Armistead found his calling as a professional soldier, even though he never fired a shot during the Quasi War. Honorably discharged from the Provisional Army in June 1800, he quickly re-enlisted in the regular service, became a first lieutenant in the corps of artillerists and engineers, and was promoted to captain of the artillery by President Jefferson. He eventually rose to command of multiple coastal fortifications in South Carolina during the War of 1812.[55]

Addison was the third-oldest Armistead brother behind John and the rarely mentioned William, the only son of this generation who never served in the military. Addison was born at Newmarket sometime between 1773 and 1776, but the precise birth year has never been verified and is omitted altogether in most published genealogies. Family records do, however, provide us with a fairly consistent order of birth—John, William, Addison, George, Lewis G.A., and Walker.[56,57]

Details of Addison's life story have faded with the passage of time, but the few surviving accounts point to him being a dutiful soldier and a trusted, if very strict, commander. Other than taking a two-month furlough in November 1804 to marry Mary Howe Peyton in Dumfries, Virginia, he was listed as present on all military service rolls for five straight years until being promoted to captain of artillery on October 1, 1806. His brother, George, also took leave to attend the wedding ceremony at Dumfries,[58] and it is noteworthy that Addison and George are linked at several key junctures in their military careers: they received their first commissions within days of one another in 1799, served together in the same regiment in the Provisional Army, and were assigned to the U.S. Regiment of Artillerists and Engineers as second lieutenants on the same day, February 16, 1801. Both men were then promoted to captain of artillery one month apart in late 1806.[59]

This was a time of relative peace for the ascendant nation, but occasional threats from both the French and British raised concerns over the safety of coastal fortifications. As far back as 1794, Congress had assigned a committee to address "the problem of defending at least the principal harbors of the Atlantic seaboard," including Charleston, Savannah, and Norfolk, the essential ports for the southern U.S.[60] Coastal operations took on an even more heightened frenzy in June 1807 when sailors from the British ship *Leopard* harassed and boarded the USS *Chesapeake* off the coast of Norfolk, stoking, at least temporarily, the threat of war with England.

One historian, addressing this period leading up to the War of 1812, wrote that the country was being defended by:

> ...a small but energetic corps of U.S. Army artillerists and engineers. These included the redoubtable Armistead brothers: Captain Walker K. Armistead, who greatly improved the Craney Island defenses guarding Norfolk, Va.; and Major George Armistead, commanding Fort McHenry, which dominated the water approach to Baltimore.[61]

Overshadowed in this case was Addison, the third "redoubtable" brother, who commanded Savannah's Fort Jackson in 1808–1809 and would later shuttle to posts at Fort Johnson, Fort Moultrie, and Castle Pinckney in Charleston from 1809–1813 which were largely responsible for the defense of these vital southern harbors.[62]

Addison's thirst for both promotion and publicity are underscored by a curious side trip to Richmond, Virginia to sit for a portrait by the famed French artist Charles Balthazar Julien Fevret de Saint-Memin. The artist was in Virginia's capital city in 1808 and drew portraits of almost 200 of the state's most influential citizens. Unfortunately, while Saint-Memin made 142 engravings during this period, he did only "crayon portraits" of 56 other subjects, including Addison. A purported reproduction of the Addison sketch appears in a later book about Saint-Memin's work in Virginia, and the uniform he wore is described in a publication about army life in the 1800s, but the original portrait has never been located and is likely lost to history.[63]

Though a stickler for discipline while on duty, Addison also took great care to look out for the personal well-being of his troops. From early 1812, when he commanded Fort Moultrie in Charleston, Captain Armistead kept up a robust correspondence with Secretary of War William Eustis to seek improved conditions at the post. In January of that year, five months before the war with England, he decried the "defenseless nature" of the local forts and complained that "at the moment I am writing there are several soldiers here in absolute want of medical care." In February, addressing his deteriorated artillery platforms, he wrote, "I had no idea that timber could have been so much rotted." In April, he requested that the lime construction of his batteries be crowned with "Palmetto logs," because otherwise, if struck by cannon balls, they "would be so scattered as to disable the men by getting in their eyes." By early June, just weeks before the U.S. declaration of war, Addison groused that "the publick buildings at this post are really suffering for want of paint," and asked Eustis to fund painters to "spruce up" the harbor command.[64]

But his ongoing quest for greater military glory was interrupted by an unidentified disease that tragically took his life less than a year into the war. He was granted a brief furlough from duty in October 1812, was noted as "sick" on the regiment's December muster roll, and passed away suddenly on February 10, 1813 at Fort Moultrie.[65] No cause of death was ever listed. Addison's obituary in the *Charleston Times* reported that "his remains were interred at Fort Johnson, on the 13th inst., with military honors," but the old fort on James Island has long ceased to exist and the specific location of his gravesite has never been found.

From the day he was born—or at least the day he was named—Lewis Gustavus Adolphus Armistead was destined to be a soldier.

Christened for the great Swedish warrior Gustavus Adolphus, Lewis carried the designation with pride throughout his life, referring to himself as "Lewis G.A." and signing with both initials on all letters and official documents.[66]

King Gustavus Adolphus commanded Sweden's military in the first half of the seventeenth century and was renowned for tactical innovations during the Thirty Years' War, hailed as both the "Lion of the North" and the "father of modern warfare." He was immortalized in Swedish lore after being killed in action during a daring cavalry charge at the Battle of Lutzen in 1632.[67] Lewis G.A. had a much less distinguished military career but rose from Virginia's militia ranks to become captain of the U.S. 1st Rifle Regiment before falling in a battle at Fort Erie, Canada during the War of 1812.[68]

Born about 1781 at Newmarket, the fifth of six Armistead sons, Lewis G.A. took a more unconventional path than his brothers but was no less determined to serve. The first military document in his name is dated October 20, 1807, shortly after a naval conflict known as the Chesapeake-Leopard affair, when he was appointed spokesman by a group of local patriots. Lewis G.A. wrote to the state's militia commander to inform him that they had formed a new

> "Volunteer Troop of Dragoons…to be styled and known by the name of 'The Northern Neck Light Dragoons,' [who] associate not only for the purpose of the defence of the country in which we reside, but will hold ourselves in readiness to march wherever the constituted authorities may direct, to protect our native land, as well as to avenge the insult (as far as we are able) that has been so recently offered to our National Flag."[69]

He identified himself as the unit's ensign and signed the letter in the manner of an official army officer, "L.G.A. Armistead."

Tempers were soon mollified on both sides of the Atlantic and the dragoons were not needed to "avenge the insult," but the headstrong Lewis G.A. continued on his unique and oddly winding path toward professional military service.

In late June 1808, his commanding officer, Major John Tayloe, sent a note to the U.S. secretary of war to "recommend L.G.A. Armistead for a [military] appointment." He wrote that young Armistead had risen to the rank of lieutenant in his corps of militia dragoons, and "if I did not think he warranted an assignment in the army, I would not speak of him in the terms I do." Concerned, however, that his argument might not be persuasive on the merits, Tayloe invoked the Armistead surname as a last resort. "He is brother to those of that name—who are now captains and spoken very highly of," the militia major said. "But if he does not [get into the army] he means to leave shortly to seek employment in New Orleans. He would prefer the cavalry but would be happy to take anything you think proper to confer on him."[70]

It was certainly because he had three brothers who were already U.S. Army officers, and not so much because of a random threat to leave for the bayou, that Lewis G.A. was appointed a second lieutenant in the Marine Corps by President Jefferson on January 16, 1809.[71] He was part of a group of three hundred Marines sent to New Orleans to man gunships the next month, but most of his activities from 1809–1811 remain a mystery. He did not reappear in military service records until February 1812 when he was named a first lieutenant in the U.S. Rifles—seemingly out of nowhere becoming an officer of sharpshooters after two unrelated stints with the cavalry and marines.[72]

His quixotic military tour had led him to the fledgling "Regiment of Riflemen," a special unit conceived in 1808 to focus on "forest warfare, skirmishing and ambushes." Its members were decked out handsomely in distinctive green uniforms with black trim.[73] Lewis G.A. formally accepted his commission on February 24, pledging to "hold myself in readiness to receive any orders that might be communicated."[74] He did not have to wait for long, however, as orders came in a frenzy to all available units when war with England broke out in June.

The riflemen played key support roles in the first two years of the conflict, and Lewis G.A. was present in May 1813 during an attack from Fort Niagara on Fort George—where his brother, George, distinguished himself with the artillery. The regiment was renamed the U.S. 1st Rifles on February 10, 1814 after Congress authorized the creation of three additional rifle units. Political leaders in Washington were so impressed by the success of these organized marksmen that they wanted a concerted push to harass the powerful British and help bring the war to a close.[75]

Lewis G.A. was promoted to captain in January 1814 and assigned to defend Sackets Harbor, New York, the lone "useful deep-water" port on the American side of Lake Ontario.[76] But with land battles roaring to the southwest near Buffalo that summer, he and his men did not stay there for long. American troops overran the British garrison at Fort Erie in what is now Ontario in early July, and the 1st Rifles were transferred later that month to help hold the vulnerable outpost in Canadian territory. The British, incensed, settled in for a siege.[77]

Periodic skirmishing followed, with the two sides exchanging manic potshots along the border. A historian wrote that "the U.S. 1st Rifles, skilled at such engagements, were ordered across the river on August 4" to harass enemy artillerists.[78] "We have been skirmishing every day in which we are generally successful," Lewis wrote on September 7 to his brother, George, at Fort McHenry. "Our corps has suffered severely since it joined the army but all the troops are in fine spirits & wish for an opportunity to give them battle."[79] Constant British pressure soon became untenable, however, and U.S. General Jacob Brown ordered an attack to break the siege on September 17.

Brown was keenly aware that British forces had sacked Washington, D.C., burned the White House, and were threatening nearby Baltimore (although results of that latter clash on September 12–14 had not yet made it to the frontier). The nation's focus was now on restoring its capital city, meaning that no fresh troops were available to help the general at Fort Erie. He would have to act on his own. Brown's plan was to launch a surprise attack "to storm the batteries, destroy the cannon, and roughly handle the brigade upon duty before those in reserve could be brought into the action." The advance element of the American column was led by two hundred marksmen from the 1st and 4th Rifles.[80]

Conditions that day were miserably wet and cloudy. An officer remembered years later that the "atmosphere was heavily loaded with vapors with, now and then, a slight shower." But the U.S. attackers, including Lewis G.A., used the cover to their advantage as they slogged through the woods to move within sight of the British line. Then, making "a total nuisance of themselves with their constant skirmishing," they announced their arrival with some man-made thunder.[81]

They captured one battery and threatened another until British resistance stiffened. It was at this crucial point that several U.S. commanders were shot down—among them Captain Armistead, who exposed himself at the head of the column as his men surged toward the guns.[82] Vicious and desperate fighting continued for almost two hours with heavy losses on both sides, until the Americans pulled back to the safety of the fort. The British quickly abandoned their position several days later—officially ending the siege and allowing Brown to claim a hollow, strategic victory—but research later showed that a withdrawal had been the British plan all along. Sadly, the American attack had been unnecessary.[83]

Armistead and other U.S. soldiers who died behind enemy lines were buried by the British in trenches dug for the siege,[84] all of them in unmarked graves. Time and the inevitable erosion of two hundred years—and modern progress—have washed away all remnants. Unmarried and without children, he left no other legacy. Brother George was already being honored as the hero of Fort McHenry and savior of Baltimore by the time news arrived in Maryland and Virginia that Lewis G.A. had been killed in action at Fort Erie, the second of two Armistead siblings to give their lives in defense of their country in the War of 1812.

Walker Keith Armistead was a trailblazer himself, the first member of his family, and one of the first in the history of the country, to receive a formal military education.

He graduated at the top of the second class from West Point in 1803, served at key coastal posts from New England to South Carolina, was engaged at Fort Niagara during the bombardment of 1812, organized the defenses of Norfolk in 1813, became the army's chief engineer, rose to the rank of brevet-brigadier general, and commanded U.S. troops in the Second Seminole War. In contrast to three of his brothers who had died by 1818, Walker lived well into the 1840s and served his country for more than forty years.[85]

Named for an uncle, Walker Baylor, who served in the Continental Army during the Revolution, and mindful of his Armistead-Baylor heritage, Walker felt the lure of military service long before his brothers marched off to war. Family genealogies generally agree that he was the youngest of six male siblings, just behind George and Lewis G.A., although misinformation over his birth year has confounded historians for years. It is likely that he was born in or around 1783.[86]

What is known for certain is that Walker was one of the original fourteen cadets assigned to "repair" to West Point in September 1801. The military-style campus on the rugged banks of the Hudson was not yet a national academy, but instruction in mathematics and other disciplines began that fall under the direction of the Corps of Artillerists and Engineers. It was "the determination of the Secretary of War that Cadets shall receive some instruction relative to their duty before they receive an appointment [to the army]and for that reason he has ordered them to West Point to attend a military school." Classes started each day at 8 a.m. on the ground floor of a two-story, wood-framed building dubbed the "Academy," followed by military drills and field sports in the afternoon.[87] Students also were responsible for keeping up the appearance of the campus, and one classmate remembered a small headquarters residence where "Cadet Armistead and myself planted twelve elm trees."[88]

President Jefferson formally created the academy as part of the Military Peace Establishment Act in March 1802. Two cadets were honored as the first graduates that summer, but Walker apparently missed so much classwork because of trips home to Virginia that he was compelled to return for the next academic year. He was nonetheless assigned to the Corps of Engineers and graduated from West Point at the top of the three-man Class of 1803, becoming the No.

3 graduate in school history.[89] On March 4, 1803, Secretary of War Henry Dearborn wrote to Jefferson:

> *Walker K. Armistead, a Cadet in the Corps of Engineers, having on examination received honorable testimonials of his progress in science and requisite qualifications to sustain a Commission in the Army of the United States, I take the liberty of proposing, to your consideration, the appointment of said Armistead as Second Lieutenant in the Corps of Engineers.*[90]

Dearborn alerted Lieutenant Armistead the next day that the president had approved his appointment.

Walker's career would eventually span two wars, five decades, and land ranging from Fort Niagara to Florida's swamps, but it began humbly enough with a three-year assignment as an engineer on the West Point campus. He was promoted to first lieutenant in June 1805 and captain of engineers in October 1806—at about the same time that his brothers, Addison and George, became captains in the artillery.[91]

Walker's final pre-war posting was as lead engineer of the Norfolk region, where he built additional batteries at Fort Norfolk and constructed an entirely new fortification on the James River.[92] He was elevated to major in 1810 and lieutenant colonel in 1812, just as war broke out with England, putting his career on a blistering fast track. Transferred north to the Niagara region as chief engineer, he saw his first battle action on November 21, 1812, when a heavy British cannonade from Fort George imperiled the garrison at Fort Niagara. The biggest danger from this "incessant storm, of projectiles" was a series of building fires ignited by "red-hot shot,"[93] but as Colonel George McFeely noted in his official battle report,

> *from the extraordinary vigilance of the officers and men, particularly [Lieutenant Colonel] Armistead of the United States Corps of Engineers, whose indefatigable exertions were extended to all parts of the garrison, the fires were got under without being observed by the enemy.*[94]

With British threats constantly evolving, Walker was dispatched again to prepare the defenses of Norfolk in March 1813. This was much to the relief of the local militia commander, who deemed him "better qualified in every respect than I am to decide upon the defects of position and structure on the forts." Walker suggested building a line of redoubts behind Fort Norfolk, digging a ditch around Fort Nelson and using artillery to fortify the weak defensive position on Craney Island.[95] The latter move—especially with the Royal Navy lurking—would have a deep-seated effect on military morale that summer in the Chesapeake region.

The most tantalizing target for the British was the USS *Constellation*, a powerful frigate anchored in the Elizabeth River between Forts Norfolk and Nelson. Its capture would have been another humiliating setback for the Americans. Local militia forces were prepared to abandon their position in the face of British firepower, convinced that a stand at Craney Island would lead to almost certain defeat, but "after a 30-year-old Army engineer, Walker K. Armistead, voiced his objections, a second council of war reversed the decision and the Americans re-committed to fighting at Craney Island."[96] Combined land and naval forces promptly repelled a British attack on June 22, achieving one of the rare U.S. victories in the first half of the summer of 1813 (and doing so, symbolically, on the sixth anniversary of the Chesapeake-Leopard affair).[97]

The war had not yet ended when Walker's life changed dramatically in another way in 1814. He married Elizabeth Stanley of New Bern, North Carolina, and within four years had purchased a three-hundred-acre farm in Fauquier County, Virginia, where they would raise nine children.[98] The army's call of duty never ceased, however, and his nomadic existence continued with new command roles as chief engineer of the Army (1818), colonel of the Third Artillery (1821), and further postings to West Point, Fort Washington, and Boston.[99]

Walker's last promotion came in 1828 when he was brevetted a brigadier general "for faithful service of ten years in one grade,"[100] the highest command level attained by the current generation of military Armisteads. The peak of his career came when he commanded all U.S. Army troops for one year during the Second Seminole War in Florida. But despite his rank and accomplishments, and despite serving honorably as a general into the mid-1840s, he would fail to match the fame of another brother, George, a *mere* lieutenant colonel.

CHAPTER THREE
"A Flag So Big"

Even in a family of accomplished U.S. military officers, George Armistead stood out from a young age for his natural leadership ability. Born on April 10, 1780 at Newmarket, the fourth of six sons, George was only nineteen years old when he became a second lieutenant in the Quasi War and had not yet turned twenty-one when President John Adams nominated him for a captaincy in the regular army early in 1801.[101] He barely had time to learn on the job.

The uncle for whom he was named, General George Baylor, served as one of George Washington's aides-de-camp in the Revolutionary War and was praised for "military ardor" and "spirited behaviour upon every occasion."[102] Promoted to command of the Third Regiment of Continental Light Dragoons, Baylor never fully recovered from a bayonet wound suffered during a British attack in 1778. He died six years later of the "fatigues of the war and the effects of wounds," leaving his own legacy of military ardor to inspire George Armistead and other descendants.[103]

The U.S. Army at the turn of the nineteenth century was woefully deficient in organization and manpower just as a new generation of soldiers was coming of age. Many veterans of the Revolution had returned to their homes and farmsteads, never to serve again, and the subject of a standing army to preserve the peace and defend the nation from attack was still a matter of fierce debate. There were those, including the great states-rights advocate, Thomas Jefferson, who believed the concept of a full-time army was a corruption of America's founding ideals. "There shall be no standing army but in time of actual war," Jefferson wrote, adding that it was neither "needful nor safe" for an army "to be kept up in time of peace."[104] But others disagreed. Among Quasi War veterans who re-enlisted in a new and more expansive U.S. defensive force in 1801, George was quickly identified as a rising star.

He became a first lieutenant in the Second Regiment of Artillerist and Engineers on February 16, 1801 and was nominated as captain a few weeks later by President Adams, whose term was just expiring.[105] As fate would have it, the promotion was never approved by the Senate, likely because of the change in administrations, so twenty-one-year-old Lieutenant Armistead was assigned instead to a company of artillerists serving on the Canadian border at Fort Niagara. He also was given the dual role of assistant military agent, charged with handling the garrison's supplies.[106]

Located at the mouth of the Niagara River where it flows into Lake Ontario, Fort Niagara was very much in the hinterlands of North America when George reported for duty in September 1801. The population was sparse and the winters unusually harsh for a soldier raised in the American south. A permanent fort had been built there by the French in 1726 and occupied by the British during the French and Indian War (1759), but controversial new boundaries drawn up in the wake of the Revolution now placed it just inside the U.S. border. Following a lengthy and acrimonious transition period, American troops took control of the fort in 1796.[107]

The British responded by erecting a rival structure, Fort George, directly across the river, but individual soldiers on both sides remained cordial enough that Lieutenant Armistead was a frequent hunting companion of British Colonel Isaac Brock, later commander of all enemy forces in Upper Canada.[108]

Armistead's service during his first term at Fort Niagara lasted six years from 1801 to 1807. Much of his surviving correspondence reflects the monotony of nineteenth century military life on the frontier—he once confined a soldier to barracks for the grievous sin of "riding a public horse without my consent or knowledge"—but it also gave the first hint of his career-long fascination with massively oversized garrison flags.[109] Unhappy that Niagara was no longer in possession of its original U.S. flag, he wrote to military agent Peter Gansevoort in Albany on October 12, 1802 to request a stand of colors "16 yards by 12 yards" as a new and official national ensign for the fort.[110]

The sheer size of the flag (thirty-six by forty-eight feet) was overwhelming, but one of his goals was to ensure that British troops on the Canadian side would have no trouble seeing it from a distance.

Promoted to captain, finally, on November 1, 1806, when he was still just twenty-six years old, George seemed destined for military greatness until a new set of instructions almost sidetracked his career.

"I have received orders to join my company at Chickasaw Bluffs on the Mississippi, a journey of about 3,000 miles," he wrote to his sister in early 1807, unaware that he actually would be heading to tiny Fort Madison in the even more remote Arkansas territory.[111] Situated on the banks of the Arkansas River about fifty miles north of its confluence with the Mississippi, the generically-named "Arkansas Post" had been in existence under French rule since 1686 but did not become part of United States territory until the Louisiana Purchase in 1803. It was still not much more than a rickety trading post and fringe frontier military establishment when Armistead departed Fort Niagara for his new assignment on March 15, 1807.[112]

A contemporary inventory taken just before his arrival detailed a "50' x 10' shingled barrack with double clay chimney [with a] prison at one end, a 20' and 12' poorly maintained kitchen with a store room for war supplies, an earthen oven, three sentry 'boxes' in poor condition, a flag staff, and the normal locks, keys, hinges and latches for (keeping) each building in proper order."[113] The population was 368, made up of "between sixty and seventy families … and about sixty Black slaves," and a wide-eyed visitor wrote that it "consists mostly of hunters and Indian traders, [and] of course it is a poor place, as settlers of this description never look for anything beyond the mere necessities of life, except whiskey."[114]

Beginning his trek in late winter, George traveled by sleigh across ice-covered Lake Erie and stopped briefly at home to visit his family in Virginia before angling to the southwest and the Trans-Mississippi Valley. Along the way he complained to his sister that he had "not heard a word" from their brother, Walker, adding, with a wink, "I presume his promotion [to captain]has been the cause of his forgetting his promises."[115] Once he arrived in the wilds of Arkansas, however, the joking ended and his outlook hardened. The little garrison at Fort Madison included only sixteen soldiers and was located as far from civilization as one could imagine.[116] George spent many idle hours on the frontier wondering if his lifelong quest for military glory would now be hopelessly overshadowed by the rapid ascent of his well-schooled sibling from West Point.

It would not. Less than a year into his tenure, he received a new assignment as justice of the peace for the New Madrid District, despite the lack of any formal legal training. A historian described the appointment as the "direct result of the need to establish American sovereignty over the Louisiana Purchase" and noted that many military officers in the region now "played a central role in settling civil disputes."[117] Most of the Founding Fathers would have decried such a dual role as an affront to U.S. civil liberties, but it was Jefferson himself who put the plan into action, opting to use military options to maintain order in otherwise unmanageable territories. Armistead became a justice on May 18, 1808, obtaining his commission from the territorial governor, Meriwether Lewis (who recently had explored the uncharted U.S. interior from Missouri to the Pacific with fellow adventurer William Clark).[118]

Judge Armistead made no lasting legal decisions and spent his brief time in that capacity settling minor disputes over land and other property, but he gained new insight into leadership and problem-solving that would help him in future assignments. The broadened perspective came in handy soon enough. A series of drastic events on the eastern seaboard threatened to pitch the young nation into war with England, including the Chesapeake-Leopard affair in 1807 and the repeated impressment of U.S. citizen-sailors by the British Navy. Promising commanders were now needed at threatened fortifications on the Atlantic coast, and Armistead told friends on November 30, 1808 that he would be leaving in a few days for a new post at Baltimore—specifically, as fate would have it, at a place called Fort McHenry.[119]

The pentagon-shaped "Star Fort" on Whetstone Point in Baltimore was the perfect place to project symbolic power and shield the nation's third-largest city from seaborne attack.[120]

Built on a peninsula jutting out past the inner harbor and between two branches of the Patapsco River, Fort McHenry dated to the late 1790s, when the U.S. first conceived of a series of coastal fortifications to protect against probing maritime powers. The walls and buildings were constructed of brick—a vast improvement over its predecessor, Fort Whetstone, which had been a mere earthen structure—and a deep, broad moat had been carved out to provide a defensive buffer while also accommodating infantry. The five bastions, or points, were arranged in such a way that cannons posted there could deliver a deadly crossfire, repelling any land-based attack.[121] The double-tiered "water batteries" were the first line of defense, protecting and controlling the harbor channel."[122]

Named for James McHenry, secretary of war under Presidents Washington and Adams, the fort was still being modified and strengthened for battle when twenty-eight-year-old Captain George Armistead reported for duty in January 1809 to serve as second in command of the First Regiment of U.S. Artillery.[123] The facilities were far advanced from anything he had experienced in rural Arkansas. Secretary of War John Armstrong described the McHenry complex as a "regular pentagon of masonry, calculated for thirty guns, a water battery, with ten heavy guns mounted, a brick magazine that will contain three hundred barrels of powder, with brick barracks for two companies of men and officers; without the fort, a wooden barrack for one company, also a brick store and gun house."[124] At the very least, it would give enemies pause before attacking.

Little is known of Armistead's military achievements during his three-year stint in Baltimore from 1809 to early 1812. Aside from noting the arrival of the first mobile horse-drawn artillery unit in U.S. Army history, the fort's records from this period are numbingly "routine and uneventful."[125] The same cannot be said for George's personal life. Having spent the previous decade stranded at lonely outposts on the frontier, he took advantage of Baltimore's thriving social scene to woo and win the hand of Louisa Hughes, daughter of a wealthy merchant, Christopher Hughes, Sr. They were married on October 26, 1810 at Otterbein Church on the city's waterfront. One of the witnesses to the wedding was George's new brother-in-law, Christopher Hughes, Jr., soon to command a company of volunteer artillerists at Fort McHenry (and later assigned to accompany U.S. peace commissioners to Ghent, Belgium to negotiate with the British).[126]

The newlyweds were virtually inseparable until April 9, 1812, when the disruptive nature of military life set in. With war looming, George was ordered to report to Bedloe's Island, located at the tip of Manhattan—known today as Liberty Island, home of the Statue of Liberty—to assist with the defense of New York harbor.[127] Louisa had just become pregnant and was forced to remain in Baltimore, fretting about his safety, especially after Congress officially declared war in June. Fortunately for George, his most heated "action" during this period was leading a procedural protest by eighteen infantry and artillery officers to overturn the appointment of an engineer to command their post.[128] The British never attacked New York, no battles took place in the harbor, and he returned home, at least briefly, for the Christmas holiday and the birth of their first daughter, Mary, on December 27.[129]

Captain Armistead was on the move again in February, when he was ordered back to Fort Niagara to take command of a company of artillerists.[130] U.S. efforts to invade Canada in 1812 had resulted in a series of humiliating defeats—veteran British troops posted there were reinforced by a loose confederation of Canadian militia and local Indians—but hope had sprung anew with a new campaign planned for 1813. Tensions ran high along the Niagara River border, where soldiers at the once-friendly garrisons of Fort Niagara and Fort George glared at one another from less than a mile apart. Armistead's role in the coming conflict was elevated further when he was promoted to major of the 3rd Regiment of Artillerists shortly after his arrival on March 3, 1813.[131]

It is curious to note that the orders from Adjutant General Thomas H. Cushing referenced "George K. Armistead," the first and only time during his military career that George was identified by a middle initial.[132] His brothers all proudly used their middle names and signed official documents with those names or initials—Walker Keith or W.K.; Addison Bowles or A.B.; Lewis G.A.—but George relied solely on his first name, signing as "George" or "Geo" Armistead. Neither his few surviving papers nor numerous published family genealogies indicate a middle name or initial.

After much careful planning and several feints to hold the enemy in place, the U.S. began its attack on Fort George when Armistead unleashed an artillery barrage at daybreak on May 27.[133] This was followed by a well-coordinated land and sea assault, as invading troops under a dashing young colonel named Winfield Scott swarmed the shoreline. Outnumbered British and Canadian defenders put up stiff resistance but eventually were forced to retreat in the face of overwhelming U.S. firepower.[134] Witnesses from both sides credited Armistead's gunners with delivering ghastly punishment from strongly-placed batteries at Fort Niagara.

One British commander noted matter-of-factly in his report that American artillerists "kept up a most galling cross-fire on us the whole morning,"[135] but another provided more context, crediting the outcome to "[fire] from the enemy's fort and all his adjacent batteries, with 16 guns, chiefly of large calibre, and three mortars… and the shot being all heated and the fire so successful that the buildings were totally consumed."[136]

He added,

> with excessive heavy firing coming from the enemy's fort and six batteries…[and with] the fort in flames and shells bursting amongst us in every direction, and very few artillery men left and no object in such a situation to be obtained, I suspended the fire…and the enemy, finding all the buildings in the fort consumed, ceased his fire about 2 o'clock.[137]

By contrast, early dispatches from victorious U.S. commanders lacked both specifics and emotion. "We took possession of Fort George and its immediate dependencies this day," Major General Henry Dearborn reported dryly to the governor of New York. "Our troops behaved like brave old soldiers. We have much more to do."[138] A week later, however, the New York *National Advocate* published a more passionate account from an anonymous battle veteran, offering additional detail and placing the rare U.S. victory in its proper context.

> *We have had another battle and our flag waves triumphant over Fort George...Our success I attribute in a great measure to the good conduct of artillerists on our side of the river, who in a short period demolished all the enemy's works. Indeed, their accurate firing and good management is beyond all praise. Major Armistead commanded during the campaign at Fort Niagara. Fort George was completely demolished and burnt.*[139]

Reports of Armistead's dazzling performance soon found their way to Washington, D.C., and the War Department. General Dearborn informed Secretary of War Armstrong in a June 8 letter that he was "greatly indebted" to Armistead and two other officers "for their judicious arrangements and skillful execution" in pulverizing the British at Fort George.[140] The thirty-three-year-old major was accorded the honor of presenting captured British battle flags to President James Madison—who was ecstatic, having endured a year of caustic taunts from anti-war advocates—and Armstrong determined that it was ludicrous to send such a capable officer back to the frontier when both Baltimore and Washington were threatened. In a seemingly-innocuous official dispatch on June 27, one that would soon find its place in the pantheon of American history, the secretary instructed Armistead to remain at home and "take command of Fort McHenry."[141]

Overjoyed as he was to reunite with his wife in Baltimore and live for the first time with his baby daughter, Mary, now six months old, George had little time to devote to family matters.

British naval forces under the ruthless Rear Admiral George Cockburn were marauding virtually unopposed across the Chesapeake, pillaging coastal towns and villages. Cockburn (pronounced "COE-burn" by the British and "COCK-burn" by the Americans) had plundered and burned the upper Maryland towns of Frenchtown, Havre de Grace, and Fredericktown in a vicious springtime tour de force.[142] On May 5 at Fredericktown, Cockburn forced the local militia commander to watch in helpless horror as furious redcoats torched his house, barn, carriage house, and other property. "How do you like the war now?" the admiral sneered.[143] A mid-June assault on Craney Island near Norfolk was foiled by Walker Armistead and his engineers, but Cockburn dispatched two companies of French prisoners three days later to loot and ravage the nearby town of Hampton, Virginia.[144]

George Armistead's first task upon arrival was to prevent such a raid from burning down Baltimore. Concerned about the lack of manpower at Fort McHenry, he quickly placed a newspaper advertisement offering bonus money and "One Hundred and Sixty Acres of Land" to each new recruit who applied directly to "GEO ARMISTEAD, Major, 3rd Artillery."[145] He then set about shoring up the fort's physical defenses. Writing on July 13 to General Samuel Smith, the local militia commander, Armistead noted that "to place this post in a complete state of defense" would require nineteen heavy guns and two ten-inch mortars, "and at least 25 spherical shot for each gun," all of which would "add considerably to the defense and safety of Baltimore."[146]

They also planned for the construction of two earthen shore batteries and the redeployment of more militia units, including the Baltimore Fencibles under Captain Joseph Nicholson, chief judge of the sixth judicial district and court of appeals of Maryland.[147]

Once it all was underway, however, Armistead reportedly had a request of his own for General Smith:

> We, Sir, are ready at Fort McHenry to defend Baltimore against invading by the enemy. That is to say, we are ready except that we have no suitable ensign to display over the Star Fort, and it is my desire to have a flag so large that the British will have no difficulty in seeing it from a distance.[148]

Armistead's obsession with mammoth banners had not changed since his earliest days at Fort Niagara. Even during his uneventful first stint at Fort McHenry in 1811, he had written to Colonel Henry Burbeck of the artillery corps, informing him "that I am getting up a new Flag staf and it will be among the handsomest now standing" and soliciting Burbeck's assistance "in getting a new flag."[149] The execution was waylaid by his assignment to Bedloe's Island and a return engagement at Fort Niagara in the first full year of the war, but Armistead never wavered in his quest for a proper stand of colors. Charged now with defending his city against the world's greatest military power, he believed the time had come for a flag that would not only identify the fort but instill pride and boost his men's morale.

An image of Mary Pickersgill from later in life. She was thirty-seven years old when she made the Star-Spangled Banner. *(Wikimedia Commons, Harris & Ewing Collection)*

The task was assigned in early July to a thirty-seven-year-old widow named Mary Young Pickersgill, a Baltimore seamstress and flag-maker of some renown. Mary was the daughter of Rebecca

Young, who had produced flags, blankets, and uniforms for the Continental Army during the Revolution (and therefore was a business rival of the more famous Betsy Ross). Mrs. Pickersgill ran a brisk business from her modest little home at the corner of Pratt and Albemarle Streets, offering "colors of every description," including flags and signal flags, to the ships and maritime merchants who docked at Baltimore's teeming port.[150] The workforce included her thirteen-year-old daughter, Caroline; three teenage nieces, Eliza, Margaret, and Jane Young; and a thirteen-year-old African American indentured servant, Grace Wisher, who was assigned to learn "the art and mystery of Housework and plain sewing."[151] It is likely that Mary's seventy-three-year-old mother helped with various projects or, at the very least, offered advice. The role of an unidentified female slave at the Pickersgill home is unknown; she probably handled household chores during this period but also may have assisted directly in the flag-making process.

Local legend holds that Armistead himself approached Pickersgill to place a rush order for two colors: a large garrison flag, measuring thirty feet by forty-two feet, and a smaller "storm flag" for inclement conditions (seventeen by twenty-five feet).[152] More persuasive evidence is that contact was made by two other officers involved in Baltimore's defense, Joshua Barney and John Stricker, both of whom had family connections to Pickersgill (although it was the army's deputy commissary, James Calhoun, who ultimately paid the bill). "My mother was selected by Commodore Barney and General Stricker to make this 'Star Spangled Banner,' which she did, being an exceedingly patriotic woman," Mary's daughter wrote.[153] The situation was tense and the timetable abnormally tight because of Cockburn's menacing presence in the bay area. One report said the flags were expected to be delivered in six weeks.[154]

Pickersgill went to work immediately on a U.S. flag with fifteen stars and fifteen stripes, the standard design of that era. The original Flag Act, passed on June 14, 1777, had decreed that "the flag of the thirteen United States be thirteen stripes, alternate red and white" and that "the union be thirteen stars, white in a blue field, representing a new constellation." But the admission of new states following the Revolution led to a second Flag Act in 1795, adding two stars and two stripes for Kentucky and Vermont. It remained that way for more than twenty years, even as more states joined the Union (there were actually eighteen states, including Tennessee, Ohio, and Louisiana, when war broke out in 1812). Not until 1818 did Congress pass a bill to reduce the flag to thirteen permanent stripes, while adding a star for each new state.[155]

Pickersgill and her co-workers put in ten-hour days, using four hundred yards of dyed English worsted wool bunting and making, by one estimate, more than 350,000 individual stitches. A singular design challenge was that the bunting was only eighteen inches wide, while each stripe had to be twenty-three inches; Mary, in essence, had to do tedious patchwork stitching on the most famous flag in U.S. history. The two-foot wide white cotton stars were then sewn into the blue union by the *reverse applique* method—cutting holes in the union to let the stars show through on both sides, saving on both weight and material.[156]

Though a veteran flag-maker, Pickersgill had never handled a task this large and was forced to innovate on the fly, given the army's stark deadline. As one of her biographers described it, Mary "gathered the fabric necessary for the two flags; calculated how to make two flags with eighteen-inch bunting; carefully cut and pieced the fabric for the strips, canton, and stars; marshaled the females in her household and other female relatives to help with the sewing, and found a large space to assemble the flag." It is noteworthy that all the sewing was done by hand, as sewing machines were not available to the public until the 1850s.[157]

The finishing touch was sewing a linen sleeve on one side of the flag, known as the "hoist." By attaching iron rings and then using a length of rope, the flag could be raised and lowered on a pole for proper display.[158]

Many years later, Mary's daughter, Caroline, wrote in a letter to one of Armistead's daughters that "my mother worked many nights until 12 o'clock to complete it in the given time.

"The flag being so very large, mother was obliged to obtain permission from the proprietors of Claggets brewery, which was in our neighborhood, to spread it out in their malt house; and I remember seeing my mother down on the floor, placing the stars; after the completion of the flag, she superintended the topping of it, having fastened it in the most secure manner to prevent it being torn away by [cannon] balls…Your father (Col. Armistead) declared that no one but the maker of the flag should mend it."[159]

The flags were delivered to Armistead at Fort McHenry on August 19, 1813. According to a receipt signed by Mary's niece, Eliza Young, she received a payment of $405.90 for an "American Ensign 30 by 42 feet first quality bunting" and an additional $168.54 for the smaller storm flag, for a total of $574.44.[160] No one thought to record the moment when the big banner flew over Baltimore harbor for the first time, but it likely was on the day of delivery, with Mrs. Pickersgill present to oversee its placement. Weighing more than fifty pounds, and perhaps as much as eighty, the flag was fastened to a ninety-foot pole that was held in position by two large hand-hewn oak timbers, anchored several feet in the ground as supporting cross braces.[161]

The British, who had probed the Chesapeake all summer and ventured as far as the mouth of the Patapsco, near Baltimore, for two weeks in mid-August, left the bay by pre-arranged plan on August 24 to avoid the "sickly season" and sail for warm winter headquarters in the West Indies.[162] But Armistead was convinced they had at least caught a glimpse of his massive new flag—or heard from others who had seen it—and deemed himself satisfied, even if his showdown with the Royal Navy would have to wait another year.

CHAPTER FOUR
War with England—Again

England had been locked in a twenty-year war with France for supremacy on the European continent when the annoying little squabble with the U.S. broke out in 1812. Few soldiers and even fewer military assets could be spared to fight the pesky Americans. But after allied troops defeated Napoleon Bonaparte at the Battle of Leipzig, forcing him to retreat to Paris and abdicate the throne in April 1814, the British were free to uncork the full wrath of their military might against the upstart former colonists.[163] "Now that the tyrant Bonaparte has been consigned to infamy," the *London Times* seethed in what amounted to a national call-to-action, "there is no public feeling in this country stronger than indignation against the Americans."[164]

From England's perspective, the War of 1812 had been a bitter outgrowth of the long and costly conflagration with France. Desperate to offset mounting casualties and bolster their ranks in the first decade of the 1800s, the British began snatching sailors from U.S. ships and forcing them to serve in the Royal Navy, an illegal tactic known as "impressment"—and a numbing affront to the young nation's sovereignty.[165] President James Madison complained to Congress in a war message on June 1, 1812 that "thousands of American citizens, under the safeguard of public law, and of their national flag, have been torn from their country, and from everything dear to them." The British were also blockading ports and severely restricting trade, choking off supplies to France at great cost to the U.S. economy, further infuriating the president. "Our commerce was been plundered in every sea," Madison fumed. "The great staples of our country have been cut off from their legitimate markets…a destructive blow aimed at our agricultural and maritime interests."[166] In the president's view, Americans were being treated "not [as] an independent people, but as colonists and vassals."[167]

The U.S. declared war on June 18, 1812, but rarely has a country been so ill-equipped to back up its words with action. Influential American "war hawks" may have dreamed of extending the nation's boundaries northward into Canada, where they might seize vast swaths of territory from the last British stronghold on the continent, but troubling deficiencies in U.S. tactics and manpower—and leadership—were evident from the start.[168] The national "army" consisted of a grand total of 11,744 soldiers, including 5,000 green recruits, and the senior-level officer corps was a toxic mix of aging veterans from the Revolution and naïve, untested firebrands.[169] It should have come as no surprise that the 1812 invasion of Canada was an unqualified disaster, repulsed at all points by well-organized British, Canadian, and Indian defenders.

The year 1813 brought more of the same, with repeated drubbings by British forces in Canada, and Rear Admiral George Cockburn's virtually unstoppable raids on the Atlantic coast. But there also were occasional glimmers of hope for the U.S. military. These included the May 27 attack on Fort George, when young commanders Winfield Scott and George Armistead proved themselves worthy adversaries for British generals, and the September 10 naval battle on Lake Erie, when Oliver Hazard Perry defeated a small but vaunted British fleet—after which Perry uttered the immortal phrase, "We have met the enemy and they are ours."[170] Frustrated by America's refusal to capitulate, England opted for a more focused approach to force a negotiated peace on favorable terms in 1814.

The first step was inserting Vice Admiral Alexander Cochrane as overall commander of the North American station, replacing the aging and ineffectual John Warren. A master of amphibious warfare and an "inveterate hater of America," Sir Alexander arrived at British headquarters in Bermuda that spring on a mission to ravage the American coastline and divert essential U.S. forces from Canada.[171]

"You are at perfect liberty as soon as you can muster a Sufficient force, to act with the utmost Hostility against the shores of the United States," he wrote to Cockburn on April 28, envisioning "their Sea Port Towns laid in ashes & the Country wasted [in] some sort of retaliation for their savage Conduct in Canada." Furthermore, U.S. citizens should know "they are at the mercy of an invading foe."[172] Cockburn was delighted by the change in strategy, having chafed the previous year under the doddering Warren. Barely one month into their North American partnership and the two admirals had the makings of a dastardly effective team.

France's defeat in April gave them another opening. Freed from the yoke of battling Napoleon, the British could suddenly bolster land and sea forces to levels unattainable by the Americans and drive their one-time subjects into submission. Cochrane believed he would add up to twenty thousand of the Duke of Wellington's best soldiers, the "Invincibles," to create a fearfully irresistible invasion force.[173] He told General George Prevost, commander of British troops in Canada, that he hoped "to be able to make a very considerable diversion in the Chesapeake Bay, to draw off in part the Enemy's Efforts against Canada" and "to Keep the Enemy in a constant alarm."[174]

One of Cochrane's most ingenious tactics was to encourage American slaves to escape to freedom—with an additional opportunity to serve in the British military if they chose. The plan, he wrote as early as March 1814, was to "facilitate the desertion of the Negroes, and their Families, who are to have their choice of either entering into His Majesty's Service or to be settled with their Families at Trinidad or in the British American Provinces."[175] Cochrane issued an official proclamation to that effect on April 2, and within a month Cockburn reported that seventy-eight "Black Refugees" were safely quartered on Tangier Island in the Chesapeake, including thirty-eight "soldiers," thirteen "Stout Effective Men...for Work," and twenty-seven women and children "belonging to and attached to above...All Volunteers to stay with us here and to assist against their former Masters."[176]

By the time hostilities broke out again, about two hundred former slaves had been mustered into their own military unit, known as the "Colonial Marines," to distinguish them, on paper, from the long-established "Royal Marines."[177] They proved to be quick learners and effective, disciplined military men, surprising Admiral Cockburn, who initially had been skeptical of the plan. "I think whenever you arrive you will be pleased with them," he wrote to Cochrane in mid-May. "They have induced me to alter the bad opinion I had of the whole of their Race & I now really believe these we are training, will neither [show] want of Zeal or Courage when employed by us in attacking their old Masters."[178]

Cochrane's program to recruit former slaves was a significant boost to British operations, in large part because of the hypocrisy it exposed in America's contradictory freedoms. Beyond the incremental addition of manpower, his troops now stood on the moral high ground. Left unstated (probably on purpose) was the fear it stoked of a slave insurrection on the American coast. "The great point to be attained is the cordial Support of the Black population," he wrote to Cockburn on July 1. "With them properly armed & backed with 20,000 British Troops, Mr. Maddison will be hurled from his Throne."[179]

But there still were two questions: Where to attack, and when?

From the start of the 1814 British campaign in the Chesapeake, the port city of Baltimore was high on Cochrane's list of potential targets, and with good reason.

The nation's third-largest city behind New York and Philadelphia, and a thriving international trade center before the war, Baltimore boasted a growing population of forty-six thousand, including shipbuilders, sailmakers, ironworkers, merchants, and craftsmen from other maritime trades.[180] It also was known for its ardent pro-war sentiment, having been judged by Cochrane to be "the most democratic town...in the Country."[181] Baltimore's reputation for brawling, raucous behavior was underscored in 1812 when ruffians attacked the offices of a newspaper that opposed the war, beating one defender to death and crippling the Revolutionary War hero "Light-Horse Harry" Lee.[182] In addition to that—and perhaps most despicable in British eyes—it was the hub of American privateering.

Britain's policy of blockading U.S. ports to suppress trade to France and other countries brought a devastating halt to American commerce in the first decade of the 1800s. As a result, maritime merchants embraced the controversial but long-accepted practice of privateering with unprecedented fervor. The U.S. government authorized hundreds of private vessels to attack British merchant ships off the coasts of both countries, seizing cargo and destroying vital equipment and supplies. Baltimore became known as a welcoming center for privateers, and its locally-built ships—the swift, two-masted "Baltimore Clippers"—wreaked havoc on British commercial shipping, confounding the Royal Navy.[183]

Among Baltimore's privateering legends was the swashbuckling Joshua Barney, who, on one famous raid, captured eighteen British ships worth approximately $1.5 million.[184] It was because of Barney and his ilk that Baltimore was tagged with a new and well-earned nickname on the streets of London: "Nest of Pirates."[185]

Much of this was on Cochrane's mind as he plotted a change in British tactics from his temporary quarters in Bermuda. He saw intriguing targets in the nearby cities of Baltimore and Washington, D.C.—although taking Washington, with a war-time population of just eight thousand, would be largely symbolic. "Should Baltimore & Washington be the primary objects, it is to be decided where the landing can be made to most advantage," Cochrane wrote to Cockburn on July 1. "To me it appears that Baltimore should be the previous object."[186] A few days later, in a more formal report to Lord Bathurst, England's secretary of state for war and the colonies, he wrote that if "the point of Attack is directed towards Baltimore I have every prospect of Success and Washington Will be equally Accessible."[187]

But for all of his verve and unconcealed hatred of America, Cochrane could not bring himself to set those plans in motion. He continued to vacillate on targets in rambling letters to subordinates and superiors, and in one message alone listed more than ten possible destinations: Boston, New York, Philadelphia, Georgetown, Alexandria, Annapolis, Richmond, Mobile, New Orleans, Charleston, Savannah—the "principal towns of America"—and, generically, North Carolina and the "Southern Coast."[188] Barely a week later, writing to another British official while still in Bermuda, he added

Rhode Island to the list and dismissed several others.[189] The lack of decisiveness was mystifying.

Even while he waffled, however, Cochrane told his U.S.-based commanders that their previous policy of hit-and-run raids should continue in the interim, terrorizing the coastal populace and embarrassing President Madison. On July 18, in a stark memo to the "Commanding Officers of the North American Station," including Cockburn, he wrote, "You are hereby required and directed to destroy & lay waste such Towns and Districts upon the Coast as you may find assailable."[190]

In Baltimore, militia General Samuel Smith and U.S. Army Major George Armistead were as confused as anyone about British intentions but proceeded with their defensive preparations as though an attack were imminent.

During the previous summer, two batteries had been constructed on the shores west of Fort McHenry to aid in the defense of the fort and the city. Battery Babcock, sometimes generously called Fort Babcock, was little more than a primitive four-foot earthwork with limited room for placing guns, but Fort Covington was a more solid structure with brick walls and a substantial ten-gun platform. A smaller three-gun platform also was built across the water on Lazaretto Point to provide a potential crossfire option.[191]

Assigning troops to man these new works was a priority that reached the highest levels of the War Department in 1814. On February 10, Major Armistead was ordered to post a new company "on duty at Fort McHenry, or Battery Babcock, as you may judge most proper."[192] Two other companies spent much of the spring and summer overseeing a chain-mast boom that stretched across the harbor to prevent unwarranted entry by enemy vessels. The goal was "to lay booms of old or new masts connected by strong iron chains, and bolts riveted through the ends of each mast" from Lazaretto Point to Fort McHenry.[193]

Wild rumors of British activity along the coast increased by June, and General Smith was spooked by a tip that Royal Navy ships had been patrolling the bay nearby. It was necessary for the booms to be adjusted on occasion to allow local merchant vessels to pass through the harbor on business, but Smith now deemed it prudent to limit opportunities for a breach by British troops. On June 20, he wrote to Armistead,

> *Sir,*
>
> *The vicinity of the Enemy makes precaution necessary. I therefore submit to your consideration the propriety of locking the Booms nightly & opening them in the morning & of prohibiting all vessels from going in or out after sunset. I ask leave to recommend your taking possession of City Barges & practicing your Sea Fencibles to the use of them. It may soon be necessary to row guard below the fort.*[194]

The U.S. caution was well-advised under the circumstances, even though, unbeknownst to Armistead and Smith, the British high command still had not settled on a plan of action.

It was sometime in mid-July that Vice Admiral Cochrane learned, to his chagrin, that a force much smaller than the twenty thousand he expected was on its way to the North American station.[195] The empire still required troops on many fronts, including in France, where peace was new and fragile. Like many military powers throughout world history, the British came to realize they couldn't be everywhere at once.[196]

As a result, only four thousand additional ground troops were sailing to Bermuda to serve as part of Cochrane's joint land-sea force (another six thousand were headed to General Prevost in Canada, where an attack from the north was being plotted on Lake Champlain). Though small in number, these newcomers to North America were some of the most skilled and battle-tested soldiers in the world, including members of the 4th Regiment of Foot, who distinguished themselves under Wellington on the Peninsula, and whose military ancestors had fought at Concord and Bunker Hill.[197] They would be under the command of Major General Robert Ross, one of Wellington's favorites, a charismatic leader who had brought on deadly results against Napoleon in Portugal and Spain.[198]

The reinforcements arrived in Bermuda on July 23, and Cochrane waited barely a week before shipping off to the American coast. His flagship, the eighty-gun HMS *Tonnant*, led the way for the invading force, accompanied by vessels carrying Ross and various contingents of soldiers, sailors, and marines.[199] Even with extra manpower, however, the indecisive Cochrane remained unsure of his attack plan. "I cannot at present acquaint their Lordships of what may be my future operations," he wrote to the secretary of the admiralty on August 11. "They will depend much on the information I may receive in this quarter."[200]

Rear Admiral Cockburn was much more focused on details when he raced out to meet the big ships as they arrived on August 14. After more than a year of pin-prick raids along the coast, he was gleeful for the chance to launch a massive overland attack to punish the ungrateful Americans—and possibly end the war. Cockburn shared none of Cochrane's ambivalence about a specific battle strategy; he already had determined that the object of their attention should be Washington, D.C.

Despite its small population and relative insignificance as a military center, Cockburn believed a successful British effort to take the nation's capital would shatter the U.S. psyche and lead to the dismantling of Madison's government. Moreover, the city was so lightly defended that it would likely surrender en masse at the first sight of redcoats marching on Pennsylvania Avenue.[201]

He devised a plan to land troops at the out-of-the-way port town of Benedict, Maryland on the Patuxent River, broaching the topic with Cochrane as far back as mid-July.

> *It is I am informed only 44 or 45 Miles from Washington and there is a high Road between the two places which tho' hilly is good…I therefore most firmly believe that within forty eight Hours after the Arrival in the Patuxent…the City of Washington might be possessed without Difficulty or Opposition of any kind.*[202]

It took all of Cockburn's persuasive skills in a tense face-to-face meeting with Cochrane, but the vice admiral finally signed off on the plan. Cockburn would lead a small fleet of boats and barges up the Patuxent on August 19 in search of Joshua Barney's American flotilla, which had hectored the British all summer. At the same time Ross and about forty-five hundred red-coated ground troops would go ashore at Benedict and await instructions.

Cockburn's sailors succeeded in cornering Barney at Pig Point along the Patuxent on August 22, but the clever U.S. commander blew up his own barges before they could be captured, allowing his men to escape to the countryside. Nonetheless, with Barney's vaunted fleet eliminated, Cockburn and Ross could reunite at Upper Marlboro and march on the capital.[203]

American militia forces scrambled to assemble under the command of U.S. Army General William Winder, a veteran of the war in Canada but another indecisive and ineffectual leader. Haunted by rumors of British activity, Winder issued a series of contradictory orders before forming his men at the town of Bladensburg, about six miles from the capital. Volunteers poured in from across the District of Columbia, including a Georgetown attorney named Francis Scott Key, who served as a civilian aide to a local militia commander, and who, at one point, helped to place some troops, despite the lack of any military training or experience. (An annoyed Winder later wrote in his battle report that, "I met several gentlemen, and, among them…Mr. Francis Key, of Georgetown, who informed me that he had thought that the troops coming from the city could be most advantageously posted on the right and left of the road near that point.") By early afternoon on August 24, with British bayonets now visible and a showdown looming, Winder's makeshift force numbered about fifty-five hundred.[204]

Despite the U.S. advantage in manpower, what happened next was a predictable rout. Veteran British troops, some of the most battle-tested soldiers in the world—and bolstered by a determined group of two hundred escaped slaves in the Colonial Marines—charged forward and scattered the American defenders, many of whom had never served in combat. (The Colonial Marines were part of the Light Brigade and suffered one killed and three wounded in the attack.) Barney and his flotillamen made a particularly gallant stand, and U.S. artillery pounded away with a fury that surprised the British, but Winder saw his ranks collapsing all around and ordered a general retreat.[205] "The contest," he conceded, "was not as obstinately maintained as could have been desired."[206] One of the novice soldiers was so unprepared for battle that he ran away to safety in a pair of dancing pumps. Key would later describe the rearward movement of U.S. troops as the "memorable flight from Bladensburg," but it became known to history by a more sinister and mocking nickname: the "Bladensburg Races."[207]

And yet this was only the start of one of the bleakest days in American military history. Ross and Cockburn allowed for a two-hour rest while troops collected prisoners and tended to the wounded, but at 6 p.m. the British began their short, historic march to Washington.[208] The Colonial Marines were again among the lead units, having been accorded "the honor of entering the capital as conquerors."[209] Ross and his men faced only a few potshots and promptly burned both of the houses that shielded the attackers. After that, Cockburn wrote, "the Town submitted without further resistance."[210]

The next course of action was debated only briefly. "Admiral Cockburn would have burnt the whole [city,]" a soldier wrote, "but Ross would only consent to the burning of the public buildings."[211] The more gentlemanly Ross knew the main British goal already had been achieved, but he wasn't above exacting revenge for U.S. atrocities in Canada. During a largely disastrous campaign north of the border in 1813, rampaging U.S. troops had burned the cities of York (where Toronto stands today) and Newark (now Niagara-on-the-Lake, Ontario). In an official proclamation in early 1814, General Prevost declared that "it became a matter of imperious duty to retaliate on America the miseries which the unfortunate inhabitants of Newark had been made to suffer." Almost as an afterthought, he added "that this departure from the established uses of war had originated with America herself, and that to her alone are justly chargeable all the awful and unhappy consequences which have hitherto flowed and are likely to result from it."[212]

The obvious targets were now the Capitol building and the White House, which had been abandoned and were wholly undefended. First in line was the Capitol, where British soldier-arsonists set fires with public documents and fired rockets into various chambers, including those housing the Supreme Court, the Senate, and the Library of Congress. Watching from afar, a U.S. naval officer called it a "sight so repugnant to my feelings, so dishonourable; so degrading to the American Character, and at the Same time, so Awful."[213]

Next up was the White House, where Madison's wife, Dolley, an elegant but stubborn hostess, had planned a business-as-usual dinner that afternoon. Tables had been set and meals prepared before everyone fled in horror. (Mrs. Madison was among the last to leave, lingering behind to help with the packing of various national valuables, including a legendary portrait of George Washington.) Exhausted British troops gleefully devoured the food and wine while an ebullient Ross proposed a toast: "Peace with America—war with Madison!" Some of the officers raced to collect souvenirs, including pictures, books, ornamental figures, and the U.S. president's small medicine chest.[214]

Painting of the White House after it was burned by the British army in August 1814, three weeks before the battle at Fort McHenry. *(Wikimedia Commons, by George Munger)*

It was not long before the White House also was put to the torch. Ravenous soldiers piled furniture in the middle of rooms and drenched bedding with lamp oil, eager to finish the destruction of American grandeur. "I shall never forget the destructive majesty of the flames as the torches were applied to beds, curtains, etc.," a British observer wrote. "Our sailors were artists at the work." For good measure, and to complete the ruination of government property, Cockburn and Ross also torched the U.S. Treasury building before ordering the weary troops to bed down for the night.[215]

A torrential storm, sometimes described as a hurricane, hammered the capital city early on the morning of August 25, adding a surreal backdrop to the devastation. Flashes of lightning magnified flames still bursting from government buildings. When the worst of the storm had passed, British troops roamed the streets to rekindle old fires as a final act of degradation. "I need scarcely observe that the consternation of the inhabitants was complete," one wrote, "and that to them this was a night of total terror."[216]

Ross agreed, believing the shocking news of Washington in flames might finally bring America to its knees. "They feel strongly the disgrace of having their capital taken by a handful of men," he wrote in a letter to his wife, "and blame very generally a government which went to war without the means or abilities to carry it on."

In an official report to the British high command filed three days later, Cockburn boasted that "I do not believe a Vestage of Public Property, or a Store of any kind which could be converted to the use of the government, escaped Destruction.

> *This general Devastation being completed during the day of the 25th, we marched again at Nine that night on our Return by Bladensburg to upper Marlborough.*[217]

Forty miles away in Baltimore, George Armistead and a panicked citizenry heard the reports and feared the worst.

The eerie glow of fires in Washington had been visible at Fort McHenry, where a soldier wrote that "as the moon went down, the luster became more clear and defined, rising and falling on the horizon like fitful coruscations of the Aurora Borealis."[218] Rumors swirled that the vengeful British would target Baltimore at first light. "All is now confusion and consternation here," a newspaper reported, "everybody moving that can get off, under the full expectation that the enemy will be here tomorrow night."[219] One local survivor from Bladensburg added to the hysteria as he careened home, allowing that "we expect every instant to hear that they have taken up the line of march for this place and if they do we are gone."[220]

Armistead had seen to it that preparations for just such a moment were in place since the summer of 1813. At the suggestion of the army's chief engineer, he had arranged for troops to dig a five-foot moat for infantry around the fort in addition to building new artillery platforms and at least three new hot shot furnaces. He'd also overseen the placement of sixty heavy ordnance guns to pound any potential attacking force.[221]

The next step was to streamline the leadership structure as battle approached. Baltimore was part of the country's Tenth Military District, and therefore under the overall command of William Winder, but senior leaders here wanted no part of Winder's indecisiveness after his desultory performance at Bladensburg. Three men—Armistead, Maryland militia commander John Stricker, and Captain Oliver Perry—approached the city's Committee of Vigilance and Safety on August 25 to ask that Sam Smith of the Baltimore militia be placed in charge. It was a bold request, given Winder's status as a professional army officer, but the nervous committee soon agreed. After receiving endorsements from Baltimore's mayor and Maryland's governor, Smith was called into federal service and took command of all troops pouring into the city.[222]

Before his demotion, however, Winder had made at least one contribution to Baltimore's defenses. Noting that there had been very little ammunition "of any description" prepared for the coming battle, he sought out Armistead to solve the problem. "I beg you will therefore apply all the force under your control to make musket cartridges & fixed ammunition," Winder said. "You will also make some for [artillery rounds]of both kinds, round and grape."[223] It was estimated that the five thousand Baltimore militia troops would require sixty-four rounds apiece, placing "a demand on you of 320,000 cartridges"—an extraordinary number—but Armistead was nonplussed by the assignment. "Old soldiers must obey orders," the thirty-four-year-old major said.[224]

The burning of Washington changed the tempo of preparations and raised fears of an immediate attack. Indeed, had Ross's infantry troops driven directly toward Baltimore from Upper Marlborough on August 26, they may have captured the city in a matter of days.

Smith and Armistead were not yet ready. But Cochrane delayed again, fearful of disease from the dreaded Chesapeake "sickly season" and still hopeful of more reinforcements from back home. He planned to sail his fleet up the coast to Rhode Island for at least the next two months.

Writing to the first lord of the admiralty on September 3, Cochrane said, "I trust [His Majesty's] Ministers will place a further reliance on my recommendation & at least double our force so as we may be able to act with vigour the moment the sickly season is over, say the 5th of Novr…"

> *"As Septr. is a fatal month even for the Inhabitants of Virginia & more so for Strangers, As soon is the Army is all reembarked I mean to proceed Northward & if possible try to surprize Rhode Island, where we will quarter…About the close of October we will move Southward…if the reinforcements arrive I propose an attack upon Baltimore the most democratic town & I believe the richest in the Country.*"[225]

It took a set of peculiar astrological conditions to intervene and change the course of U.S. history.

Cochrane reversed his travel plans on September 7, deciding that "the approaching Equinoxial new Moon" made it "unsafe to proceed immediately out of the Chesapeake."[226] He knew that those conditions would produce the highest tides and strongest tidal currents of the year, creating treacherous conditions for any ships trying to leave the bay.[227] The safest bet was to turn around and wait several weeks near Baltimore before heading off to Rhode Island. Under the circumstances, he and Ross "resolved to occupy the intermediate time to advantage, by making a demonstration on the City of Baltimore; which might be converted into a real attack should circumstances appear to justify it."[228]

Back at Fort McHenry, Major Armistead grew increasingly worried about the safety of his family. Still believing the British might attack at any moment, and unaware of Cochrane's frenetic maneuvering up and down the bay, he decided to send his pregnant wife, Louisa, and one-year-old daughter, Mary, sixty miles away to a little-known farming community in south central Pennsylvania. The

Armistead ladies arrived in Gettysburg sometime before September 7, likely staying at the York Street dwelling of Mrs. Margaret Stewart, whose late husband, William, had owned a grain storage business in Baltimore (the precise connection between the two families is unknown, but the Baltimore business ties are intriguing).[229] In a letter written early on September 10 and addressed to Louisa in "Gettysburgh," George spoke longingly of "my sweet Mary...our dear Mary" and asked his wife to "present my respects to Mrs. Stewart."[230] He also acknowledged Mrs. Armistead's dismay at being sent away on such short notice to a strange location, especially with no battle being fought.

> *"My Dear Louisa's letter of the 7th I have just read. I am really sorry to find you so dissatisfied. I wish to God you had not been compeld to leave Baltimore but you now must be contented as it is impossible from your present situation to attempt a return...We cannot correctly ascertain what [British] intentions are but should they depart from the Bay, I will be with you immediately so be not alarm'd if I should pop in on you."*[231]

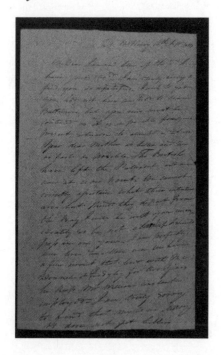

George Armistead corresponded with his wife, Louisa, in Gettysburg, Pennsylvania, where he sent her for safety just days before the battle. *(Photos by Colleen McMillan, taken at the former Maryland Historical Society, currently the Maryland Center for History and Culture)*

Later that same day, the outlook changed drastically. U.S. scouts posted along the coast spotted dozens of British ships heading menacingly toward the mouth of the Patapsco with little doubt that the rest of the fleet was on the way. At Fort McHenry, Major Armistead received reports that they were "Ships of the line, heavy Frigates and Bomb vessels, amounting in the whole to [at least] 30 Sail… with every indication of an attempt on the City of Baltimore."[232] One local militia private racing to his post found the fort in a state of preparatory frenzy, with "matches burning, the furnaces heated and vomiting red shot…and every thing ready for a gallant defense."[233]

Armistead wouldn't be making a side trip to Gettysburg after all.

CHAPTER FIVE
A Most Gallant Defense

British troops were sailing toward Baltimore with the renewed vigor of successful foreign invaders when they were intercepted on September 7 by, of all things, an American truce ship.

Led by attorney Francis Scott Key, the U.S. mission sought the release of a civilian prisoner, Dr. William Beanes, who had been seized from his estate in Upper Marlboro, Maryland on August 28.[234]

The case became an unexpected pivot point in U.S. history. Back on August 22, just as the British began their drive to Bladensburg, Beanes welcomed Major General Robert Ross and other officers under a flag of truce, offering his home as their headquarters and providing food, wine, and other amenities. Five days later, in the aftermath of battle, he violated their trust by capturing several British stragglers on his property. Ross was apoplectic at the turnabout. He made manic inquiries, decided that the sixty-five-year-old Beanes had "acted hostilely" toward his soldiers, and sent a detachment to seize him in the middle of the night. He was no doubt pleased to hear that the old man had been handled roughly by his captors.[235]

One British officer recalled that "the inhabitants of that village, at the instigation of a medical practitioner called Bean *(sic)*, had risen in arms as soon as we were departed; and falling upon such individuals as strayed from the column, put some of them to death and made others prisoners." Offended British troops, he said, "pulled the doctor out of his bed (for it was early in the morning) and compelled

him, by a threat of instant death, to liberate his prisoners, and…
brought him in triumph to the camp."[236]

Beanes's friends were horrified by the news, fretting he would be
sent to Canadian territory in Halifax, never to see his family again.
They recruited Key, a fellow Marylander and friend of one of Beanes's
close associates, to negotiate a release. Using connections in Washington, Key sought presidential approval for the mission and was
assigned by Madison to work in tandem with John S. Skinner, the
American prisoner-of-war agent who was well-acquainted with the
British, especially Rear Admiral George Cockburn.[237] Key described
it in a September 2 letter to his mother after returning briefly to
Georgetown to pack his belongings.

> …*I am going in the morning to Balt. to proceed in a
> flag-vessel to Genl Ross. Old Dr. Beanes of Marlbro'
> is taken prisoner by the Enemy, who threaten to carry
> him off. Some of his friends have urged me to apply for
> a flag [of truce]& go & try to procure his release. I hope
> to return in about 8 or 10 days, tho' it is uncertain, as
> I do not know where to find the fleet…*[238]

Key and Skinner received their formal instructions from General
John Mason, the U.S. commissary general of prisoners. Mason wrote
a letter claiming that Beanes had been "taken from his bed, in the
midst of his family and hurried off almost with no clothes," and
called it a "departure from the known usages of civilized warfare."[239]
But if playing on Ross's better nature wouldn't work—and they knew
it might not—they also had a receipt for a future prisoner exchange
to secure the doctor's release.

As a final good-faith gesture, Key collected packets of letters
from wounded British prisoners at Bladensburg and other sites,
expressing thanks for humane treatment by American doctors.[240]

The two men left Baltimore on Monday, September 5 aboard
a sixty-foot sloop (probably the *President*, although that has never
been confirmed) and entered the Chesapeake Bay. Where they might
find the Royal Navy was anyone's guess, but Vice Admiral Alexander
Cochrane's decision to turn back toward the city brought the British
within range sooner than expected. It allowed Key and Skinner to
hail them under a flag of truce near the mouth of the Potomac River

two days later. At precisely 2:10 p.m. on Wednesday, September 7, according to the log of Cochrane's flagship, *Tonnant*, a small boat was sent to bring the Americans aboard.[241]

Skinner soon realized their timing could not have been worse. Cockburn had been his best and most accommodating British contact during the war, but the admiral was clearly preoccupied with preparations for an "expedition against Baltimore" and had no time for bureaucratic niceties.[242] When a stiffly formal mid-afternoon meeting between the two sides failed to make any progress, Skinner gambled by pulling Ross aside for a one-on-one chat, delivering the letters Key had gathered from Ross's wounded soldiers. Only then, after much soul-searching, did the defiant general soften.[243]

Ross said he believed that Beanes deserved "more punishment" but felt "bound to make a return for the kindness which had been shown to his wounded officers…and upon that ground, and that only, he would release him."[244]

Against all odds, Key and Skinner had succeeded.

The men and their crew were elated, rejoicing in the moment, surrounding and hugging Dr. Beanes—that is, until Key inquired about a return to Baltimore. He was told "that neither he, nor anyone else, would be permitted to leave the fleet for some days; and must be detained until the attack on Baltimore, which was then about to made, was over."[245] The Americans were transferred under guard to two different ships, and eventually back to their own truce ship, as the entire fleet headed up the bay. Skinner waited until the eve of battle on September 11 before approaching Cochrane to renew their request. "Ah, Mr. Skinner," the admiral responded, "after discussing so freely as we have done in your presence our purposes and plans, you could hardly expect us to let you go on shore now in advance of us."[246]

Key, Beanes, and Skinner would have to watch from a distance.

A sneering hodgepodge of British foot soldiers, sailors, and marines sailed into the Patapsco River on Saturday, September 10 and headed toward Baltimore, intent on destruction. For all his indecisiveness, Cochrane believed that the Americans, "like Spaniels, must be treated with great severity before you ever make them tractable," and he foresaw a blistering land-sea attack that would eviscerate Baltimore and bring Mr. Madison to his knees.[247] About forty-seven hundred troops under the joint command of Ross and Cockburn would land on a narrow strip of land at North Point on Monday, September 12, overrunning the U.S. militia and driving ten miles to the city. Cochrane would then unleash the navy's bomb ships at Fort McHenry, pounding it into submission before swarming through the streets and burning the public buildings.[248]

As British troops rowed toward the shore in the wee hours of Monday morning, another naval officer, Rear Admiral Edward Codrington, captured the emotions in a letter to his wife:

> *The work of destruction is now about to begin, and there will probably be many broken heads tonight. I do not like to contemplate scenes of blood and destruction; but my heart is deeply interested in the coercion of these Baltimore heroes, who are perhaps the most inveterate against us of all the Yankees.*[249]

U.S. General Sam Smith had assumed correctly that the British would launch their ground attack from North Point. Accordingly, he amassed a force of more than ten thousand men at Hampstead Hill, on the eastern approach to the city, and sent out his best militia unit, the thirty-two-hundred-man City Brigade under General John Stricker, to harass the redcoats as they drew near. Stricker, a hard-nosed veteran of the Revolutionary War, was determined above all else to avoid a Bladensburg-type collapse in his hometown. His plan here was to meet the British halfway and at least stall their advance while the rest of the army dug in behind him in a series of defensive lines.[250]

Ross and Cockburn unloaded at North Point and started their long trek to Baltimore before all the troops had come ashore, anxious to be in position for a full assault against the city by Tuesday. Several miles into the march they paused for breakfast at a farm owned by local citizen Robert Gorsuch, who had no choice but to serve up a feast of eggs, meat, and country butter.[251] Stricker, curious at the delay, dispatched two hundred and fifty men to sneak ahead and observe the British, ascertain their immediate intentions, and take a few potshots. Fearing a nighttime bayonet attack that would have spooked his volunteer militia, he wanted the battle started now, out in the open, with many hours of daylight left.[252]

But Ross wanted action, too. His advance party left the Gorsuch place shortly after noon and was well in front of the main body when it stumbled into the probing American force. Impatient as he was—Ross had said he would "eat in Baltimore tonight, or in hell"—he feared that his troops had moved too far forward and risked losing touch with the rest of the army.[253] Brave to the point of recklessness, Ross rode out to check on sounds of gunfire and foolishly made himself an inviting target. History hung in the balance as three American riflemen took aim.[254]

A shot smashed into Ross's right arm. He slumped in the saddle, swaying slowly from his horse, and was cradled to the ground gently by several petrified aides. The bullet from an unknown (and, centuries later, still unidentified) marksman had pierced his chest, likely puncturing a lung and breaking some ribs. Realizing before anyone that the wound was mortal, wanting to formally pass on command of British ground troops, a military man to the end, Ross called immediately for his top subordinate, Colonel Arthur Brooke[255]—but the impact of his death on the invasion plan was incalculable.

Brooke was a skilled, steady, competent leader who had served well in Europe and Africa, but he had none of Ross's battlefield *elan*, and, more to the point, had not been privy to high-level strategy sessions with Cochrane and Cockburn.[256] Some of the men barely knew him. Thrust into command with no time to prepare, he now was responsible for the most important land-based attack of the War of 1812. "Imagine if Eisenhower had been shot the day before D-Day," one historian said to put it in perspective for a modern audience. "That's really what happened here."[257] But British troops, sullen at the loss of their general, many weeping, still moved forward in good order, and it is to Brooke's everlasting credit that he had them in position to attack Stricker's brigade by mid-afternoon.

The Battle of North Point erupted with a fury at 3 p.m. Veteran British regiments were again bolstered by the presence of a small group of Colonial Marines, the escaped U.S. slaves fighting for their freedom.[258] Leadership change or not, Brooke and Cockburn expected another mismatch with militia, a virtual repeat of the Bladensburg Races, but Stricker's volunteer infantry held firm and American artillery thundered away, opening gaping holes in the lines, stunning the British.[259] The fire of the Baltimore troops was "very active and uncommonly certain," wrote the correspondent for the local *Niles Weekly Register*. "The men took deliberate aim, and the carnage was great—the 'invincibles' dodging to the ground, and crawling in a bending posture, to avoid the militia—the 'yeomen' they were taught so much to despise."[260] Even Brooke conceded that the fire "was so destructive…and thinning our ranks so much."[261]

Bloodied unexpectedly, the great British army reformed and resumed its attack with even more determination. "Napoleon has affirmed that he never witnessed anything more terrific than the fire of a British line of infantry," said Lieutenant George Gleig of the Light Brigade (later adding that "the ex-emperor was perfectly correct").[262] Indeed, it was only a matter of time before the invaders gained an advantage, pushing the Americans back, inflicting casualties—but there was none of the chaotic retreat that had marked the disaster at Bladensburg. Stricker's men fell back in reasonably good fashion, retaining their cohesiveness as fighting units until they reached the safety of the next defensive line.[263] "They retired in better order than could have been expected under a galling fire," Niles wrote, "and they retired reluctantly at the repeated command of their officers."[264] There was, in fact, no panicked race to the rear.

The British had won a tactical victory, seizing valuable territory on the bloody slog from North Point, but they still had several miles to go when Brooke called off the attack to let his troops recover and rest. "The day now being considerably advanced," Gleig wrote, "and the troops somewhat fatigued by their exertions, our new leader determined to halt for the night on the field which he had won."[265] There was little doubt, however, that the Americans had fought tenaciously and frustrated the redcoats with a brilliant defensive strategy. Brooke had been stymied on his first day in command; he would not be in position to attack Baltimore at first light on Tuesday, which was the original plan; and more British blood would have to be spilled just to reach the city limits.

The focus now shifted to Fort McHenry, at the tip of the inner harbor, where Cochrane and the bomb ships would try to batter

Major Armistead into submission with a withering frontal assault. Control of the fort meant control of the city and harbor, regardless of what happened in the ground war to the east. Late on the afternoon of Monday, September 12, just as Brooke broke off his attack, Cochrane announced his intentions to the new army commander in a note that was superb in its simplicity: "At daylight, we shall place the bombs and begin to bombard the fort."[266]

Armistead had foolishly let his guard down two days earlier, allowing eighty militia volunteers under Judge Joseph Nicholson to march home from Fort McHenry for a breather, but he quickly saw the error of his ways.[267]

As darkness fell on September 10, with the Royal Navy racing up the Patapsco, Armistead dashed off a note ordering Nicholson to "return with your company without a moment's notice—the British are in sight!"[268]

The fort soon became a swirl of frenzied activity. By mid-day on September 12, sounds of gunfire from North Point added a surreal backdrop to last-minute defensive preparations. Armistead had one thousand men at his disposal, including six hundred regular infantry troops posted in the dry moat around the fort, ready to meet the enemy head on if it should come to that. More than three hundred others were assigned to work McHenry's big guns. Flotillamen, messengers, medics, and musicians scurried about. Small units of gunners also settled in at the shore batteries—Fort Covington, Battery Babcock, and Lazaretto Point—hoping to catch the British in a crossfire.[269]

In one final defensive maneuver, the Americans began sinking merchant ships and barges across the Northwest Branch of the Patapsco, clogging the entrance to the inner harbor.[270]

Armistead was certain an attack was coming soon. At 4:30 p.m., he informed General Smith that "from the number of barges and the known situation of the enemy, I have not a doubt but that an assault will be made this night upon the fort."[271] Concerned about British deception after nightfall, he even worked out a series of code words with the commander at Lazaretto Point (the signal would be "William," the answer "Eutaw").[272] But Admiral Cochrane had a different idea, delaying any action until the following morning, insisting he needed more time to arrange the sixteen ships in his attacking force.

Crucial to the operation were five inelegant, stubby "bomb ships"—fearsome vessels capable of launching two-hundred-pound cast-iron bombs that could explode on impact, or in mid-air, depending on the length of the fuse. The mighty British Navy had only eight such ships in its worldwide arsenal, and five of them were now anchored in the Patapsco off Baltimore harbor.[273] The "bombs," as they were known, had been arrayed at sunrise by Cochrane "in elegant order...forming a half-circle" two and a half miles from the fort.[274] Meticulous British record-keeping shows that it was 6:30 a.m. on Tuesday, September 13 when the lead ship, *Volcano*, fired the first shots of the naval Battle of Baltimore.[275]

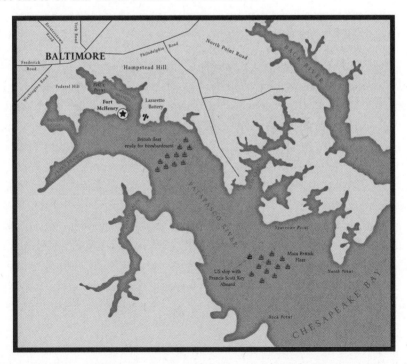

The Battle of Baltimore took place here from September 12-14. British soldiers landed at North Point (lower right) on September 12 and started their drive toward the city. The British Navy began a twenty-five-hour attack against Fort McHenry on the morning of September 13. Francis Scott Key's "truce" ship may have been moved closer to the British bomb ships during at least part of the battle. *(Courtesy of National Park Service and Rick Deckard)*

They fell short, causing consternation among the British fleet. Eager to get at the Americans, the crews of the bomb ships advanced to within a mile and a half, accompanied by the frigate *Cockchafer*, which fired a cheeky broadside at Fort McHenry's walls. *Volcano* and the four other bombs soon joined the assault.[276] But Cochrane, in his zeal to win the contest early, had gambled by moving Britain's most valuable naval vessels to within range of the U.S. guns, virtually negating an advantage in firepower.

Armistead countered immediately. As Private Isaac Munroe described it,

> *Major Armistead mounted the parapet and ordered a battery of 24 pounders to be opened upon them and immediately after, a battery of [36-pounders] followed, and then the whole Fort let drive at them. We could see the shot strike the frigates in several instances, when every heart was gladdened, and we gave three cheers, the music playing Yankee Doodle.*[277]

Armistead knew the maximum range of his artillery here was only a mile and a half. Several months earlier he had requested bigger guns for such a situation but was turned down by the secretary of war.[278] Cochrane discerned the U.S. weakness and adapted quickly, pushing the five bomb ships to a safe distance two miles from the fort, where they could pound away at the Americans unchallenged. *Meteor, Terror, Aetna* and *Devastation* all hurled massive exploding shells from their ten and thirteen-inch mortars. *Volcano* also fired a unique projectile called the carcass, a hollow cast iron shell filled with combustible materials and designed to set large buildings on fire.[279] The rocket ship *Erebus* brought an additional inventory of flame-trailing missiles known as Congreve rockets, which, while notoriously inaccurate, lit up the sky and sowed fear in the hearts of an awestruck enemy.[280]

Armistead urged his men to squeeze more distance out of their guns by raising the barrels to full elevation, but even he knew those efforts were futile and largely symbolic.[281] American shells splashed well short of their marks, bringing hoots of derision and other taunts from British sailors. The frustrated major could do little to respond "to the incessant and well directed Bombardment" than to have his troops lob periodic shots at random, if only to show the public—and the British themselves—that the fort had not capitulated. As Armistead put it later,

> *We immediately opened Our Batteries...but unfortunately our Shot and Shells all fell considerably Short of him; this was to me a most distressing circumstance as it left Us exposed to a constant and tremendous Shower of Shells without the most remote possibility of our doing him the slightest injury. It affords me the highest gratification to State, that although We were left thus exposed, and thus inactive, not a Man Shrunk from the conflict.*[282]

Judge Nicholson, from his perspective with one of the batteries, had a harsher assessment of the morning's action: "We were like pigeons tied by the legs to be shot at."[283]

Baltimore citizens watching the spectacle from rooftops of downtown buildings strained to see the results, fearing the worst. Out on the water, Key, Beanes, and Skinner paced the deck of their own truce ship, nervous and fretting, guarded by British sailors with no better insight than their own.[284] "The attack on Fort McHenry was terribly grand and magnificent," the *Niles Weekly Register* reported. "Four or five bombs were frequently in the air at a time, and, making a double explosion, with the noise of the *foolish* rockets and the firings of the fort, Lazaretto and our barges, created a horrible clatter."[285]

But the paper also noted with hometown bravado that "Armistead, the gallant commander, and his brave garrison fired occasionally to let the enemy know the place was not given up!"[286]

Cochrane, facing the Americans in battle for the first time and hoping to make quick work of the fort, was stunned by the level of obstinance. He knew that only a few weeks earlier, during a British expedition up the Potomac, U.S. troops had fled without firing a shot from Fort Washington near Mount Vernon.[287] As Skinner overheard it, the admiral expected to silence McHenry quickly and turn his guns on Hampstead Hill, allowing his army to advance "to a position from which the town might be laid under contribution or burnt."[288] But despite the one-sided naval barrage to open the battle, the fort held firm and casualties were light, scuttling the original plan. This would take longer than expected.

At 9:30 a.m., barely three hours after the first shot from *Volcano*, Cochrane sent a note to Cockburn and Brooke informing them that it would be "impossible for the Ships to render you any assistance."[289]

Stubborn resistance from Armistead's makeshift force wasn't the only challenge facing Cochrane that morning. Fire from the British fleet had been woefully ineffective, spewing terror and rattling eardrums but doing surprisingly little damage to the fort or its occupants. Fuses were timed incorrectly. *Niles* reported that each time one of the massive bomb ships fired, "they were forced two feet into the water by the force" of the discharge, creating a constant churn in the water, vessels bobbing up and down.[290] The wind was picking up and conditions became more perilous as a nor'easter blew in toward Baltimore.[291] Aiming the shells was difficult.

Another obstacle was the series of merchant ships sunk by the Americans to block the entrance to the inner harbor—making an alternative attack impossible.[292]

But the bombs kept coming, "the hissing rockets and fiery shells…threatening destruction as they fell," according to a British midshipman.[293] Armistead reported that "a large proportion burst over Us, throwing their fragments among us" although "many passed over."[294] By noon, according to its log book, *Volcano* alone had fired seventy-three projectiles.[295] Cochrane found no reason to stop, especially with minimal return fire coming from the Americans, and Private Munroe of the Baltimore militia lamented that they were "reduced to…facing by far the most tremendous bombardment ever known."[296]

A VIEW of the BOMBARDMENT of Fort McHenry.

Contemporary painting of British bomb ships attacking Fort McHenry in September 1814. *(Wikimedia Commons)*

The battle almost ended at one point in the afternoon when a British shell ripped violently through the roof of the fort's powder magazine (which, as only Armistead knew until then, was *not* bomb-proof).[297] It is not a stretch to say that the history of the United States changed when the shell did not explode, because three hundred powder barrels had been stacked in three neat tiers inside the magazine's brick walls. "This was the main powder magazine for the defense of Baltimore itself," explained Scott Sheads, long-time historian at the Fort McHenry National Monument and Historic Shrine. "If this goes, the entire fort will go. If the fort goes, the city may very well fall."[298] But the fuse was doused, disaster somehow averted. The powder never exploded. Armistead ordered the men to remove the barrels and place them at intervals behind the fort's rear walls, an assignment that was carried out with life-saving swiftness and verve.[299]

At 2 p.m., the long-expected storm whipped in from the northeast with "heavy showers of rain" soaking the troops and reducing visibility.[300] It was at about this time that another British shell screamed over the ramparts, striking the southwest bastion where Judge Nicholson's fencibles were posted. The first major direct hit of the battle killed Lieutenant Levi Claggett, wounded four other men nearby and spun their twenty-four-pounder gun off its carriage, breaking a wheel. Momentarily, another bomb burst overhead, the British having finally found the range after eight hours, and Munroe was standing just inches away when a piece of shrapnel "the size of dollar, two inches thick" killed Sergeant John Clemm.[301]

American troops rushed to assist their injured comrades and repair the damaged gun, touching off a flurry of activity that was misinterpreted by the British. "The bustle necessarily produced in removing the Wounded and remounting the Gun probably induced the Enemy to suspect that We were in a state of confusion," Armistead said.[302] Admiral Cochrane indeed sensed a moment of U.S. weakness, ordering his ships to move forward within a mile of the shore and finish the destruction of Fort McHenry.[303] With this, Armistead's eyes widened.

"I immediately ordered a fire to be opened," he said, "which was obeyed with alacrity through the Whole garrison."[304]

"The balls now flew like hail stones," *Niles* reported.[305]

It was during this firefight at mid-afternoon, with rain teeming down and wind swirling, that Armistead's gunners gained a measure of revenge after so many long hours of forced restraint. *Devastation*, now an inviting target, sprung a small leak when a U.S. cannon shot struck her port bow. *Volcano* took five straight hits and began to rock briefly from side to side (fitting, perhaps, for the ship that had started the onslaught at daylight).[306] Cochrane, realizing his mistake, ordered the fleet back to its original position beyond the range of American firepower. "In half an hour those intruders again sheltered themselves by withdrawing beyond our reach," Armistead sneered. "We gave three Cheers and again ceased firing."[307]

Both sides continued to be puzzled by silence to the east, where a British infantry attack on U.S. forces at Hampstead Hill was expected since at least mid-day.

In his first full day on the job, Colonel Arthur Brooke had indeed wanted "to proceed at about twelve or one to work our destruction,"

TOM McMILLAN

but an early morning survey of the strong U.S. position gave him pause.[308] With maybe fifteen thousand Americans dug in on the hill, fortified by earthworks and glowering artillery, Brooke thought his outnumbered army would need support from Cochrane's big naval guns to have any chance of success.[309] "[Y]our fire I should think on the Town would be of infinite service to us," he wrote in a hopeful note to the vice admiral.[310]

That wasn't possible. Cochrane made his position clear in the reply he sent at 9:30 a.m., but British communications this day were painfully slow and inefficient.[311] Couriers had to travel across the choppy river in a rainstorm, then pick their way through unfamiliar terrain, including soggy woods—all while potentially under fire, and in danger of capture. It took long hours. Cochrane's note did not arrive until 8 p.m., when darkness fell and Brooke had already adjusted his plans.[312]

During the frustrating period of daylight silence, Brooke determined that his best hope was a nighttime attack, coming well after midnight, when the U.S. would least expect it (and when its advantage in artillery would be negated). The idea was to push forward at 2 a.m., ideally with support from the bomb ships and other guns.[313]

But the tone of Cochrane's note changed everything. "This was a blow not easy to explain," Brooke said.[314] Wracked by indecision on whether to proceed anyway, the jittery colonel called a council of war among his senior leaders and heard arguments on both sides of the debate before deciding to call off the infantry attack. "I had made all my arrangements for attacking the enemy…but from the situation I was placed in [the council] advised I should Retire," he wrote in a final message to the admiral. "I have therefore ordered the Retreat to take place to Morrow morning."[315]

Given the state of rampant British confusion that night, it is somehow fitting that Brooke's note never made it to Cochrane on time. The navy was still not sure whether the army would attack. Choosing to err on the side of caution in the growing darkness, Cochrane arranged for a small fleet of boats to stage a diversion at 1 a.m. on the Ferry Branch of the Patapsco, just to the west of Fort McHenry, creating chaos for the American defenders.[316] No one had a clue what might happen next.

On the water facing Fort McHenry, the British bomb ships pulled back to a safer distance and resumed their fire at 3 p.m., albeit "more furiously than before."[317] The rain fell in sheets and the wind blew wildly, frustrating gunners, playing havoc with fuses. From several miles away, thirty-five-year-old Francis Scott Key could still make out a waterlogged U.S. flag flying brazenly from a pole on the McHenry grounds. Given the conditions, it would have been the smaller (seventeen by twenty-five feet) storm flag that Mrs. Pickersgill had sewn as part of Armistead's order the previous summer, rather than the majestic (thirty by forty-two feet) garrison flag. "The garrison flag was too big to fly in such a raging storm," author Steve Vogel wrote in his book, *Through the Perilous Fight*. "The weight of such a large, sopping-wet wool flag might snap the flagpole."[318] Fort McHenry historian Scott Sheads believes that the garrison flag had been raised that morning, as U.S. Army regulations required, and endured at least part of the battle but was replaced by the storm flag when inclement weather blew in.[319]

Key wouldn't have made the distinction anyway. A friend who spoke to him only days after the battle wrote that Key, Beanes, and Skinner "thought themselves fortunate in being anchored in a position which enabled them to see distinctly the flag of Fort McHenry from the deck of the vessel."[320] The sight of the Stars and Stripes thrilled him, regardless of size, especially after nine hours of relentless British bombing, but as day turned to night and the onslaught continued, he had to wonder if his fellow Marylanders could hold on through the darkness. From about 9 p.m., only glare from the rockets or bursts from the bombs—or lightning from the storm—could enable him to catch a glimpse of the besieged fort.

British Midshipman Robert Barrett, aboard HMS *Hebrus* in the Patapsco, confirmed as much when he described what happened next:

> *All this night the bombardment continued with unabated vigor…the fiery shells glittered in the air… whilst to add solemnity to this scene of devastation, the rain fell in torrents—the thunder broke in mighty*

*peals after each successive flash of lightening that for
a moment illuminated the surrounding darkness.
This was the period, fast and approaching midnight,
selected for the boats of the squadron to make a diversion in favour of our army.*[321]

Still unsure whether ground troops would attack Hampstead
Hill at 2 a.m., Cochrane ordered Captain Charles Napier to take a
mishmash fleet of twenty vessels up the Ferry Branch of the Patapsco, on the west side of the fort, with the "intention of drawing
the Notice of the Enemy."[322] Napier would have barges, launches,
gigs, and at least one rocket boat at his disposal.[323] The plan was
to maneuver around the bomb ship *Meteor* and use the western
shoreline as a guide, rowing with muffled oars until they passed Fort
McHenry and came within range of the smaller U.S. batteries. There
they were to "remain perfectly Quiet" until 1 a.m., when Cochrane
advised "the Bombs will open upon the Fort and Sky Rockets will be
Thrown up"—creating a diversion for the diversion.[324]

It was an effective strategy in theory; less so in practical application. The big British mortars stopped firing at midnight, their first
brief ceasefire since 6:30 a.m., giving U.S. troops a sense that something was coming. But eleven of Napier's ships then rowed the wrong
way in the soggy darkness, depriving him of more than half his firepower. A bright blue rocket fired at 1 a.m. was the signal to begin the
diversion, followed by a thunderous cacophony of shot and shell from
the bomb ships and *Erebus*.[325] Napier and the remaining nine barges
actually slipped past Fort McHenry unnoticed, but Sailing Master
John Adams Webster at Battery Babcock spotted "small glimmering
lights" that must have been "matches on board the barges."[326] With
that, the guns at Babcock and Fort Covington—and eventually Fort
McHenry—let loose on the British.

"We once more had an opportunity of opening our Batteries
and Kept up a continued blaze for nearly two hours," Armistead said
later. "Had they ventured to the same situation in the day time, not
a Man would have escaped."[327] The assault may have been overkill
against just nine barges and 128 men, but U.S. troops were elated
to finally have some targets and could not be deterred after so long
under fire. They pounded away. "The houses in the city were shaken to

their foundations," *Niles* reported, "for never, perhaps from the time of the invention of cannon to the present day, were the same number of pieces fired with so rapid succession."[328] Armistead offered special praise for Webster and Henry Newcomb, the naval commander at Fort Covington, who "during this time Kept up an animated and I believe a very destructive fire, to which I am persuaded We are much indebted in repulsing the Enemy."[329] Napier had no choice but to slither back to the fleet, his mission now pointless and futile, because the British army never attacked.

The night fell briefly silent again. It was about 4 a.m. when Napier's barges returned to the safety of the main force, allowing the bomb ships to unlimber and fire again—although *less* furiously than at any time since the previous morning.[330] Long intervals between mortar shots made combat-weary U.S. soldiers at Fort McHenry and others on Hampstead Hill hopeful that the worst was now over. Out on the water, however, removed from the sounds of battle and unable to see the flag in the darkness, Francis Scott Key wondered what it all meant.

Key, Beanes, and Skinner checked their watches closely. It was sometime after 5 a.m. on Wednesday, September 14 when the first faint glimmers of sunlight broke through the cloud cover. They had paced the deck "in painful suspense" all night, Key told a friend, "watching with intense anxiety for the return of day."[331] The firing had slowed by now, the rain had stopped altogether and an unseemly calm settled over the harbor. In the haze and morning mist, Key grabbed his spyglass to scan the horizon toward the fort, hoping to learn if "our flag" was still there.

He had seen it on occasion during the pitch-black night, whenever a well-placed bomb or rocket lit up the sky, but only for a few seconds at a time. Who knew what the battle had wrought? According to Armistead, the British bombardment lasted twenty-five hours with two brief intervals, firing more than fifteen hundred bombs and seven hundred rockets, the kind of terrific onslaught that could easily bring down a fort and a city.[332] Key and the others could only watch and wait, counting off the minutes until sunrise, uncertain as to whether "the stars and stripes or the flag of the enemy" would be flying over Fort McHenry.[333]

They had their answer shortly after day broke. Key saw a flag hanging limply from a pole, but at first couldn't tell if it was American or British, until a beam of sunlight hit the harbor, giving it some life—the stars and stripes of the storm flag announcing the outcome to the world. Key was overcome with "the warmest gratitude" and called the sight of the flag over the fort "a most merciful deliverance."[334] Years later, recounting the thrill of the moment in a speech at Frederick, Maryland, he declared, "Through the clouds of war, the stars of that banner still shone in my view."[335]

It was about this time that Admiral Cochrane decided to give up the fight. By about 7:30 a.m., with the sun now rising over an exultant Baltimore, he signaled the British attack squadron to weigh anchor and pull out. *Erebus* went first at 8 a.m., followed by the bomb ships. Within the hour, the supporting frigates, including *Surprize*, with Cochrane aboard, headed down the Patapsco toward the Chesapeake.[336] They were still within sight of the battle scene at 9 a.m., when, in accordance with army regulations, a flag-hoisting ceremony was held at Fort McHenry, and Major Armistead's massive garrison flag replaced the smaller storm banner.[337]

Midshipman Robert Barrett, glancing back from the British frigate *Hebrus*, knew it was a signature moment for the victorious U.S. troops.

> *After bombing the forts and harbour of Baltimore for twenty-four hours, the squadron of frigates weighed, without firing a shot, upon the forenoon of the 14th, and were immediately followed by the bombs and sloops of war. In truth, it was a galling spectacle for the British seamen to behold. And, as the last vessel spread her canvas to the wind, the Americans hoisted a most superb and splendid ensign on their battery, and fired at the same time a gun of defiance.[338]*

Gallant defenders of Fort McHenry, exhausted but running on adrenaline, were too delirious with joy to know it was history in the making. An army band added to the merriment, striking up patriotic songs with an "ear-piercing fife and spirited drum."[339] Private Munroe, drenched and fatigued after twenty-five hours under fire, but having finally found his second wind, described the occasion thusly:

> *At this time our morning gun was fired, the flag hoisted, Yankee Doodle played, and we all appeared in full view of a formidable and mortified enemy, who calculated upon our surrender in 20 minutes after the commencement of the action.*

The big flag flapped in the breeze. Elation, relief, and defiance were rampant emotions of the day. Watching from the river, detached from the battle but indelibly linked to this moment at Fort McHenry, Key reached for some paper and jotted down his thoughts.

FRANCIS SCOTT KEY.

Francis Scott Key *(Wikimedia Commons)*

CHAPTER SIX
"O Say Can You See?"

Francis Scott Key was virulently opposed to this second war with England on religious and moral grounds. Pious enough to have once considered entering the clergy, Key feared "divine punishment" for an ill-conceived conflict and was mortified that U.S. troops would invade Canada, a faultless and uninvolved neighbor, in an attempt to spite the British crown.[340]

The future author of "The Star-Spangled Banner" even rejoiced in the fall of 1813, when British and Canadian troops defeated the U.S. Army in two battles near Montreal. "The people of Montreal will enjoy their firesides for this, and I trust many a winter," Key wrote to his friend John Randolph, the anti-war congressman from Virginia. "This I suppose is treason, but, as your Patrick Henry said, 'If it be treason, I glory in the name of traitor.' I have never thought of those poor creatures without being reconciled to any disgrace or defeat of our arms."[341]

And yet it was a different matter entirely when England invaded his native state. Key came from sturdy military stock—his father, John Ross Key, served with Washington in the Revolution—and he was apoplectic in 1813 when Cockburn plundered Maryland's shoreline, torching seaport towns and scattering citizens from their homes.[342] On three different occasions over the next two years, Key joined the local militia to help respond to British threats, albeit never serving longer than twelve days, and never firing a gun. At Bladensburg in August 1814, he accompanied a militia general as his civilian aide, for a time even helping to place the U.S. troops, although it was unlikely the British knew about this when Key arrived two weeks later at the mouth of the Potomac to seek the release of Dr. Beanes.[343]

Once that mission was accomplished, Key, Beanes, and Skinner were transferred to HMS *Surprize* on September 8 and placed under the care of Admiral Cochrane's son while the Royal Navy prepared for battle.[344] "They were very kindly treated by Sir Thomas Cochrane," wrote Key's friend and brother-in-law, Roger Taney, "until the fleet reached the Patapsco and preparations were [being made] for landing the troops."[345] On that day, September 10, the elder Cochrane moved his headquarters operation from the massive *Tonnant* to the lighter, quicker *Surprize* and sent the three men back to their own truce ship under a guard of marines.[346]

The precise location of the truce ship during the bombardment remains a source of mystery even after two hundred years. Early estimates that it was eight miles from Fort McHenry are preposterous, given limited visibility from that distance, especially in a rainstorm. A much more plausible theory is that it was placed just behind the bomb squadron, roughly three miles from the fort on the Patapsco River. The ship also may have been moved several times during the twenty-five-hour attack, including to a position directly alongside the "bombs," where it appears in a contemporary sketch of the battle by a Maryland soldier on Hampstead Hill. It is possible that Cochrane wanted someone with government credentials nearby in the event of a U.S. surrender.[347] Unfortunately, the only relevant testimony from Key himself is a second-hand quote, via Taney, that they were "anchored in a position which enabled them to see distinctly the flag of Fort McHenry."[348]

Key's emotion would have been palpable on the morning of September 14, 1814 when, unsure of the outcome of the overnight battle, he focused his glass through the "mist of the deep" and was roused by the sight of the American flag. Watching defeated British sailors retreat to their ships and inspired by the patriotic fervor of the moment, he scrawled some "brief notes" to memorialize the occasion.[349] Only once, later in life, would Key speak publicly about it— at a political event in Frederick, Maryland in 1834—but in doing so, he offered us a glimpse into his soul at this transcendental moment in American history. "In obeying the impulse of my own feelings," Key said,

> "I have awakened yours...I saw the flag of my country waving over a city—the strength and pride of my native State—a city devoted to plunder and desolation by its assailants...I heard the sound of battle; the noise of the conflict fell upon my listening ear, and told me that 'the brave and the free' had met the invaders...though I walked upon a deck surrounded by a hostile fleet, detained as a prisoner, yet was my step firm, and my heart strong...I saw the discomfited host of its assailants driven back in ignominy to their ships. Then, in that hour of deliverance and joyful triumph, my heart spoke...Does not such a country, and such defenders of their country, deserve a song?"[350]

Key, Beanes, and Skinner were released by the British on Friday, September 16 and sailed past Fort McHenry into Baltimore harbor, greeted as conquering heroes by a relieved and joyous citizenry. Key promptly took a room at the Indian Queen Hotel and, following a much-needed bath and a change of clothes, sat down to complete his composition on a clean sheet of paper, using notes he'd taken while aboard the truce ship.[351]

Though Key had written only a few songs before this, it is clear that he had a specific melody in mind.[352] "The Anacreontic Song," also known as "To Anacreon in Heaven," was a lively and well-known tune of that era, renowned for challenging a singer's skill and vocal range. It was composed in 1775 for the Anacreontic Society, a London-based gentlemen's club, and had gained widespread popularity on both sides of the Atlantic by the early nineteenth century. The ancient Anacreon was a legendary Greek poet known for odes of love, wine, and revelry, and his spirit clearly lived on in the upscale society's London meetings. After a sumptuous dinner and classical music concert, with fine wine flowing freely, members would be feted with a rousing rendition of the club's constitutional song:[353]

To Anacreon in Heav'n, where he sat in full glee,
A few sons of harmony sent a petition,
That he their inspirer and patron would be:
When his answer arriv'd from the Jolly Old Grecian
"Voice, fiddle and flute, no longer be mute
I'll lend you my name and inspire you to boot,
And, besides I'll instruct you like me, to entwine,
The Myrtle of Venus with Bacchus's Vine."[354]

The Englishmen who crafted the music—composer John Stafford Smith and lyricist Ralph Tomlinson—could not have imagined the impact they would have on American history over the next two hundred-plus years.

The societal concept spread quickly to the U.S., and chapters were formed in several cities, including the Columbian Anacreontic Society in 1795, hailed as "one of the most important musical organizations in New York City."[355] The song's influence grew as it was adapted to numerous political and social causes, its lyrics rewritten to fit the issue of the moment. The most prominent new version was Robert Treat Paine's "Adams and Liberty," a politically-charged number touting the virtues of President John Adams in 1798. Paine's lyrics were clunky at best—Adams's name wasn't even mentioned until the *ninth* verse—but they captured the public's fancy and helped ensure that Smith's music retained its popularity well into the nineteenth century.

Let Fame to the world sound America's voice;
No intrigues can her sons from their Government sever;
Her pride is her ADAMS—her laws are his choice,
And shall flourish till Liberty slumbers forever!
Then unite heart and hand, like Leonidas' band,
And swear to the God of the ocean and land;
That ne'er shall the sons of Columbia be slaves,
While the earth bears a plant, or the sea roll its waves.[356]

By one estimate, American songwriters reworked the words and had those songs published more than eighty times by 1820.[357]

There can be no doubt that Key himself was aware of the "Anacreontic" melody at least nine years before the Battle of Baltimore. In November 1805, he wrote his own lyrics for a song with the same tune, "When The Warrior Returns," celebrating the heroism of U.S. sailors in the First Barbary War at Tripoli Harbor.[358] Though far from elegant songwriting, the first of Key's four verses aligned better with the tempo of the music than the original stanza of "To Anacreon in Heaven." It was a promising start.

> *When the warrior returns, from the battle afar,*
> *To the home and the country he nobly defended,*
> *O! warm be the welcome to gladden his ear,*
> *And loud be the joy that his perils are ended!*
> *In the full tide of song, let his fame roll along*
> *To the feast-flowing board let us gratefully throng,*
> *Where, mixed with the olive, the laurel shall wave,*
> *And form a bright wreath for the brows of the brave.*[359]

We can now see the first faint hints of the national anthem as Key rhymed "wave" and "brave" in the final two lines, which were repeated in this manner throughout the song. But it was not until the beginning of the third verse that he experimented with a deft and soon-legendary turn of phrase for the first time.

> *In the conflict resistless, each toil they endured,*
> *'Till their foes fled dismayed from the war's desolation:*
> *And pale beamed the crescent, its splendor obscured*
> *By the light of the star-spangled flag of our nation*

Key's 1805 song was greeted warmly by the audience and published in several newspapers but left no lasting impression at the time.[360] It took a surreal convergence of circumstances, starting with the arrest of Dr. Beanes, to put him in a position where those words had new meaning. Key's journey back to Baltimore on September 16, with Major Armistead's giant flag in full view at Fort McHenry, gave him time to gather his thoughts and consider proper context. He had written dramatically of a battle before, but never one he had seen in person, or with the survival of his country threatened.

The "star-spangled" banner, indeed.

Key got down to work now in the Indian Queen Hotel, referring to notes from the truce ship to guide him, although, as it was related later, "for some of the lines, as he proceeded, he was obliged to rely altogether on his memory."[361] His four verses portray the intensely personal feelings of one who witnessed a seismic turning point in the country's history. The first verse (the one sung today before every professional sporting event, and assumed by many to be the entire anthem) is often described as "one long question," but, according to Key's original version, it actually is a pairing of two questions.[362] He does *not* end the verse with an emphatic statement of victory. Writing in the moment, transporting himself back to the early-morning darkness of September 14, an unsettled Key could not be sure if Major Armistead's flag yet waved.

> O say can you see by the dawn's early light,
> What so proudly we hail'd at the twilight's
> last gleaming,
> Whose broad stripes and bright stars through the
> perilous fight
> O'er the ramparts we watch'd were so
> gallantly streaming?
> And the rocket's red glare, the bomb bursting in air,
> Gave proof through the night that our flag was
> still there;
> O say does that star spangled banner yet wave
> O'er the land of the free and the home of the brave?[363]

Even today, at many sporting events, angry citizens and U.S. military veterans approach team officials to object about the question mark appearing at the end of that verse on the stadium's video boards. "Are you saying we're not the home of the brave?" is the common complaint. In reality, many Americans do not know that Key's song has four verses, and it is not until the second verse that he draws his conclusion and celebrates the triumph.

Key wrote about his experience sequentially. At the start of the second verse, still uncertain about the battle's outcome, he recounted the nerve-wracking scene aboard the truce ship as morning broke. There had been little firing for at least an hour—"the silence was awful," *Niles* reported—but the three men could still not determine which flag flew over the fort.[364] Adding to the confusion, both the Union Jack and the Stars and Stripes were red, white, and blue. The rain-soaked flag they saw from afar was visible only briefly, inconclusively. Key's next question was pensive.

> *On the shore dimly seen through the mists of the deep,*
> *Where the foe's haughty host in dread silence reposes,*
> *What is that which the breeze, o'er the towering steep,*
> *As it fitfully blows, half-conceals, half discloses?*

With the rising of the sun and increased visibility, however, Key soon had his answer. Using stirring rhetoric to complete the second verse, he proclaimed victory for the U.S. and supplanted his three earlier question marks with an exclamation point.[365]

> *Now it catches the gleam of the morning's first beam,*
> *In full glory reflected now shines in the stream,*
> *'Tis the star-spangled banner—O long may it wave*
> *O'er the land of the free and the home of the brave!*

Each verse of Key's song had its own purpose and tone. More than two centuries later, it is important to remember that he finished it just two days after the British attacks on Baltimore, surrounded by battle damage and within sight of horribly wounded U.S. soldiers. He was writing in the context of the times in September 1814, merely describing what he had seen and felt, not imagining his words would become a national song. That was *never* his aim.

Key's contempt for the invading British pours out in the third verse. He explained those feelings later in a note to a friend, writing that the despised Admiral Cochrane had "intimated his fears that [Baltimore] must be burned, and I was sure that if taken *it would have been given to plunder…it was filled with women and children!*" Key felt particular disdain for British officers he encountered on the mission to free Dr. Beanes. "With some exceptions," he wrote, "they appeared to be illiberal, ignorant and vulgar, and seemed filled with a spirit of malignity against everything American."[366]

Although the third verse was printed and sung with regularity for decades following the battle, musicians began to remove it from song sheets early in the twentieth century, after England became a staunch U.S. ally during World War I.[367] As a result, it is rarely heard and virtually unknown by most Americans today. But an angry, defiant Key chided the British for their defeat at Fort McHenry in 1814, taunting the world's most powerful military as "the band who so vauntingly swore…a home and a country shall leave us no more," and mocking their "foul footstep's pollution." He also noted their use of "hirelings" (apparently paid professional soldiers, or, perhaps, mercenaries) in contrast to the volunteer American militia.[368]

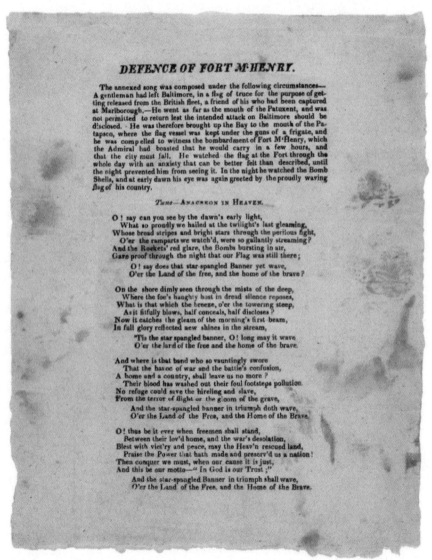

This broadside of Key's lyrics was printed on September 17, 1814, three days after the battle. It is believed that his brother-in-law originally called it the "Defence of Fort M'Henry," because Key never gave his song a title. Note that the tune is "Anacreon in Heaven." *(Wikimedia Commons)*

Most controversially, however, by writing that "no refuge could save, the hireling and slave, from the terror of flight or the gloom of the grave," he likely was condemning the Colonial Marines, the escaped slaves who bravely joined the British to fight for their freedom in the "land of the free." Francis Scott Key is one of the most contradictory figures in American history; though demonstrably pious and patriotic, he came from a long line of slaveholders, owned slaves himself, espoused racist views, opposed full abolition, supported the colonization of freed Blacks to Africa, and had a complex record on slavery as an attorney, arguing cases both for and against slaves. It is reasonable to assume that, in the immediate aftermath of battle, he focused his lyrical venom on the several hundred former slaves who had just fought for the enemy in the land war in Maryland—and not all slaves, as some have charged—but we are left to interpret the exact meaning, as he never broke down his composition line-by-line. [369]

Here is Key's full third verse, following his declaration of victory for the U.S.:

And where is that band who so vauntingly swore,
That the havoc of war and the battle's confusion.
A home and a country shall leave us no more?
Their blood has wash'd out their foul footstep's pollution.
No refuge could save, the hireling and slave,
From the terror of flight or the gloom of the grave,
And the star-spangled banner in triumph doth wave,
O'er the land of the free and the home of the brave.

According to one report, the Colonial Marines suffered two killed, two missing, and "several" wounded in the Baltimore attack. Overall, British casualties were forty-six killed and three hundred wounded. [370]

Key's religiosity set the theme for his fourth and final verse, as he offered praise to God for blessing the "heav'n rescued land." (Earlier in 1814 he had briefly considered entering the ministry at St. Paul's Parish in Baltimore.)[371] He underscored his belief in American exceptionalism—"then conquer we must if our cause it is just"—and, rather unwittingly, wrote the precursor of the national motto. Key's quote at the end of the sixth line, "In God is our trust," has since been condensed to "In God We Trust," printed on U.S. currency and elsewhere.[372]

> *O thus be it ever when freemen shall stand,*
> *Between their lov'd home and the war's desolation,*
> *Blest with vict'ry and peace may the heav'n rescued land*
> *Praise the power that hath made and preserved us a nation!*
> *Then conquer we must, when our cause it is just,*
> *And this be our moto—"In God is our trust,"*
> *And the star-spangled banner in triumph shall wave,*
> *O'er the land of the free and the home of the brave.*

Key somehow fit all four verses on one page of clean paper, although he had to cram the final verse to do so. The next morning, Saturday, September 17, he went to check on Judge Nicholson, his wife's brother-in-law, who had been in the thick of the fighting, and presented him with the composition.[373] Nicholson was over-whelmed. If Key had any doubts as to the impact of his song on citizen-soldiers who defended Fort McHenry against the British Navy, his encounter with the teary-eyed battle veteran erased them. "The Judge had been relieved from duty, and returned to his family only the night before Mr. Key showed him his song," Taney wrote. "And you may easily imagine the feelings with which, at such a moment, he read it and gave it to the public."[374]

Nicholson decided that the song should not stay in private hands. Perhaps with assistance from Skinner, he sent Key's manuscript to the office of the *Baltimore American* that afternoon. Businesses were just reopening following the battle, and a teenaged apprentice at the paper helped set the type for a handbill, carefully picking out each letter, a tedious but necessary process in the early nineteenth century.[375] Key had not thought to provide a title, so someone, most likely Nicholson, came up with the bland but efficient "Defence of Fort M'Henry." He also wrote a preamble for the readers, identifying Key only as a "gentleman" who had been "compelled" to watch the bombardment "with an anxiety that can be better felt than described."

To confirm that it was written as a song, and not merely a poem (as many have incorrectly theorized), Nicholson added the note "Tune—ANACREON IN HEAVEN."[376]

At least one thousand handbills were printed, and some were taken immediately to Fort McHenry to distribute to the soldiers.[377] "It was, no doubt…favorably received," Taney wrote. "In less than an hour after it was placed in the hand of the printer, it was all over town, and hailed with enthusiasm."[378]

The song was published in a newspaper for the first time by the *Baltimore Patriot* on September 20. (The *American*, for some reason, declined to carry it in the September 20 edition but corrected the error on September 21 after being scooped.) The *Patriot's* introduction noted, quite perceptively, that "The following beautiful and animating effusion" was "destined long to outlast the occasion, and outlive the impulse which produced it."[379] Other papers followed their lead and soon the song was published in New York City, Philadelphia, Washington, D.C. and up and down the Atlantic seaboard. On September 24, as waves of patriotism swept the country, Key's hometown newspaper, the *Frederick Town Herald* (of Maryland), was the first to identify the author, crediting the handiwork to "F.S. Key Esq. formerly of this place."[380]

"Our good Frank's patriotic song is the delight of everybody," Key's aunt wrote to his mother in October.[381]

Though it had been sung many times in private settings during the first month after the battle—in parlors and at firesides, and no doubt in pubs and dining establishments—the first advertised public performance of the new song came on October 19 at Baltimore's Holliday Street Theater. A "Mr. J. Hardinge" was the soloist. Shuttered for almost two years because of the war, the theater had reopened only one week earlier, and its owner, William Wood, worried that the featured play, a five-act tragicomedy translated from German, would not be enough to attract a large audience. He took out the following ad in local papers:

> *After the play, Mr. Hardinge will sing a much admired NEW SONG, written by a gentleman of Maryland, in commemoration of the GALLANT DEFENCE OF FORT M'HENRY, called THE STAR-SPAN-GLED BANNER* [382]

It was the first known reference to the song by its now official title. Whether the credit is due to Wood or the soloist or another individual—perhaps Thomas Carr, who had a music store in town—is unclear. By early November, Carr's store had published and was selling sheet music for "THE STAR SPANGLED BANNER," a "PATRIOTIC SONG" played to the tune of "Anacreon In Heaven." It soon appeared in songbooks in New York, Hagerstown, Maryland, and Newburyport, Massachusetts.[383]

The immediate appeal of the song startled Key, who had no way of knowing it would one day become the national anthem. (It did not receive that formal designation until 1931, 117 years after the battle and more than eighty years after his death.)[384] Remarkably, he never wrote again about his experience in Baltimore harbor and never granted an interview to a reporter. In his only public address on the matter, he professed surprise and gratitude that his "fervor of the moment" had made such an impact. "The song, I know, came from the heart," Key said, "and if it has made its way to the hearts of men whose devotion to their country and the great cause of Freedom I know so well, I could not pretend to be insensible to such a compliment."[385]

He always believed he was a mere witness to history, not a participant, regardless of the song's popularity. During his comments, he paused twice to pay tribute to the brave soldiers who had risked their lives to defend the city and the fort against the Royal Navy. "I was but the instrument in executing what you have been pleased to praise," Key said. "It was dictated and inspired by the gallantry and patriotism of the sons of Maryland. The honor is due, not to me who made the song, but to the heroism of those who made me make it.

"I will therefore propose a toast—The real authors of the song, 'The Defenders of *The Star-Spangled Banner*.'"[386]

One of the defenders, probably the most important of all, endured a miserable first week after victory in the Battle of Baltimore. Major George Armistead, who had worked almost nonstop since the British were spotted in the Patapsco on September 10, collapsed at Fort McHenry on the evening of September 15, "taken violently ill with a chill and fever."[387] Judge Nicholson said he was in a "high state of delirium."[388] These may have been the first hints of a medical condition, probably related to his heart, that would plague Armistead on and off for the next four years, but the circumstances of his post—under fire, drenched with rain, burdened by the weight of command, with little or no sleep—all contributed to his state of fatigue.

Nicholson was his most ardent supporter while he convalesced at home in Baltimore, not far from the fort. "I trust that the noble Armistead will receive the thanks and the rewards of his government," the judge wrote to Secretary of War James Monroe on September 18. "We were like pigeons tied by the legs to be shot at, and you would have been delighted to have seen the conduct of Armistead...I entreat you not to let him be neglected."[389]

Brigadier General William Winder, the regular army officer who at least nominally oversaw the Ferry Branch defenses, and was a veteran of battles in Canada and at Bladensburg, filed an official report in praise of the stricken major.

"The garrison of fort M'Henry, under the command of Major Armistead, are entitled to and receive the warmest acknowledgements and praise from the brig. gen. for their steady, firm and intrepid deportment," Winder wrote. He singled out Armistead for "his able, vigilant and exact arrangements," for the "zeal, vigor and ability he has discovered in his preparations for defence," and for the "prompt and efficacious manner in which he has complied, under great and perplexing difficulties, with demands from all quarters."[390]

Sam Smith, who shouldered overall responsibility for defense of the city, also made it clear in a September 19 letter that Armistead's role was essential and exemplary. "The successful defense of Fort M'Henry by Major Armistead...is beyond all praise. His gallantry and intrepidity enabled them to defend the Fort against every effort of the enemy, and there is no doubt that this intrepid officer will be rewarded by the Government."[391]

Word soon reached President Madison in Washington, D.C. The city's great buildings were still in ruins, painful scars from the British incursion three weeks earlier, and Madison, noting the contrast with Baltimore, was eager to give the hero of Fort McHenry a promotion. The commission he signed on September 20 made Armistead a brevet lieutenant colonel for meritorious service at the Battle of Baltimore, "and I do strictly charge, and require all officers and soldiers under his command, to respect and obey him accordingly." (The original commission was displayed in the home of a proud Armistead descendant before being donated to the Smithsonian in 2021.)[392]

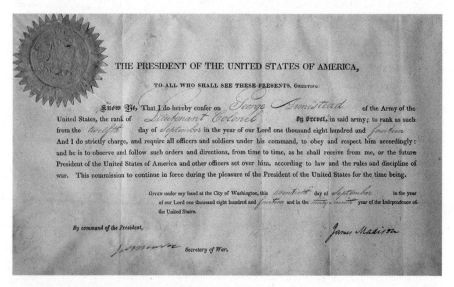

President James Madison promoted Armistead to lieutenant colonel less than two weeks after the battle. *(Courtesy of Harry, Liz and George Armistead)*

The citizens of Baltimore and soldiers at Fort McHenry agreed with the president, and the city's *Federal Gazette*, perhaps prompted by Judge Nicholson, rushed the news into print:

> *We are much gratified by having it in our power to announce, that the President of the United States has evidenced his approbation of the gallant conduct of Major George Armistead of the corps of artillery as commander of Fort M'Henry, during the late attack and bombardment, by giving him a brevet appointment of Lieut. Colonel in the Army of the U. States.*[393]

It was the highest rank Armistead would ever achieve, higher than any of his brothers except Walker, but at least one U.S. Army officer, General James Wilkinson, thought he deserved even more. "The defense of Ft. McHenry was of no ordinary character, for the passive resistance of danger is the test of valour," Wilkinson wrote. "It was sustained with firm, manly resolution, and the merits of

Major Armistead, who commanded here, on that and other occasions, combined with his long services, and his intrinsic excellence as an officer, gave him an indisputable right to preference over many."[394]

But the new lieutenant colonel had little reason to quibble. His life had changed dramatically for the better in the six days since the British retreat. Beyond news of his promotion, word arrived from Gettysburg that his wife, Louisa, had delivered their second child, a daughter named Margaret, on September 15, the day after the battle.[395] The chance to reunite with his family and meet Margaret Hughes Armistead for the first time was motivation enough for him to hasten his recovery, resume his role at the fort, and prepare for a trip to Gettysburg in a few weeks.

"We have just dined, and I have smacked my Chops over a brace of blue wings," he wrote in a hilariously rambling note to Louisa on September 22. "I shall visit [Fort McHenry] this evening but will not remain there…I am pestered out of my life with visitors…I want to see you and my Dear babys, which will, I…hope, be soon." If Nicholson had told him about Key's song by this point, he never mentioned it.[396]

It was two days later, on Saturday, September 24, that Armistead filed his formal battle report with Secretary of War Monroe. He apologized for the delay, due to "a severe indisposition," then recounted in painstaking detail his two-day ordeal under fire from the Royal Navy. According to his best calculation, "from fifteen to Eighteen hundred Shells were thrown by the Enemy," about 400 of which, "fell within the Works." He seemed happiest that "our loss amounts only to four Men Killed and twenty four Wounded" and noted that "every Officer and Soldier under my Command did their duty to my entire satisfaction."[397]

But by now his thoughts had turned to Gettysburg and Louisa, and to a future made brighter by his performance at Fort McHenry. The president's promotion, sent with a "very handsome compliment," as he told her, gave him a status he never imagined and seemed to place him on a fast track to even greater military success.

"[A]t least your husband has got a name and standing that nothing but divine providence could have given him," Armistead wrote. "We must soon all meet and talk the War over."[398]

CHAPTER SEVEN
Fame Interrupted

Navy Commodore John Rodgers, who took temporary command of Fort McHenry after Armistead fell ill, was the first to report the victory to U.S. military authorities. "The enemy has been severely drubbed, as well his Army as his Navy, & is now retiring down the river," Rodgers wrote with great excitement to Secretary of the Navy William Jones on September 14. He added, wryly, "I shall give you a more particular acct. as soon as I get a little rest."[399]

General Sam Smith scrawled a similar note to Secretary of War Monroe, confirming the enemy's "unsuccessful attempt by both land and water." The Washington-based *National Intelligencer* rushed it into print under the headline "HUZZA FOR BALTIMORE," touching off celebrations across the region.[400]

More good news arrived on September 18 with stunning reports that the U.S. had scored simultaneous victories in upstate New York—over the vaunted Royal Navy on Lake Champlain and the British infantry at Plattsburgh—effectively ending an invasion from the north.[401] Momentum was with the Americans for the first time since the war began in June 1812. The thought of such a turnabout had seemed impossible just three weeks earlier, when the British rampaged through Washington and briefly seized the capital city. At noon, General Smith ordered a federal salute to the New York victors, and celebratory guns banged away from Forts McHenry, Covington, Babcock, and Hampstead Hill.[402]

The departing British still were close enough to hear the fireworks, even if only faintly, and the man-made Baltimore thunder caused their hearts to sink. Midshipman Robert Barrett was one of many who once dreamed that "the port might have been graced with the colours of Old England, and the numerous merchant-vessels and shipping within the harbor our lawful prizes." Writing his memoirs thirty years later, Barrett still winced at the unexpected sting of defeat. "I will proceed to state that it was with the batteries biding us defiance—the weather scowling with a thick drizzling rain upon our proceedings—whilst our hearts and spirits were depressed to the extreme—that we retired down the Patapsco River with far different sensations from those we experienced on entering it…"[403]

An agonized Vice Admiral Alexander Cochrane wrote his formal report to British authorities on September 17. Refusing to admit defeat in an official forum and applying some astounding PR spin, Cochrane said "the primary object of our movement had been already fully accomplished" and a withdrawal took place only because additional attacks "might risk a greater loss than the possession of the Town would compensate for." He tried to minimize the obvious outcome by calling the battle a mere "demonstration." Listed among the handful of fanciful British achievements were "causing them to remove their Property from the City and… producing a total Stagnation of their Commerce and heaping upon them considerable expenses."[404]

But in a private letter written to a different government official on the same day, Cochrane confessed to many errors and misgivings. He claimed that the attack on Baltimore was made "Contrary to my Opinion" and scolded himself for following the advice of General Ross, essentially blaming the martyred army officer for the defeat. "I reluctantly consented to preserve Unanimity between the two services [but] I now exceedingly regret my deviation from My Original plan." He even complained that the powerful and well-equipped British military suffered from a "Want of Many essentials, to place us upon a par with the Enemy in the stile (*sic*) of Warfare they pursue"—ridiculous as that sounds in retrospect.[405]

No American would read Cochrane's papers or become aware of his self-doubt for many decades, but all who witnessed the withdrawal from Baltimore had a sense that the enemy was, indeed,

wounded and war-weary. The gunfire from Fort McHenry and spon-
taneous celebrations up and down the east coast reflected a growing
sense of optimism that the makeshift U.S. military had withstood
England's best shots. "The invincibles of Wellington are found to
be vincible, and are melting away by repeated defeats," a Virginia
legislator named William Wirt wrote to his wife. "A few more such
repulses as they met in Baltimore…and we shall have a peace on
terms honorable to us."[406] It was a heady time for the young nation.

George Armistead's victory over the British at Fort McHenry went
a long way toward forcing a peace treaty to end the war, but the
impact was not immediate. Given the plodding pace of communication early in the nineteenth century, battle reports took weeks to
cross the ocean and reach their intended recipients in Europe.

As a result, talks between British and American diplomats at
Ghent, Belgium proceeded in such a time warp that the Battle of
Baltimore was already over before they learned the "old" news that
the British had burned Washington three weeks earlier. Leverage
shifted back and forth based on out-of-date dispatches and madden-
ingly-delayed newspaper headlines, giving peace commissioners on
both sides an almost impossible task.

The U.S. had been seeking an honorable end to the war as far
back as January 1814, when an anxious Madison assembled his
five-man negotiating team. It stands as one of the most distinguished diplomatic delegations in American history, even with the
test of time after two centuries. The roster included John Quincy
Adams, Madison's minister to Russia, and son of a former president;
Henry Clay, who resigned as speaker of the House of Representatives to take the job; James Bayard, a seventeen-year veteran of the
house and senate; Albert Gallatin, secretary of the treasury and a
former senator and congressman; and Jonathan Russell, ambassador
to Sweden and Norway and former acting minister to England. In
another of the war's many quirks of fate, one of the group's secretaries
was Christopher Hughes, Jr. of Baltimore, a former militia captain at
Fort McHenry and George Armistead's brother-in-law.[407]

The Americans settled in at Ghent in the spring of 1814 but waited for almost four months before their British counterparts arrived. Adams, who was the chairman by virtue of his international experience, knew immediately that the tardiness was by design. Victory over Napoleon in Europe had freed the British to send additional troops and equipment to the U.S., giving them one last chance to squash the former colonials, seize more territory, harden borders to impede westward expansion, and force diplomatic concessions. "I can imagine no other motive for their studied and long protracted delays," Adams said, "…than the intention of waiting for the effect of their forces upon our fears."[408] Gallatin was even more dramatic when he wrote, "We should have to fight hereafter not for 'free trade and sailors rights,' not for the conquest of the Canadas, but for our national existence."[409]

The two teams met for the first time in a formal setting on August 19, just five days before the attack on Washington. Aware that Cockburn had been raiding the Atlantic coast all summer, stoking more terror, the British made some outrageous demands to test American resolve. In addition to proposing an Indian buffer state in the upper Midwest, they wanted territorial concessions in Maine and Minnesota, a reduction of U.S. naval presence on the Great Lakes, and a restriction on fishing privileges in British/Canadian waters (unless they could bargain for a territorial "equivalent"). The very issue that touched off the war—the impressment of U.S. sailors—wasn't even discussed. For Adams and his partners, it was a discouraging non-starter.[410]

The danger in a prolonged stalemate was that British troops would inflict more damage on the battlefield, demoralizing the defender and leading to even more stringent demands at Ghent. It had been so long since a significant U.S. victory that visions of a resurgence seemed hopelessly naive. "I tremble indeed whenever I take up a late newspaper," Clay conceded. "Hope alone sustains me."[411] To the surprise of no one, the talks went nowhere for several weeks before suddenly taking a turn for the worse.

Cockburn and Ross invaded Washington and torched the White House on August 24, but it was not until a month later, on September 26, that reports of this signature British achievement reached England's shores. (Keep in mind that the courier had left the U.S. three weeks before the attack on Baltimore, so all of that was still unknown—a news blackout that is hard to fathom today.) British overconfidence grew exponentially, and the next few days brought a series of celebratory war bulletins from the *Times* of London:

> *We stop the press to announce the receipt of the following most important intelligence from America—the CAPTURE and DESTRUCTION, by his Majesty's Forces, of the CITY OF WASHINGTON, on the 24th ult., after a severe, but brilliant action, in which they enemy was defeated with great loss.*

> *"…Washington captured, its dock, its arsenal and all its public buildings destroyed, the heads of the faction beaten, disgraced and flying for their lives—these are indeed impressive lessons, which we fervently hope and trust will produce their proper effect on the people of the United States"*[412]

Sensing that the conflict was nearing its end, Lord Bathurst, secretary of state for war and the colonies, wrote Ross to announce that even more troops were on the way. Checking his maps and noting the proximity to Baltimore, Bathurst begged the general to show no mercy and bring the rebellious city to its knees. If Britain could "make its inhabitants feel a little more the effects of your visit than what has been experienced at Washington, you would make that portion of the American people experience the consequences of the war, who have most contributed to its existence."[413] Bathurst had no way of knowing that the mortal wounding of Ross on September 12 had already struck a debilitating blow to his military hierarchy on the Chesapeake Bay.

British diplomats were predictably elated when word of Washington's demise reached Ghent. They had offered no response to the rejection of their original peace terms, and now there was little chance for wiggle room on the U.S. side of the table. Bathurst told his men to put on a "face of compress'd joy" when they delivered the news to the Americans, but, beyond that, they were to employ a strategy of silence. Lord Liverpool, the British prime minister, was so certain of victory that he couldn't keep himself from a condescending quip. "Let them feast in the meantime on Washington," he said.[414]

Imagine the shock, then, when the next set of reports in October turned the peace talks upside down.

U.S. victories at Baltimore and Plattsburgh and the incomprehensible death of General Ross, all within a matter of three days, "materially counteracted" the previous stance.[415] The impact at Ghent was immediate and profound. "If we had either burnt Baltimore or held Plattsburgh," a British official groused later, "I believe we should have had peace on [our own] terms."[416] But the world—and the future of the world—had changed forever

"The Capture of Washington was a source of great triumph and exultation and inspired a belief that their troops could not be resisted," American commissioner James Bayard wrote to his cousin on October 26. "This error has been sadly corrected by the repulse in the attack upon Baltimore, by the destruction of their fleet on Lake Champlain, and by the retreat of [General] Prevost from Plattsburg."[417]

For at least one member of the U.S. negotiating team, news of the success at Baltimore was uniquely personal. Secretary Christopher Hughes was the brother of Armistead's wife and had served with the militia at Fort McHenry as recently as 1813. He also was married to the daughter of Sam Smith, overall commander of the city's defenses. In a celebratory entry in his diary, Hughes praised "the brave and honourable conduct of my brother in law Major Armistead" and allowed that the "exemplary behaviour of my Townsmen in Baltimore, under the management of Genl. Smith, afforded me the sincerest satisfaction."[418]

The two teams haggled over various points during the next two months, but it was clear now that a grudging peace was attainable. Remarkable as it seems, the final agreement failed to resolve earlier issues and called for all borders to revert to *status quo ante bellum*, meaning "the state existing before war."[419] Neither side would gain or lose territory despite two-plus years of fighting. To mitigate all doubt, a provision specifically stated that "all territory, places and possessions whatsoever, taken by either party from the other during the war" would be "restored without delay."[420] Minor border disputes would be resolved by future joint commissions.

The formal document to end the War of 1812 was signed by U.S. and British commissioners on December 24, 1814. As one author described it, "the carillon at St. Bavon Cathedral was ringing for Christmas by the time the delegates sat at a long table at 6 p.m. to sign, seal and exchange the treaty."[421] And yet the challenge remained to get three copies overseas to Washington as quickly as possible, because the countries would technically remain at war until the treaty was ratified by both seats of government. Hughes was one of three men selected for the journey, each of them traveling by a different route to ensure that at least one would make it safely.[422]

In the meantime, neither British nor American soldiers had any idea that peace had been reached, so battles continued to rage on U.S. soil. Admiral Cochrane, still smarting from his setback at Baltimore, focused his attention on New Orleans, where he aimed to seize control of the city and, with it, the Mississippi River. But on January 8, 1815, U.S. forces under General Andrew Jackson battered the British in the Battle of New Orleans, inflicting more than two thousand casualties. "Such a disproportion in loss, when we consider the number and the kind of troops engaged, must, I know, excite astonishment," Jackson wrote.[423] Indeed, news from New Orleans galvanized the nation and set off celebrations in major cities, including Baltimore, where a general order was issued from Fort McHenry on February 5:

> Lieut. Col. ARMISTEAD, commanding at Fort M'Henry, will cause a national salute to be fired to-morrow morning at ten o'clock, from the guns of the Fort, in honour of the splendid victory obtained by the arms of the United States under Major General Jackson, over the enemy in the attack made by the latter on the defences of New Orleans...[424]

Many modern-day Americans still believe that Jackson's victory in the Battle of New Orleans "won" the War of 1812, oblivious to the fact that peace terms had been settled by that point, awaiting only travel and ratification. Armistead's brother-in-law departed Ghent in late December, sailed directly from France to the U.S. coast, and endured much "foul weather" off the Virginia capes before arriving in Washington in early March, only to learn that another emissary, Henry Carroll, had beaten him by several weeks. It was February 16, 1815 when the Senate ratified the treaty by a 35–0 vote and Madison signed his copy, exchanging it with a British secretary to formally end hostilities.[425] The date was exactly five months after Key had completed "The Star-Spangled Banner."

The treaty spoke of "terminating the war which has unhappily subsisted between the two countries" and called for a "firm and universal peace between his Britannic Majesty and the United States, and between their respective countries, territories, cities, towns, and people of every degree."[426]

In pure military terms, the U.S. had neither won nor lost—it was, at best, a draw—and one of the key causes of the war, the impressment of U.S. sailors against their will, was not even addressed. Canada remained in British hands. And yet the monumental effort that cost so many lives and treasure was far from pointless. Challenged by a foreign rival, Americans had stood up for their sovereignty. They had defended their homeland against the world's most powerful military and announced their growing presence on the international stage, gaining, in the process, a new symbol, motto, and national song.

Madison, in his post-war address to the nation, spoke of victory resulting from "the patriotism of the people, the public spirit of the militia, and the valor of the military and naval forces of the country," but it was left to one of the peace commissioners, Albert Gallatin, to provide the best perspective for future generations.[427]

"The war has renewed and reinstated the national feelings and character which the Revolution had given, and which were daily lessening," Gallatin wrote. "The people now have more general objects of attachment, with which their pride and political opinions are connected. They are more American; they feel and act more as a nation; and I hope that the permanency of the Union is thereby better secured."[428]

Three years after this second war of independence threatened to tear the country apart, the Star-Spangled Banner yet waved.

Aside from the fact that he was now a local hero, recognized and feted on every street corner, George Armistead's life returned to normal shortly after the Battle of Baltimore. He resumed command of Fort McHenry by the end of September 1814 and made plans to travel to Pennsylvania to reunite with his wife and two young daughters. "I proceed to Gettysburg tomorrow," he wrote to a friend on October 11, "to bring my wife and children home whom I have not seen for nearly two months."[429] It was a joyous moment for the family after long weeks of strife and upheaval.

Activity at the fort soon resumed its mundane routine, with Armistead and his troops building seawalls and conducting drills, but memories of the war remained constant and vivid, especially among local citizens. Proud of their city's resistance, they proposed building a monument on Calvert Street to commemorate the U.S. victory and honor its fallen heroes. Approvals came quickly, and plans were set for a ceremony to begin construction on September 12, 1815, the one-year anniversary of the infantry battle at North Point. Armistead was one of three invited guests on hand to help lay the cornerstone and take part in a suitably "grand procession," along with fellow commanders Sam Smith and John Stricker.[430]

The fifty-two-foot "Battle Monument" was completed in 1822 and became the city's official emblem in 1827. (It still stands today in Baltimore's Monument Square.) A classical figure of "Lady Baltimore" faces the harbor, clutching a laurel wreath to symbolize victory and flanked, symbolically, by a cannon ball. The base sits on eighteen layers of marble, representing the eighteen states at the time of the battle. Armistead is one of four prominent leaders listed on the bronze plaque at its base, alongside Smith, Stricker, and Baltimore's mayor, Edward Johnson.[431]

Awards, honors and similarly grand ceremonies became commonplace in the years following the war. Indeed, in contrast to his anonymity today, it was impossible to underestimate Armistead's popularity in Maryland and along the Atlantic coast during this time period. As early as February 8, 1815, before the peace treaty was even ratified, the committee of Military Affairs in the U.S. House of Representatives recommended that President Madison present a "Reward of Valor"—a commemorative sword—to acknowledge "a high sense of the merit of lieut colonel Armistead."[432] Similar tributes were offered by various governmental bodies, including the Maryland General Assembly, which on January 10, 1816 had its attention "irresistibly drawn to the brave commander of Fort McHenry, whose invincible constancy in maintaining that important post entrusted by his country to his gallantry and military experience during the tremendous bombardment...[added] another laurel to his country's fame and entitled him to the admiration of all his countrymen."[433] The assembly also gave him a sword.

The most memorable ceremony came at Fort McHenry on May 11, 1816, when a committee of the "Citizens of Baltimore" presented Armistead with a silver punch bowl in the form of a thirteen-inch British mortar shell, etched with scenes of the bombardment. His brief acceptance speech, published three days later in the *American and Commercial Daily Advertiser* (of Baltimore), marked the only time he spoke in public about the battle that shaped his legacy.

Gentlemen—I cannot adequately express the high sense of the obligation I feel myself under to you, for presenting this flattering testimony of my services on the 13th and 14th September 1814, at this post. As the offering of free born citizens, cherishing the pure principles of independence and civil liberty, it is the richest boon that could be bestowed upon a soldier emulous of fame: As such I am proud to receive it, and glory in this opportunity of transmitting to my posterity, so distinguished a mark of a country's gratitude; giving thereby, to that country, an indisputed claim to their talents and exertions in support of that free and happy constitution and laws, under which we live. I do not claim to myself an exclusive right to this rich reward: great merit is due to the officers and soldiers with whom it was my good fortune to be associated, in the important occasion you have sought to commemorate; and to their united, cordial and patriotic exertions, aided by the interposition of Divine Providence, in a great measure do we owe the safety and prosperity of our beloved city.

I beg you, gentlemen, to accept for yourselves and the citizens of Baltimore, the assurance of my regard and esteem.[434]

Later that day, the *American* reported that Armistead, Smith, and Stricker would sit for a series of specially-commissioned portraits by the artist Rembrandt Peale, and, once "finished and framed," the portraits would be placed in the city's Council Chamber "until a suitable building is procured or erected for their accommodation."[435] (They are on display today at the Maryland Center for History and Culture in downtown Baltimore, and another original copy of the Armistead portrait, showing George with ruddy cheeks and a shock of curly black hair, was recently donated to the Smithsonian by Armistead descendants.)

When he wasn't traveling the region to receive awards or pose for portraits, George resumed his post at Fort McHenry, at one point working alongside his brother, Walker, the noted U.S. Army engineer. They built a massive stone seawall to protect the vulnerable shore batteries and planned for a seven hundred-foot brick and masonry wall to secure the fort's northern boundary. His family also grew exponentially, as Louisa gave birth to two more children in nineteen months. Their first son, Christopher Hughes Armistead, was born in April 1816, and a third daughter, Georgiana Louisa Armistead— born on the Fort McHenry grounds, and named in honor of both parents—came along in November 1817.[436]

It was also sometime during this early post-war period that George came into possession of the large fifteen-star, fifteen-stripe flag that flew over Fort McHenry on the morning of September 14, 1814—the original Star-Spangled Banner. Precisely how this happened has never been officially recorded. If he received it as a gift from the army, as family legend held for years (his granddaughter, Margaret Appleton Baker, was often quoted to that effect), there is no record or receipt to confirm that. The more likely scenario is that he simply took it. "I do not know how the flag came into my father's possession," his youngest daughter, Georgiana, admitted years later, when the flag was in *her* possession. "I was not five months old when he died, and always accepted the ownership as a fact without question—just as I did with any property. It might have been *a usual or granted right for a commander to take a trophy of success.*"[437] Whatever the process, George's action helped save a national icon, preserving it for viewing by future generations, even if he did it in defiance of army policy. The smaller storm flag, however, was never recovered and is lost to history.

Lieutenant Colonel George Armistead died suddenly on April 25, 1818, less than four full years after his heroic stand at Fort McHenry. Just thirty-eight years old, he left behind a wife and four young children, and, from a military and political standpoint, a legacy unfulfilled.[438]

"It is interesting to speculate on what his career would have been had he lived longer," wrote the late Lonn Taylor, a historian at the Smithsonian Institution in Washington D.C. and one of the nation's foremost experts on the flag and its origins. "As a contemporary of his fellow Virginians Winfield Scott and Zachary Taylor, he might have risen to high command in the Mexican-American War, or even been elected to high office."[439]

There is no contemporary document describing the cause of Armistead's death, which is remarkable in itself, given how the news blindsided the city. Newspapers ran adoring obituaries and thousands of citizens turned out for what became the largest funeral procession in Baltimore's history. Speculation now centers on a heart attack, because Armistead was still commanding Fort McHenry at the time of his death in April 1818, and there had been no reports of a long or debilitating illness. It is possible that the first signs of a heart condition appeared after the Battle of Baltimore, when he collapsed from exhaustion and fell into "a high state of delirium," but the only published hint we have is a pension application filed by Louisa Armistead in 1856, stating that he died "in consequence of disease contracted while in service in the line of his duty."[440]

Newspapers scrambled to rush stories into print. Under the headline, "A HERO FALLEN," the *American* wrote that "the recollection of the ever memorable 14th September naturally occurs to our mind—when the Star-Spangled Banner waved in proud defiance to a formidable foe…then it was that Baltimore was saved, and a wreath of never-fading laurel encircled the departed hero's brow."[441] The *Niles Weekly Register* was only slightly less dramatic, reporting that the death of "our gallant friend" was met "with every testimonial of respect that a grateful people could bestow." *Niles* also noted that "the procession was the largest ever witnessed in this city on a similar occasion" and that "several respectable strangers attended."[442]

From two hundred miles away, the *New York Columbian* showed that sorrow had not been limited to Baltimore or Maryland, publishing the following poem in an early May edition, titled, "ON THE DEATH OF COL. ARMISTEAD, The Hero of Fort M'Henry:"

> *The soldier falls!—a nation weeps*
> *While glory lulls to rest*
> *How sweetly then, that warrior sleeps*
> *Upon her peaceful breast!…*
> *Yet at that hour, to dress his grave,*
> *Unearthly forms repair—*
> *He's gone, where dwell the good and brave—*
> *His brethren greet him there!*[443]

George Armistead was buried in the Hughes family vault at Baltimore's Old St. Paul's Cemetery, marked only by a small military nameplate and a bronze plaque saluting "the illustrious men interred within this enclosure" on the cemetery's outer wall.[444]

Honors kept accumulating even years after his death. The first of several city monuments dedicated solely to Armistead was authorized in 1827 and built in 1828 at the Old City Spring on Calvert and Saratoga Streets. Described as a "marble tablet flanked by two marble cannons and surmounted by a flaming bomb"—a dramatic design by early nineteenth century standards, it thrilled visitors for more than thirty years before falling into disrepair by the time of the Civil War. Surviving remnants, including the marble cannons, were placed in temporary storage for twenty years and incorporated into a new monument on Eutaw Place in 1882. But after local residents complained that it did not "harmonize with the loftiness of their homes," it was moved in 1886 to Federal Hill where it still stands today, overlooking the city and harbor Armistead defended. Fittingly, two cannons had fired from near this same spot during the famous funeral procession in 1818.[445]

This nineteenth century monument to Armistead stands today on Baltimore's Federal Hill. *(Author photo)*

A much more humble presentation came in January 1839, just before the twenty-fifth anniversary of the battle, when George's only son, Christopher Hughes Armistead, traveled to Annapolis to accept a ceremonial sword from the Maryland General Assembly, "in testimony of the high sense of approbation the legislature entertain of the gallant conduct of his Father in the late war."[446] Not to be outdone by a rival state, the governor of Virginia, Thomas Gilmer, invited Christopher to Richmond for a similar ceremony in 1841. George had been born at Newmarket in Caroline County, Virginia and—though a Marylander at the time of his death—was hailed by Virginians as a native son. Gilmer spoke of the "high esteem and admiration entertained by his native State for the courage and solider-like conduct of Lt. Colonel Armistead." Christopher, who was born two years after the battle and had just turned two years old when his father died, caught the patriotic fervor of the moment, noting that George had "kept that flag flying, the stripes and stars of which shone brightly amidst the 'rockets' red glare and bombs bursting in air.'"[447] The swords became family keepsakes.

Decades later, on the one hundredth anniversary of the battle in September 1914, the City of Baltimore dedicated a towering bronze statue of Armistead on the grounds of Fort McHenry. Funded by the city and the War of 1812 Society of Maryland, the statue featured George gazing out toward the Patapsco River, hand on sword, with a huge inscription—ARMISTEAD—at the base. An audience of more than 5,000, including national and international dignitaries, watched as the commander's grandson, sixty-five-year-old George Armistead Jr., pulled the cord to reveal sculptor Edward Berge's handiwork. At the same time, 6,500 Baltimore schoolchildren, arranged in the shape of a human flag, and accompanied by a 250-piece orchestra, sang "The Star-Spangled Banner" in Armistead's honor, "adding a colorful display and musical note."[448]

Modern visitors to Fort McHenry are greeted by this monument to Armistead, dating to the 100th anniversary of the battle in 1914. *(Author photo)*

Fort McHenry had been leased by Congress for use as a municipal park by the time of the ceremony, but it was repurposed as a military hospital during World War I and was not turned over to the National Park Service until 1933. Originally, the Armistead statue was located on the outer battery earthworks overlooking the Patapsco, but it has since been moved twice—when the park's first visitor center was built in 1964, and when a new center replaced it in 2012.[449] It is the first sight that greets visitors to the fort in the twenty-first century, with "Armistead" perpetually searching for British ships on the water, framed against the backdrop of a large fifteen-stripe flag.

CHAPTER EIGHT
Guardians of the Banner

From the day he took the original Star-Spangled Banner home from Fort McHenry after the battle, George Armistead and his descendants guarded it zealously for more than ninety years.

Following George's death in 1818, ownership passed to his wife, Louisa Hughes Armistead; then on to their daughter, Georgiana Armistead Appleton; and, eventually, to their grandson, Ebenezer Stuart (Eben) Appleton, a New York stockbroker and the final private owner.[450] It was an astounding and unprecedented chain of hand-me-down custody for a legitimate national heirloom.

The old flag was unfurled on occasion for local events in the Baltimore region, but it was not well known to the American people and did not gain national attention until 1873, when Georgiana allowed it to be photographed for the first time. There was more news coverage with an appearance at the centennial anniversary of the Flag Act in Boston on June 14, 1877, but the intensely private Eben, who took possession on the death of his mother in 1878, kept it largely out of public view for almost thirty years until donating it to the Smithsonian Institution early in the twentieth century.[451]

Aspects of that journey have rarely been explored in depth, but they offer a remarkable window into the triumphs, struggles, and improbable coincidences of the early history of the United States.

There is no record that George Armistead displayed his "precious relic" in the few years before his death, or even that it was used at his funeral procession, which was covered extensively by the Baltimore and national press. No story mentioned it.[452]

The flag did not reappear in public for another six years, until October 1824, when the Marquis de Lafayette visited Baltimore on a celebratory tour of the United States. The French aristocrat, who commanded American troops during the Revolutionary War and became an indispensable ally of George Washington, was still an immensely popular figure in the U.S. following the War of 1812.[453] "Lafayette in Baltimore!" blared the headline in the *Baltimore American*, which noted that "citizens of both sexes [were] anxious to enjoy the honor of being among the first to greet the arrival of the General among us."

The overflow crowd buzzed in anticipation as a steam ship on the Patapsco River "communicated the pleasing intelligence that the 'Nation's Guest' was approaching the city." According to the *American*, "it was immediately announced by a discharge of three guns from Fort M'Henry, and succeeded by a salute of thirteen guns, fired by a detachment of the First Brigade of Artillery, which was stationed on Federal Hill…

"The discharge of Artillery was a signal for the display of the national flag, which was now to be seen on all the public buildings and vessels in the harbor; and first of all was seen rising to its elevated station on the flag-staff of Fort M'Henry, the same 'STAR SPANGLED BANNER' which waved in triumph on that spot during the awful bombardment of 1814.

"The barge intended for the General was handsomely cushioned, carpeted and otherwise ornamented, and at the head was an eagle bearing in its beak this appropriate motto—'WELCOME LAFAYETTE—to the land of the free and the home of the brave.'"[454]

Transported to Baltimore for the occasion were several items from the Washington family's war era collection, including the general's iconic campaign tent, which arrived in silk bunting and was set up on the parade ground at Fort McHenry to host a reception, with the Star-Spangled Banner draped over it.[455] Louisa Armistead also brought along the distinctive silver punch bowl in the shape of a British mortar that had been presented to her husband in 1816 by the citizens of Baltimore.[456] Colonel John Eager Howard, a local veteran of the Revolution, addressed the crowd with a speech that "evinced much emotion" and caused "every eye" to be "suffused with tears," but after spending much of his allotted time on the unique bond between Lafayette and Washington, he closed with an acknowledgement of the fallen hero of Fort McHenry.

> *This Fort, not distinguished in your day, garrisoned principally by citizen soldiers, many of whom are now present, has recently and successfully sustained a formidable bombing. If its commander had been permitted to have sojourned longer with us, he would have been fully rewarded for every toil and danger by an interview with you on this joyous occasion.*[457]

The Lafayette ceremony, coming ten years and one month after the Battle of Baltimore, marked the first time since George's death that the Star-Spangled Banner had traveled the short distance from the Armistead family home to Fort McHenry. Sadly, for posterity, it was also the last. Louisa would agree on several occasions to lend the flag to local "Defenders' Day" events, honoring the anniversary of the Battle of North Point on September 12 each year, but it never again returned to the ramparts of the old Star Fort or hung from the famous flagpole.[458] She guarded her husband's legacy by limiting the flag's appearances to what she considered appropriate celebrations, often spreading them out over several years.

There is a noteworthy news account from Defenders' Day in 1828, when it was carried with Louisa's approval to Hampstead Hill, where Baltimore infantry troops had set up their main defensive line against the British. "On the staff we saw the old flag of Fort McHenry…amidst the joyous shouts of those who recognized its tattered folds," a reporter wrote. "A holy relic never disgraced, and receiving now the homage of friends, as in 1814, it commanded the respect of foes."[459]

On the sixteenth anniversary in 1830, the flag was made available for public viewing at Rembrandt Peale's art museum downtown, advertised with the following note in *Baltimore Patriot*: "SPLENDID ILUMINATION—THIS EVENING, September 13, 1830—Mrs. Armistead having politely loaned 'THE FORT McHENRY BOMBARDMENT FLAG,' it will be exhibited in the Salon."[460] Adding to the splendor of the moment, the museum also displayed a "splendid illuminated picture" of the Battle of North Point, which measured almost 150 square feet.[461]

Nine years later, on the morning of the twenty-fifth anniversary in 1839, a local militia unit marched to Georgiana's home in the Mount Vernon neighborhood to borrow the flag for a monument dedication at North Point.[462] These appearances were so rare—just once every few years—that newspaper reports often contained excessively flowery language and tried to outdo one another with tributes to the flag and heroes. As the *American & Commercial Daily Advertiser* of Baltimore wrote:

> *Previous to taking their station in line, the Independent Blues repaired to the residence of the widow of the late Col. George Armistead, and received from her hands the flag which waved over Fort McHenry during the bombardment…*

> *The procession then repaired to a shady and retired spot in an adjacent wood, where a handsomely decorated rostrum had been erected on one side of which hung, in all its pristine glory, the very Star-Spangled Banner which floated triumphantly over Fort McHenry… which as it fluttered in the midnight breeze, visible only by the glare of the bursting shells, convinced the ruthless invader how vain were his efforts to conquer a free people.*[463]

The flag was dusted off and brought out again in 1841, hanging from the speakers' platform to welcome President-elect William Henry Harrison to Baltimore (possibly without anyone knowing that Harrison was one of Armistead's distant relatives), and made its only other political appearance at the Young Men's Whig National Convention in 1844. A pamphlet detailing the Whig event said that "from the premises of Christopher Hughes Armistead, just above Charles Street, was displayed the identical Star-Spangled Banner...whose waving through 'that perilous night' suggested the thought of that most beautiful of all our National songs—'The Star-Spangled Banner.'"[464]

Curiously, however, it was not used for Francis Scott Key's funeral in 1843. Louisa Armistead's brother-in-law offered it to Key's family, but there is no mention of it in newspaper accounts of the funeral. The family apparently declined.[465]

Most printed references to the Fort McHenry flag in the first half of the nineteenth century referenced phrases from Key's song, and it soon became clear that the flag and the music were linked inseparably in American history.

Indeed, it was not long after the battle that "Star-Spangled Banner" became a widely accepted nickname for all U.S. flags, the first sign of the song's growing appeal.

George Templeton Strong, a New York attorney whose diary offered an intriguing window into American life during this period, noted as much when he wrote that "a lot of tipsy loafers are just going past, screaming out 'The Star-Spangled Banner,' at the top of their lungs, and in all sorts of diabolical discords. But it sounds glorious. It's a glorious thing altogether—words and music—no matter how it's mangled."[466]

"The Star-Spangled Banner" gained in popularity and was published in at least twenty regional songbooks between 1814–1842, including one titled *National Hymns*. It started to compete with two Revolutionary era favorites, "Yankee Doodle" and "Hail, Columbia," as candidates for the title of unofficial national anthem. When another melodious contender, "Columbia, The Gem of the Ocean," came along in the 1840s, the first verse even started with a Key-like phrase: "O Columbia! The gem of the ocean/The home of the brave and the free."[467] But the best indication of the song's influence came when parody writers co-opted the tune to deliver other contemporary messages.

Musical parodies were a common practice at the time, described by anthem historian Marc Ferris as "writing new, topical verses to existing music, a church tactic dating back to the Reformation."[468] Eighteenth-century Americans often rewrote lyrics to "To Anacreon in Heaven," sometimes for political favor—including "Adams and Liberty" for the country's second president, John Adams—and nineteenth-century writers weren't about to be outshone. The 1840 election brought a flurry of partisan parodies about William Henry Harrison that were organized into a campaign songbook called *The Harrison Medal Minstrel*. Two of the most popular selections were "The Harrison Banner" and "Harrison and Liberty," both set to the beat of "The Star-Spangled Banner."[469]

Harrison commanded U.S. troops in the western theater during the War of 1812, which explains why the third verse of "Harrison and Liberty" praised his victory over the British in the Battle of the Thames in Canada:[470]

> *Oh! say, ye brave sons of the far-spreading West*
> *Where is the lov'd chief who met the foe's dread invasion?*
> *His name both in peace and in war will be bless'd,*
> *While the "stars" still in friendship unite us a nation.*
> *Then hold it no shame, that he led you to fame,*
> *When the lion, subdued, lay crouch'd on the Thame.*
> *Then inscrib'd on our flag be Harrison's name,*
> *And liberty, union and law we proclaim.*[471]

Temperance activists soon found a home in the music, adopting it to promote their nationwide campaign for abstinence from alcohol. They believed it served their purpose more than any other because "To Anacreon in Heaven" was chided as a bawdy British drinking song, toasting the virtues of wine and bacchanalian behavior. The American Temperance Society, which formed in Boston in the 1820s, emphasized the "value of sobriety and industry" with the goal of ensuring a "disciplined and sober work force." The concept caught on quickly, and, by 1833, there were more than six thousand local societies in the U.S., including the Washington Temperance Society (founded, oddly, in Baltimore), which "attempted to convert drunkards to the pledge of teetotalism."[472]

During a ten-year period starting in the 1840s, these groups delighted in writing five different parody versions of "The Star-Spangled Banner" for magazines and songbooks. One of the most popular was "Oh! Who Has Not Seen," published in *Cold Water Magazine* in 1843:[473]

> *Oh! who has not seen by the dawn's early light,*
> *Some poor bloated drunkard to his home weakly reeling,*
> *With blear eyes and red nose most revolting to sight;*
> *Yet still in his breast not a throb of shame feeling!*
> *And the plight he was in—steep'd in filth to his chin,*
> *Gave proof through the night in the gutter he'd been,*
> *While the pity-able wretch would stagger along,*
> *To the shame of his friends, 'mid the jeers of the throng.*[474]

It came as no surprise, then, that abolitionist groups joined the growing trend, seizing on the opportunity to attack slavery by repurposing Key's song. Some members may have been aware that Key was a slave-owner himself and helped to found the American Colonization Society in 1816, but their anger in the 1840s was channeled more toward his contradictory description of American ideals: "Land of the *free*."

To be fair, abolitionists rewrote the lyrics to a number of patriotic songs, including "My Country, 'Tis of Thee" and "Hail, Columbia," but the most chilling was a graphic adaptation of "The Star-Spangled Banner" that focused on slavery's raw brutality. Released in 1844, it was titled "Oh, Say Do You Hear:"

> *Oh, say do you hear, at the dawn's early light,*
> *The shrieks of those bondmen, whose blood is now streaming*
> *From the merciless lash, while our banner in sight*
> *With its stars, mocking freedom, is fitfully gleaming?*
> *Do you see the backs bare? Do you mark every score*
> *Of the whip of the driver trace channels of gore?*
> *And say, doth our star-spangled banner yet wave*
> *O'er the land of the free, and the home of brave?*[475]

Given the sheer number of parodies in the mid-nineteenth century, it is astonishing that Key's original lyrics not only survived but thrived during this period, growing stronger and more popular in the face of cluttered competition. "Despite numerous alternatives circulating in popular culture," Ferris wrote, "'The Star-Spangled Banner' sold briskly and, in practice, evolved into the national anthem long before the Civil War."[476] Even writers who chose different melodies still managed to borrow a phrase or two from Key's now-famous work. One example was an 1860 campaign song for Abraham Lincoln, "Lincoln and Liberty," using flag-waving patriotism as its theme:

> *Then up with the banner so glorious*
> *The star-spangled red, white and blue*
> *We'll fight 'til our banner's victorious*
> *For Lincoln and liberty too.* [477]

During the forty-plus years that Louisa Armistead cared for the flag, from 1818 until her death in 1861, she made numerous small deletions and at least one addition—sacrilegious by modern standards but considered very commonplace in her day. Still visible on the back side of the flag is a distinct red chevron, or upside-down V, sewn onto the third white stripe from the bottom. Lonn Taylor, historian for the Smithsonian's Star-Spangled Banner preservation project, and author of two books on the flag, believed it was intended to be the letter A (for Armistead), but the crossbar "was either never on, or it fell off." There also is a small B on to the chevron, but its purpose and meaning are unknown. "Baltimore," perhaps? There are only guesses.[478]

Those who see these acts as desecration of U.S. history should know that George himself scrawled his name on the flag, along with the date "September 14, 1814," according to Armistead family tradition. His granddaughter, Margaret Appleton Baker, told an interviewer in 1895 that "it bears upon one of its stripes his name and the date of the bombardment in his own handwriting."[479] If true, however, the signature has faded over time.

Smithsonian conservators in the early twenty-first century even found a partial inscription by Georgiana on one of the damaged stars, reading *"this precious relic of my father's fame [large hole where fabric has been roughly cut out]??? day of Octr 1861 Georgiana Armistead Appleton."* This may have been to stake her own claim to ownership of the flag following her mother's death earlier that month.[480]

A much more common practice in the mid-to-late-1800s was the act of cutting small pieces from the flag to present to friends and dignitaries or to honor fallen heroes. Fully embracing the custom, three generations of Armistead ladies, starting with Louisa, trimmed more than eight feet of material from the end of the Star-Spangled Banner—mostly in small, uneven pieces, one at a time, over a period that spanned decades. In addition to wind damage on the "fly end" of the flag, this reduced its size from thirty by forty-two feet at the time of the battle to its current, irregular dimensions of thirty by thirty-four feet.[481]

"Snippings from flags would be anathema now, considered very disrespectful," said Marilyn Zoidis, curator of the flag at the Smithsonian from 1999 to 2006, "but doing so was part of the mentality of the nineteenth century. Souvenirs from flags became especially common during the Civil War period, with people giving them out as mementos. Louisa and her daughter, Georgiana, were very kind to people who asked."[482]

Another historian said citizens of that time period were fascinated with pieces of history, noting that "a glove, a gorget, a lock of hair, or a battle map connected by memory with great men or great deeds" could arouse "the appropriate emotion of awe and…a condition of moral sensitivity and reflection."[483]

The first inquiry is believed to have come from the widow of one of the Baltimore citizen-soldiers who defended Fort McHenry under Armistead's command. According to Margaret Appleton Baker, "I remember hearing from my mother that a brave soldier—who had served under her father—on his death bed wrote and requested Mrs. Armistead to let him have a piece to wrap around his dead body. The request was complied with."[484] As time passed, numerous others—battle veterans, widows, politicians, civic leaders, and historians—asked for and received small pieces of the flag. The most remarkable deletion during this period was a large white star cut from the bottom of the blue field, leaving a prominent ragged hole in the middle of the flag—although where that star went, and to whom, remains a frustrating mystery after all these years.

"Pieces of the flag have occasionally been given to those who deemed to have a right to such a memento," Georgiana wrote in 1873, "[and] indeed, had we given all that we have been importuned for little would be left to show. My impression is that the star was cut out for some official person. The red A was I assume sewn on by my mother. My father's name is in his own handwriting. The bag [that holds the flag] is the same in which I always remember it, I therefore feel sure that it is the identical one in which it was placed after the bombardment."[485]

Georgiana Armistead Appleton, daughter of the hero of Fort McHenry and long-time custodian of the flag. *(Courtesy of Christopher Hughes Morton and Karen Morton)*

The family's generosity during this period became well-known, and, as a result, Georgiana and her siblings were often flooded with appeals from random citizens across the country, asking for small swatches of the flag. Most of the letters were mundane, straightforward requests, but one of the most remarkable came in 1845 from a youngster in Chicago, Charles Bonney, who thought he was being especially bold in writing to Georgiana.

I presume that out of the Forty Million people in the United States (Chicago Boys included), not one of them has yet been forward as to request a single thread of the original 'Star-Spangled Banner,' which I believe is in your possession. But if you will pardon this Chicago boy's presumption, I would like to request that, if you could conveniently spare me just one short thread of this memorable token of older times, it would be most highly esteemed and appreciated.[486]

Georgiana was surprisingly accommodating to these inquiries, and in 1873 she sent an image of her father and a photo of Key's autographed copy of the song to Stephen Salisbury of Worcester, Massachusetts, along with a small red-and-white fragment of the flag. But she soon learned that gestures of kindness often begat more requests and led to an endless cycle. In early 1874, Salisbury wrote that "a friend had a framed piece of fragments…I saw that he had a scrap of blue, which I have not, and this gave me a sentiment and hope that I could have a blue fragment to go with my white and red. I therefore cannot refrain from asking you to send me a piece of blue 2 inches square, or 2 ½ inches by 1 ½ inches."[487]

There is no evidence of Georgiana's response. Much of the story of the most famous flag in U.S. history was never officially documented and was passed down through generations of the Armistead family only by word of mouth.

The death of Louisa Hughes Armistead on October 3, 1861, six months after the start of the Civil War, devastated the family but ushered in a new era for the Star-Spangled Banner.

By the terms of her will, Louisa "bequeathed" the flag to her youngest daughter, Georgiana—a decision that did not sit well with her only son, Christopher, who assumed he was next in line.[488] Family legend holds that he was furious after reading the will for the first time, shouting angrily and demanding shared custody.[489] As a consolation prize, he received a much less valuable memento, his father's commemorative silver punch bowl set. That no doubt added to the sibling tension, leading Christopher to threaten legal action, but they soon worked out their differences and reached an acceptable truce.[490] Georgiana and her husband, William Stuart Appleton, even moved in with Christopher and his wife on West Monument Street in Baltimore for a brief time during the early part of the Civil War, bringing the flag with them.[491]

The move was an economic necessity, because William and Georgiana had fallen on hard times. In an April 15, 1861 letter to an uncle in Boston, Georgiana described her family as "destitute and suffering" and wrote that "until my husband and sons can find some settled employment, the united efforts of my daughter and I will indeed be futile, even admitting that the state of the country will allow us to carry out our design of opening a school." She knew from news reports that the first attack of the Civil War took place three days earlier, when Confederate troops bombed Fort Sumter in South Carolina. "Age and wisdom are now disregarded," she seethed, "and politicians will not see the suicidal policy they are now pursuing."[492]

Much later in life, Georgiana detailed the custody of the flag during this tumultuous period:

> At the breaking out of the war it was in our house, but Mr. Appleton immediately broke up house-keeping and our furniture was stored. The flag was then taken for safekeeping to my brother's house in Monument Street…

My mother shortly after went with him and his family to Virginia, where she shortly died, but on his return he was, after some angry words, for he thought the flag should have been his, forced to give it up to me…and with me it has remained ever since, loved and venerated…

[My mother's reasons] were that I was called after my father and was the only one of the children born at Fort McHenry. There is a legend that at the time of my birth this banner was raised and the disappointment was great that it was a girl.[493]

The flag was still at Christopher's house in late November 1861, when the famed historian Benson J. Lossing toured the city to research a book on the War of 1812. Lossing, who was noted for his groundbreaking work on the history of the Revolution, and would later write extensively about the Civil War, obtained a rare profile sketch of George Armistead for his *Pictorial History of the War of 1812*, but the most memorable highlight of his trip was seeing the original Star-Spangled Banner for the first time:

I called upon Mr. Christopher Hughes Armistead, son of Colonel George Armistead, the commander of Fort McHenry in 1814, who kindly showed me the identical flag of which Key inquired, 'O, say, does that star-spangled banner yet wave…Mr. Armistead spread it out on his parlor floor. It was a regular garrison flag, faded and worn by exposure to storms and missiles. It had eleven holes in it, made by the shot of the British during the bombardment.[494]

Lossing's visit came almost fifty years after the Battle of Baltimore. During that time, as the flag's condition deteriorated with improper storage and handling, many observers assumed that the visible damage had been caused by British bombs. It has since been established that the garrison flag did not even fly during major portions of the battle in inclement weather on September 13, 1814, replaced by the smaller storm flag, and was not raised again until 9 a.m. on September 14, when Key saw it. There was a lone account, however, written in the 1870s, of a soldier who recalled the Fort McHenry flag being hit by a shell.[495] We can never know for certain, but modern historians believe that most, if not all, of the damage to the big garrison flag took place when the Armistead women and their relatives—uneducated in formal preservation techniques— shared it with the public.

Following the brief period when they lived with Christopher on Monument Street, Georgiana and her husband found living quarters "at the corner of Madison and Hargrove Alley" in November 1861, giving the flag yet another new home.[496] This was a relief for Christopher's wife, Agnes Gordon Armistead, who viewed the national heirloom as little more than a burden for her small family. "I am glad to be rid of it," Agnes wrote in her diary. "More battles have been fought over that flag than ever were fought under it!"[497]

Georgiana's continuing interest in guarding the flag during the Civil War was critical to its continued existence as an American icon. Ironically, aside from her oldest sister, Mary, who was described in a letter as a "Patriotic Unionist," most members of the family had Southern sympathies.[498] One of Georgiana's sons was arrested while trying to join the Confederate Army, and she would have known that four of her first cousins were serving as Confederate soldiers. But Georgiana continued to protect and care for the flag during this time of national upheaval, keeping it safe from ill-meaning relic hunters and rabid secessionists, who might have defaced or destroyed it.

CHAPTER NINE
Civil Unrest/Civil War

In early September 1861, five months into the Civil War—and just as Baltimore was ready to celebrate the forty-seventh anniversary of George Armistead's victory over the British—local authorities swooped in to arrest twenty Southern sympathizers boarding a ship to Richmond.

One of them was George Armistead Appleton, the eighteen-year-old grandson of the hero of Fort McHenry, who had in his belongings a Confederate flag.[499]

"IMPORTANT ARRESTS" screamed the headline in the September 9 edition of Baltimore's *American and Commercial Advertiser*. "TWENTY BALTIMORE SECESSIONISTS ON THEIR WAY TO VIRGINIA." Working on a tip, local police had dispatched eleven officers to North Point to await the arrival of a "party of recruits for the Confederate army." The unsuspecting traitors were arrested as they disembarked from wagons near a rendezvous point at the Battle Monument House, and many of their possessions were confiscated, including Appleton's rebel flag, several "uniform jackets and pantaloons" and a stash of letters intended for Confederate officials in Richmond. The paper reported that "the vigilance of the Police on Saturday and yesterday broke up a scheme of our city Secessionists to carry men and arms to Virginia."[500]

The name "George A. Appleton" was listed sixteenth on the roster of detainees printed in small type on the front page. Reporters apparently were not aware that he was George Armistead's grandson, or that he went by his middle name, "Armistead," instead of "George." (Had they done even a modicum of research, they would have learned that he was the son of Georgiana Armistead Appleton and had direct ties to the original Star-Spangled Banner.) The prisoners were shuttled to the newly-established Union prison at Fort McHenry—talk about irony—before being shipped out to more permanent quarters at Fort Columbus in New York and Fort Warren in Boston.[501]

The few surviving letters from Appleton's five months in captivity are filled with requests for every-day necessities ("a blanket," "woolen gloves," "soap," "tobacco"), although there is one detailed missive where he debates his pro-Union clergyman. "If you allow me to differ with you," he wrote, "I think Maryland is no more loyal than she was in the beginning of this contest, and one of these days it will be shown which one of us is right."[502] Unfortunately, he left no other record of his views on the war or details of his clear Southern sympathies.

The same could not be said for another descendant of Baltimore's Fort McHenry royalty. Frank Key Howard, grandson of Francis Scott Key, was editor of a pro-Southern newspaper, *The Daily Exchange*, and found himself swept up in a massive series of arrests on Friday, September 13. Government agents targeted multiple members of the Maryland legislature and other openly "disloyal" citizens, including Howard, who were agitating against the government's war policy.

The Union Army hierarchy was well aware of President Abraham Lincoln's fear that the state might try to secede. Losing Maryland would cripple the Union, cutting it off from the capital in Washington, D.C. and forcing government officials, including Lincoln, to flee. As far back as April, Lincoln had even suspended the writ of habeas corpus, a flagrant violation of civil rights deemed necessary to keep order in the streets. In a historic missive dated April 27, he reminded his generals that "you are engaged in repressing an insurrection against the laws of the United States" and that if resistance rendered it necessary "to suspend the writ of habeas corpus, you…are authorized to suspend that writ." But continuing unrest, particularly in the teeming port city of Baltimore, prompted acts of further repression.[503]

The main focus was on legislators with Southern leanings who threatened to tip the balance in favor of the Confederacy at the state's pending secession vote on September 17. Lincoln wanted to leave *no doubt* that Maryland would remain in the Union. On September 11, his secretary of war, Simon Cameron, ordered that "the passage of any act of secession by the Legislature of Maryland must be prevented," and, if necessary "all or any part of the members must be arrested."[504] On September 12, the army followed Lincoln's directive and called for the detention of disloyal state legislators.[505]

Anti-secession efforts didn't stop there, however; officials working at the government's behest also seized the mayor of Baltimore, a U.S. Congressman, and several opposition newspaper editors.[506] Lincoln's postmaster general, Montgomery Blair, heard from sources that "a majority of the Union men in Baltimore desire to suppress all the opposition presses in the city." Blair passed the word to the army, saying "I believe the *Exchange, Republican* and *South* should be suppressed. They are open disunionists."[507]

Federal officials justified Howard's detention because he was "known to be in deep sympathy with the rebels and his paper advocated zealously for their cause." During a midnight search of his home, they claimed to have found "articles for his paper, correspondence, lists of names pledged to favor the recognition of the Confederate States and drafts of proceedings for the legislature—most of decided secessionist character."[508]

Howard's paper, the *Exchange*, took a decidedly contrarian view, reporting that his arrest was "of the most brutal and outrageous character" and that government intruders "behaved most lawlessly and indecently." Specifically, it said, "The ruffians demanded the keys of the house and commenced a thorough search. Beds were turned upside down, closets and bureaus ransacked, cupboards opened, and where keys could not be found, locks were forced."[509]

As had happened with Confederate recruits one week earlier, these new prisoners were taken into Federal custody and transferred temporarily to Fort McHenry—the irony of which was not lost on Key's grandson. From a cramped holding room on the second floor, he noted that his arrest and arrival at the fort came on September 13, the same date, more than four decades earlier, when Key had watched bombs bursting in air from a perilous perspective behind the invading British fleet.

When I looked out in the morning, I could not help being struck by an odd, and not pleasant coincidence. On that day, forty-seven years before…my grand-father, Mr. F.S. KEY…had witnessed the bombardment of Fort McHenry. When, on the following morning, the hostile fleet drew off, defeated, he wrote the song so long popular throughout the country, 'Star-Spangled Banner.' As I stood upon the very scene of that conflict, I could not but contrast my position with his, forty-seven years before. The flag which he had then so proudly hailed, I saw waving, at the same place, over victims of as vulgar and brutal a despotism as modern times have witnessed.[510]

More than any other city in a border state, Baltimore was a cauldron of civic unrest from the earliest days of the war. This was due largely to the unique nature of its location, thirty miles south of the Mason-Dixon Line and forty miles north of the nation's capital. It was once called America's "northernmost Southern city and southernmost Northern city."[511] Radical sentiments on both sides ran deep.

On April 19, only a week after the Rebels bombed Fort Sumter, Union Army troops traveling through Baltimore to Washington had been accosted by an unruly mob of Southern sympathizers, hurling bricks and other projectiles. The "Pratt Street Riot," as it came to be known, left four Union soldiers dead and more than thirty wounded, the first battle casualties of the Civil War. Noting the historic date (and the irony that Union soldiers involved were from Massachusetts), Southerners hailed it proudly as the "Lexington of 1861."[512]

More arrests came in dramatic bursts throughout the spring and summer, including on July 1, when a Union general controversially ordered the detention of four Baltimore police commissioners. One of them was Charles Howard—Key's son-in-law, and father of Frank Key Howard.[513] Charles was hauled off to Fort McHenry before being transported to Fort Lafayette in New York, where he was reunited with his son in September, and, ultimately, to Fort

Warren in Boston.[514] The Howards were among a large group of detainees who wrote an angry letter in October to "His Excellency, the President of the United States," protesting "the inhumanity of their confinement and treatment," but it did nothing to alleviate their situation, and they remained in custody for more than a year.[515]

Another Baltimore prisoner at Fort Warren was granted a reprieve, however. In late November 1861, after about ten weeks of captivity, Armistead Appleton agreed to sign an oath of allegiance to the United States, clearing the way for his unconditional release.[516] The process took several more months—he would not go free until late February—but no one was more relieved than his mother, Georgiana, who held staunch pro-Southern feelings and had been apoplectic at news of the arrest in September. She recorded her emotion in a stunning letter, eviscerating the Lincoln administration and predicting, rather remarkably, that they would soon have support from the British:

> *It is an outrage that you should be left a prisoner, but the British lion will growl might soon…and then we shall see a fuller display of the weakness of this administration. They shall come to a speedy destruction…I hate to think of them and yet I have no ill or personal feelings for any of my friends who differ in personal opinion from me. I have (thank God) no drop of Puritan blood in my body and can therefore be as tolerant as I am, and besides the South can afford to be magnanimous at all times and more particularly now…I told a 'Federal' high in authority a few days since when accounting for the quiet of the city all the 'Rowdies' have enlisted in the Federal Army and all the Gentlemen, God save the mark, are gone to Virginia."* [517]

Armistead Appleton was transferred to authorities back home in Baltimore on January 16, 1861, and it was only then that they publicly acknowledged the surreal connection to his grandfather. Union Army General John Dix committed it to print for the first time, describing several items seized in the original North Point raid, including Appleton's "secession flag," which was being donated to the Massachusetts Historical Society:

This flag was taken from the party of men near North Point, where the British Army landed in 1814. They were on their way to the insurgent States. The flag was found in the carpetbag of Mr. George A. Appleton, a young gentleman of this city, about eighteen years of age, a grandson of Colonel Armistead, who defended Fort McHenry at the time the Star Spangled Banner was written. Young Appleton was sent out of Fort McHenry on the anniversary of the battle of North Point for infidelity to the same flag, and was imprisoned for some time at Fort Columbus, in the Harbor of New York, and more recently at Fort Warren, in the Harbor of Boston. He is now in [Baltimore] awaiting the action of the Government in his case.[518]

Armistead Appleton was granted parole and released from Federal custody on February 20, 1862, after promising to "render no aid or comfort to enemies in hostility to the United States."[519]

George Armistead Appleton, Armistead's grandson who was briefly held at Fort McHenry when he tried to join the Confederate Army during the Civil War. *(Courtesy of Christopher Hughes Morton and Karen Morton)*

The grandson and son-in-law of Francis Scott Key remained in federal captivity at Fort Warren until November 27, 1862, when, as Frank Key Howard remembered, "we left our prison for our homes."[520] Frank wasted little time resuming his pro-secession diatribes, both in the newspaper and in a book, *Fourteen Months in American Bastiles*, published early in 1863. Each of the political prisoners, he said, had "determined at the outset to resist, to the uttermost, the dictatorship of ABRAHAM LINCOLN, and having done so, each had the satisfaction of feeling, as he left Fort Warren, that he had faithfully, and not unsuccessfully, discharged a grave public duty." Moreover, "we came out of prison as we had gone in…and with a stronger resolution than ever to oppose it by every means."[521] As if to accentuate the point, five of his brothers, including the astoundingly named McHenry Howard, had joined the Confederate Army to fight against the U.S.[522]

Just across town, however, young Armistead Appleton apparently underwent a change of heart. Still unnerved by his time in prison—and despite the secessionist leanings of his mother and extended family—he fulfilled the terms of his oath of allegiance and never again offered his services to the rebel military. Instead, because he was a male citizen of a Union state between the ages of twenty and forty-five, he was compelled by the U.S. Enrollment Act of March 1863 to register for the Union Army draft.[523] Military records at the National Archives show that Armistead and his younger brother, Eben, indeed registered for the draft in the spring of 1863, shortly before the Battle of Gettysburg. A remark next to Armistead's name on the registration form notes that he "is said to be in the Junior Artillery," a likely reference to Battery A, Maryland Junior Light Artillery, which was organized in Baltimore for six months' service in July 1862, but there is no indication that he or his brother ever served.[524] Eben went on to become the guardian of the original Star-Spangled Banner in his later years.

As war broke out and the young country split along geographic lines, battlefields weren't the only places where the conflict was being waged.

In the chaotic early months of 1861, a sectional tug-of-war erupted over patriotic songs such as "The Star-Spangled Banner" and even over the flag itself.

North and South had fought together to gain independence from England in the Revolutionary War and to affirm it in the War of 1812, and Southerners believed they had equal rights to ownership of Key's song and other historic tunes.

"I never could learn to get entirely over a certain moisture of the eyelids that always come to me listening to the sweet and stately melody of the 'Star Spangled Banner,'" a Louisiana reporter wrote in January 1861. Noting similar feelings about *Yankee Doodle* and *Hail, Columbia*, two stalwarts from the late 1700s, he said "these tunes and anthems all rightfully belong to the South. Instead of abandoning them, let us claim them as our legitimate property."[525]

The *Richmond Examiner* agreed in its April 4 edition, barely a week before the attack on Fort Sumter, exhorting readers to "never surrender to the North the noble song, the 'Star-Spangled Banner!'"

A similar emotional battle was being fought out in print over custody of the national flag. Some of the most radical Southerners believed that their claim to Key's song also extended to the banner it represented. The *Savannah Republican* (of Georgia) urged the newly-formed nation to "re-erect the stars and stripes as their own national flag," while resuming "upon Southern lyre those glorious old tunes, 'Hail, Columbia' and the 'Star-Spangled Banner.'"[526] Aware that Southerners had borrowed concepts from the U.S. flag to create a new Confederate design, the *Richmond Dispatch* wrote that, "indeed, as we were maintaining the principles it was intended to represent, and the North had abandoned them, we were honestly entitled to the whole flag."[527]

None of this sat well in the North, where the stature of the flag had grown exponentially in the half-century since the War of 1812, inspired in large part by Key's lyrics.

At a flag-raising ceremony at Chester Square in Boston on April 27, Edward Everett, the former U.S. senator and governor of Massachusetts, said, "We set up this standard not as a matter of display, but as an expressive indication that, in the mighty struggle which has been forced upon us, we are of one heart and one mind that the government of the country must be sustained." He noted that the flag was now floating "as never before, not merely from arsenal and masthead, but from tower and steeple, from the public edifices, the temples of science, the private dwellings, in magnificent display of miniature presentiment."[528] Four days later, at a similar rally in Chicago, U.S. Senator Stephen A. Douglas of Illinois thundered that "Every man must be for the United States or against it. There can be no neutrals in this war—only patriots or traitors. I express it as my conviction before God that it is the duty of every American citizen to rally round the flag of his country."[529]

But politicians weren't alone in harnessing support for the Union war effort. Thanks to the volunteer efforts of church groups and neighborhood organizations, massive flags flew from the steeple of New York's Trinity Church on Wall Street; over the portico of St. Paul's Church on Broadway; from the rooftop of the Brown High School building in Newburyport, Massachusetts; and at the revolutionary summit of Boston's Bunker Hill. In Cincinnati, witnesses said a ninety-foot-long flag ("well-proportioned," they claimed) was unfurled from the spire of a Roman Catholic cathedral. Even in Baltimore, a newspaper reported that "a 'star-spangled banner' was raised with great demonstrations of enthusiasm, over the post office and custom-house…greeted with tremendous applause, waving of hats, and cheers for the Union."[530]

The North was not going to yield the national flag.

Far from battlefields and the sound of the musket fire, combatants in this sideshow of Civil War competition turned to parody song-writing to make their points to the masses.[531] Writers with distinctly different points of view could cleverly comment on current events and help bolster their side of the debate by creating new lyrics for original pieces of music that were well-known to the general public. The familiarity of chords and melodies made it easier for the often-irreverent new words and rhymes to resonate.

Given its widespread popularity and historic underpinnings, "The Star-Spangled Banner" was a prime target for parody writers on both sides of the debate. In the early months of the war, Northern lyricists were particularly sensitive to Southern attempts to co-opt the flag. One of the first to address the topic was William Allen, who penned "Our Country's Free Flag" in May 1861, completing and publishing his work before the armies had even clashed on a major battlefield.[532] In the second verse, adapting new imagery to the song Key made famous, Allen skewered Southerners for a bogus claim to the banner, mocking them as traitors who rely on slavery for success.

> *Do you think that to rebels our flag we shall yield,*
> *Those rebels, the despots who thrive by enslaving?*
> *In their madness they call us, the free, to the field;*
> *We'll teach them, we trust, very soon they are raving.*
> *We are strong in the right, and we welcome the fight,*
> *Which quickly the aims of the traitors shall blight.*
> *For we bear not a flag all defiled and unjust,*
> *And not in ourselves, but in God is our trust.*[533]

Physician and poet Oliver Wendell Holmes Sr. released his own version of the song on the most patriotic of days—July 4, 1861—but, unlike many others, Holmes never intended his work to be a parody. Instead, he proposed two new verses for "The Star-Spangled Banner," bringing relevance and contemporary context to its historic value. One of them gained instant national attention and "was widely disseminated, often as a fifth verse appended to Key's lyrics and even in government-affiliated publications," according to the Star Spangled Music Foundation's *Poets & Patriots: A Tuneful History of "The Star-Spangled Banner."*[534]

Holmes, whose son, Oliver Jr., fought for the Union and became a Supreme Court justice early in the twentieth century (and is often mistakenly credited with writing these verses), was "upset by a country torn in half" and "professed his belief in the ultimate liberty and glory of the nation." His message to the country was boldly defiant and hard-edged in its tone, lashing out at "a foe from within" and denouncing the Southern traitor "who dares to defile" the flag. Like Allen before him, he focused on slavery as the root cause of the conflict and foresaw a day when all slaves would gain their freedom and become U.S. citizens.

> *When our land is illumined with Liberty's smile,*
> *If a foe from within strikes a blow at her glory,*
> *Down, down with the traitor who dares to defile*
> *The flag of her stars and the page of her glory!*
> *By the millions unchained who our birthright have gained,*
> *We will keep her bright blazon forever unstained;*
> *And the star-spangled banner in triumph shall wave,*
> *O'er the land of the free, and the home of the brave.*[535]

There was no dearth of enraged response from the South, where secession-minded authors and composers also took pen to paper with revolutionary fervor. The first stanza of an early New Orleans version of the song, "The Stars and Bars," ended with the vindictive, "Oh! say has the star-spangled banner become/The flag of the Tory and Vile Northern Scum?" Another Louisiana entry rewrote the chorus with a cold-hearted sectional taunt: "For this flag of my country in triumph shall wave/O'er the Southerners' home and the Southerners' grave."[536]

The most biting of the early Southern parodies was probably Frederick Pinkney's "The Flag of Secession," which mocked two of Key's most legendary phrases ("Oh, say *can't* you see" and "the land of the *freed*") and called out the U.S. president by name.[537] Conceding that an established country would never relinquish ownership of its flag, Pinkney identified the "palmetto flag" of South Carolina as a temporary symbol while rebel officials argued over the design of a new flag of their own. South Carolina had gained a mythical status among secessionists as the first state to secede from the Union in December 1860, and the choice of its state flag was well-received in the South. Pinkney wrote:

> *Oh, say can't you see by the dawn's early light*
> *What you yesterday held to be vaunting and dreaming?*
> *The Northern men routed, Abe Lincoln in flight,*
> *And the palmetto flag o'er the Capitol streaming.*

The pumpkins for fare, the foul feted air,
Gave proof through the night that the Yankees
were there.
Now the Flag of Secession in triumph doth wave,
O'er the land of the freed and the home of the brave.[538]

There was even a group of rabid secessionists who rejected anything resembling "Union" music; instead, they created new and different melodies to frame their defiant lyrics. A Richmond publishing house, J.W. Davies & Sons, produced sheet music in 1862 for "Farewell to the Star Spangled Banner," a collection of five verses with a repeating chorus that "jettisoned Key's song and its flag entirely." One of the later verses vowed that Virginia would "break down the iceberg of northern coercion/And rise in her glory of freedom and right," but the more popular first verse paid tribute to South Carolina and its palmetto symbolism.

Let tyrants and slaves submissively tremble,
And bow down their necks 'neath the Juggernaut car,
But brave men will rise in the strength of a nation,
And cry, "Give me freedom, or else give me war!"
Farewell forever, the Star spangled banner,
No longer shall wave o'er the land of the free,
But we'll unfurl to the broad breeze of Heav'n.
Thirteen bright stars round the Palmetto tree

It was not long before most Southerners accepted the harsh reality that neither the national flag nor Key's song would become official symbols of the Confederacy. The flag was burned and buried in public ceremonies throughout the South (including one in the town of Liberty, Mississippi, "in the presence of a crowd of spectators, who would not tolerate such a memento of the Federal Union"),[539] and two songs in particular, "Dixie" and "The Bonnie Blue Flag," became the newest musical standards.[540]

In early September 1862, as Confederate troops entered Maryland for their first invasion of the United States, anxious Union soldiers went door-to-door in Baltimore to canvas for recruits.

Two of them stopped at the home of Elizabeth Phoebe Key Howard—Key's daughter—and asked about the availability of the seven Howard men who were listed in the 1860 census. She took a deep breath, because all were either in prison or in active service with the Confederate Army.

As McHenry Howard recounted it in his memoir:

"One day two men came to the house and…insisted on seeing my mother. They said, 'Madam, we are enrolling officers and have come to get the names of male members of your family—have you a husband or sons capable of bearing arms?' She said, 'Yes, a husband and six sons.'

"'Your husband, what is his name and where is he?' 'Charles Howard, he is a prisoner in Fort Warren.'

"'And your eldest son?' 'Frank Key Howard, he is also in prison with his father.'

"'And your next son?' 'John Eager Howard, he is a captain in the Confederate Army.'

"'And the next?' 'Charles Howard, he is a major in the Confederate Army.'

"'And the next?' 'James Howard, he is a lieutenant-colonel in the Confederate Army.'

"'And the next?' 'Edward Lloyd Howard, he is a surgeon in the Confederate Army.'

"During this, the men had become more and more flustered and faltered out, 'And your youngest son?' 'McHenry Howard, he is also in the Southern Army and with Stonewall Jackson, and I expect he will be here soon.'

"And she shut the door in their faces."[541]

McHenry Howard was a twenty-two-year-old law student who had passed the bar in Baltimore shortly before he enlisted as a Confederate soldier. He made a name for himself as a staff officer for Generals Edward Johnston, Isaac Trimble, and George "Maryland" Steuart, and he served under the overall command of legendary Thomas "Stonewall" Jackson, taking part in Jackson's legendary Valley Campaign. Young Howard also was present for the battles of First Manassas, Gaines's Mill, White Oak Swamp, Malvern Hill, Cedar Run, Payne's Farm, the Wilderness, and Spotsylvania until being taken prisoner by Union troops.[542] Many years after the war, he wrote a precisely detailed memoir of his Confederate service and acknowledged his ancestral connection to Francis Scott Key.

"On my mother's side," Howard said, "my great grandfather was a Revolutionary soldier and his son, my grandfather, was the author of 'The Star Spangled Banner' and one of the founders of the African Colonization Society. He died as late as 1843, and in 1861 there were upwards of sixty descendants living, and I think of them also every man, woman and child was Southern."

Almost as a footnote, he added, "Of all these…I cannot recall that any owned slaves in 1861."[543]

Another family with extended ties to the Star-Spangled Banner and Fort McHenry also took up the Confederate cause with great enthusiasm. Lewis Armistead, George's nephew, who had attended West Point and served for twenty-two years in the U.S. Army, commanded a brigade in Robert E. Lee's Army of Northern Virginia, and achieved the deepest penetration in Pickett's Charge at Gettysburg, often called the "high water mark" of the Confederacy. Given the widespread study of the Civil War and its popularity in American culture, Lewis became the most famous of all the Armisteads during the twentieth century, feted with paintings and monuments on the Gettysburg battlefield. A little-known fact is that his three younger brothers and teenaged son also served as Confederate soldiers.

CHAPTER TEN
The Rebel Armistead

Lewis Addison Armistead was destined for military service from the day he was born on February 18, 1817. Named for two uncles, Lewis and Addison, who gave their lives during the War of 1812, he was the son of a rising star in the U.S. Army and a nephew of the hero of Fort McHenry, linked by blood and legacy to the story of the Star-Spangled Banner.

Lewis Armistead, nephew of the hero of Fort McHenry who led a Confederate brigade in Pickett's Charge at Gettysburg. *(Wikimedia Commons)*

Lewis never had a chance to meet his Uncle George, who died shortly after his first birthday, but he and his younger brothers grew up regaled by tales of the flag, the song, and the historic stand at Baltimore harbor.

Their father, Walker Keith Armistead, was the embodiment of military doctrine and one of the most accomplished professional soldiers of his era. After becoming the third man to graduate from West Point in 1803, he was named chief engineer of the army in 1818 and promoted to brigadier general in 1828. Walker dutifully shuttled to army posts on the east coast during this period while his wife and nine children settled in at his three-hundred-acre plantation in Fauquier County, Virginia, where slaves handled much of the farm work. Young Lewis did preparatory work at Georgetown College and was completing studies at a school in Winchester, Virginia when his acceptance letter from West Point arrived in 1833.[544]

It was the start of a long and eventful U.S. Army career that spanned parts of four decades, including meritorious service in the Mexican-American War, where he was brevetted twice for gallantry and led a storming party in the final attack on Chapultepec. But his early days at West Point were known mostly for hijinks, irreverence, and repeated classroom struggles, contrary to his pedigree. Lewis spent three raucous years on campus and somehow never got out of the freshman class.

The academic charade ended in January 1836, when "Cadet Armistead [was] placed in arrest, charged with disorderly conduct in the Mess Hall...and was promptly confined to his room."[545] Numerous academy records were destroyed in an 1838 fire, but the most commonly-accepted story is that Lewis brawled with another cantankerous cadet, the future Confederate general, Jubal Early.[546] A fellow officer wrote in 1870 that it was "a youthful escapade...I have been told, the partial cracking of Jubal A. Early's head with a mess-hall plate," and an Armistead relative once referred to a cryptic "boyish frolic" on campus, but there is no other evidence to explain exactly what happened, or why.[547]

No matter. The indiscretion was serious enough that Lewis, at his father's urging, submitted a letter of resignation rather than risk a court martial and expulsion. The letter was accepted only as courtesy to the revered family name.[548] Lewis waited quietly for three years, perhaps attending classes at a small southern military school, then took advantage of his lineage (again) to receive a U.S. Army commission as second lieutenant in the Second Seminole War. He served briefly in combat at the start of his deployment in 1839 before being added to the staff of the newly-appointed commander of all U.S. troops in the Florida theatre—Brigadier General Walker K. Armistead.[549]

Lewis spent the next twenty-two years in sustained service to the U.S. military, including a two-year stint in the Mexican War from 1846–48, when his unique blend of leadership, fearlessness, and battlefield moxie made him one of the army's young stars on the rise. At the Battle of Churubusco, fellow soldier Cadmus Wilcox wrote that "The Sixth Infantry charged down the causeway as ordered, Lieut. Lewis A. Armistead at the head of the leading platoon." A few weeks later, in the decisive attack on Chapultepec, Wilcox said, "The ditch was at length reached, Lieut. Lewis Armistead, Sixth Infantry, being the first to leap into it under artillery and musketry fire."[550] Lewis received two brevets for "gallant and meritorious service" and came out of the war as a brevet major, seemingly destined for future greatness. Few made mention that when the U.S. flag was raised in triumph over Mexico City on September 14, 1847, it was thirty-three years to the day—and almost to the moment—that Uncle George Armistead had defeated the British at Fort McHenry.[551]

But the upward curve of his career flattened after that, in large part because of an unimaginable series of personal tragedies during his post-war service on the frontier. In a five-year period between 1850 and 1855, Lewis suffered the deaths of two wives and two of his three children, including an infant son with the haunting name of Lewis B. Armistead, who lived for less than one year and does not even appear in family genealogies. His own doting father had passed away in 1845, depriving Lewis of the most influential figure in his life, and a fire destroyed his mother's house and ravaged the family farm in 1852, endangering his younger siblings.[552] He requested, and received, a lengthy leave of absence, noting in a letter to army headquarters that "my father's estate was left in an unsettled condition and from mismanagement is still in a very unsatisfactory state…I think I could be of some service to my mother & to the younger children of the family if at home."[553]

Lewis provided great comfort for his family back in Fauquier County, but the weight of relentless trauma took a toll on his life and outlook. Fellow officers said he was noticeably more bitter and withdrawn by the time he returned to duty at his frontier post in Kansas, and it was only by throwing himself back into his work that he was able to put those tragedies in the past. Still, that kind of discipline came with a cost; he went almost three years without seeing his only surviving son, also named Walker Keith, in honor of his grandfather.

A respite came late in 1859, when, as a veteran officer with a famous family name, he manipulated the system for a year-long leave of absence.[554] Lewis spent the first nine months of 1860 back home in Virginia, reconnecting with his son and younger siblings, and took time on occasion to visit with old friends and neighbors, including the future Confederate cavalier Turner Ashby.[555]

Ashby commanded a local militia unit, the Fauquier Mountain Rangers, who had been called to service during the John Brown Raid in October 1859 and were present for Brown's hanging in Charles Town. As such, he had a gnawing realization that the country was tearing apart. Ashby told Armistead about this, talked about his growing fears of a civil war, but his fellow Virginian had been away for so long—detached for years from Southern life and politics—that he couldn't quite grasp the reality. Lewis thought Ashby was being too negative.

"Turner, do not talk so!" he said at one of their meetings in the summer of 1860. "Let me sing you a song, and wipe away your gloom."

With that, the nephew of George Armistead began to belt out the first few lines of "The Star-Spangled Banner."[556]

Lewis Armistead resumed full-time U.S. Army duty in December 1860, when he reported to his new post at San Diego, California.

South Carolina had seceded by the time he took command on December 26, and other Southern states were planning to join the exodus and form their own breakaway nation. Conflicted as to his future—should he side with his home state, Virginia, or remain with the United States?—Armistead sought advice from his old army friend, Winfield Scott Hancock, now serving as a quartermaster in Los Angeles.

Hancock didn't make it any easier. "I can give you no advice," he said, "as I shall not fight upon the principle of State-rights, but for the Union whole and undivided…I cannot sympathize with you; you must be guided by your own conviction, and I hope you will make no mistakes."[557]

An agonized Armistead continued to wrestle with his decision. He was a proud native Southerner who descended from a long line of slaveholders, grew up on a farm with nineteen slaves, and had owned at least one slave himself; deep down, he wholly supported the Rebel cause. And yet his family's legacy was linked by blood and deed to the United States Army and the original Star-Spangled Banner, one of the most iconic pieces of early American history. To underscore that point, the big fifteen-stripe flag that flew over Fort McHenry was still in the private possession of his Aunt Louisa at her home in Baltimore.

In the end, Lewis chose the Confederacy, explaining in a letter that he "left to fight for my country, and for, and with, my own people,"[558] but the emotion spilled out in a surreal farewell get-together with Hancock and other army friends, held at the Hancock home in Los Angeles before they all went off to fight one another in the Civil War.

As Hancock's wife, Almira, described it, "The most crushed of the party was Major Armistead, who, with tears which were contagious, streaming down his face, and hands upon Mr. Hancock's shoulders, while looking him steadily in the eye, said, 'Hancock, good-by, you can never know what this has cost me, and I hope God will strike me dead if I am ever induced to leave my native soil, should worse come to worst.'"[559]

Joining another army turncoat, the future Confederate General Albert Sidney Johnston, Armistead made his way across the country during the blazing hot summer months of 1861, passing through Arizona, New Mexico, and Texas before reaching New Orleans and angling his way to the Confederate capital in Richmond. He was commissioned colonel of the Fifty-Seventh Virginia regiment in September, joining his three younger brothers—Walker Jr., Franck, and Bowles—who were already serving in the Confederate Army. His teenaged son, Walker Keith, who went by "W. Keith," or, simply, "Keith," would become the fifth member of the family to volunteer early in 1862.[560]

There was perhaps no better example of the shifting sands of the national divide than the astounding case of W. Keith Armistead, the great-nephew of the hero of Fort McHenry.

In July 1860, just nine months before the start of the Civil War, he applied for an appointment to the U.S. Military Academy at West Point, hoping to follow in the footsteps of his father and grandfather. Lewis then tried to move the application along, writing a letter to the U.S. Secretary of War to ask that the application be viewed favorably, based on the family's long history of military service.

> *Upperville, Fauquier Co., Va.*
> *July 25, 1860*
>
> *Sir,*
>
> *I have the honor to apply for the appointment of cadet, to the U.S. Military Academy, for the year 1861, for my son, W. Keith Armistead.*
>
> *W. Keith Armistead will be sixteen years old next December—and, I believe, is fully qualified for the appointment.*
>
> *Twenty one years of my life have been [spent] in the service, on the frontier; I have therefore had little, if any, opportunity of becoming acquainted with the great or influential men of my country. I do not know, how, if I had the inclination, to request their influence in obtaining the appointment for which I now apply.*
>
> *If I, or any of my family, have ever done anything deserving of the favor of the War Dept., or of the Executive, it should be on record—it is to that record alone that I can appeal...*

Very Respectfully,
Your Obedient Servant,
Lewis A. Armistead
Bvt. Maj, 6th Infy.[561]

West Point records do not indicate whether Keith's application was accepted or rejected, but it became a moot point when Virginia seceded from the Union in May 1861. By September, as the academy's fall semester was starting, his father and three uncles were already serving in the Confederate Army, and the young man was making his way back to Richmond from an unidentified preparatory school in the North.[562]

On December 2, 1861, just ten days before Keith's seventeenth birthday, Lewis wrote another letter applying for a cadetship "for my son," this time in a prospective *Confederate* officer program. The rarely published letter is the most valuable of all existing Armistead family documents, because it reveals Lewis's reasons for joining the Rebel cause and highlights his fatherly concern for Keith's education and military future. It was addressed with personal flair to Confederate Adjutant General Samuel Cooper, one of his old U.S. Army comrades from the Seminole and Mexican Wars.

Camp Belcher, near Richmond, Va.
Dec. 26, 1861

Sir,

I have the honor to apply for the appointment of cadet for my son, W. Keith Armistead.

I have been a soldier all my life. I was an officer in the Army of the U.S., which service I left to fight for my own country, and for, and with, my own people—and because they were right, and oppressed. My resignation was forwarded in the month of May last, but I was unable to leave California until late in June, which I did with Genl. A.S. Johnson (sic), and other resigned officers of the U.S. Army, and arrived in the City of Richmond, Va. about the 15th of September last.

I never was a man of any wealth, and the little I had was all sacrificed when I left the U.S. Army. I wish it had been more. I am not able to continue my son's education. He is willing to take a musket, but I think he has capacity to do better, and that he is of the right age to begin a military education. He will be seventeen on the 12th inst.

Altho' my services were rendered under a different flag from that which I now acknowledge, I can recall them with pleasure and pride, and I believe they are still remembered by some, perhaps none better than the Adjt. Genl. Of the C.S. Army.

Your (Obedient Servant)
Lewis A. Armistead
Col. 57th Va. Vol.[563]

Having never rendered service to the U.S. Army or flag, Keith reached his decision to join the Confederacy with far less emotion than his father. He was anxious to improve his chances for officer training and took it upon himself to write letters to various Rebel authorities in March 1862, requesting additional support. One of them even reached the desk of General Robert E. Lee, who at the time was a senior military advisor to the Confederate president, Jefferson Davis.[564]

Remarkably, Lee responded within three days, writing to the Confederate Secretary of War to endorse Armistead for the appointment. Much of Lee's support was based on his familiarity with the young man's father, but another Rebel official added a note to Lee's letter that "Mr. (W. Keith) Armistead has been, in this office, since arrival, most assiduous in the performance of duty, correct in habits, and eager" to prove his worth.

In full, Lee wrote:

My personal acquaintance with W. K. Armistead is but of recent date; but the impressions formed of him in this short period are of favorable character; and I hear good accounts of him...

I know him to be the son of a brave solider and worthy man, Brig. Genl. Armistead, in the service of the Confederate States.[565]

It was an understandable effort on the part of Lewis, Keith, and General Lee, but the searing demands of war left little time for the Rebels to form an academy; they could not afford such a luxury. Keith enlisted in Company A of the Sixth Virginia Cavalry on May 6, became an aide to the famed General J.E.B. Stuart in August and joined his father's staff as a first lieutenant and aide-de-camp in April 1863.[566]

Lewis Armistead was promoted to brigadier general in April 1862 and fought for the first time against the U.S. flag on June 1, at the Battle of Seven Pines.[567] It must have been a jarring experience.

His brigade performed poorly during an ill-advised attack, although fellow officers praised him for personal bravery during the Confederate defeat. "Armistead's men fled early in the action," wrote D.H. Hill, who commanded a nearby division, "with the exception of a few heroic companies, with which that gallant officer maintained his ground against an entire brigade."[568] Several others also praised his "gallantry" in a losing effort at Malvern Hill on July 1, reminiscent of his days fighting for the U.S. in the Mexican War, when he won regular plaudits as one who embodied the home of the brave.[569]

With those two battles as his only significant action, however, Armistead's Confederate military career was unremarkable in the first two years of the war. It did not reach its crescendo until the third day of the Battle of Gettysburg on July 3, 1863, when he and his men played a pivotal role in the most famous frontal attack ever launched on U.S. soil.

Following two days of bloody but inconclusive fighting, Robert E. Lee called for a risky, straight-forward movement over almost a mile of open farmland to attack the Union center. George Pickett's division formed the right side of the alignment, with Armistead's brigade in a supporting second line. It is likely that Armistead knew he would be attacking troops commanded by his old friend, Hancock, who had been posted there and fought fiercely on July 2, but this was no time for sentimentality.

One of the enduring images of the Civil War came minutes later in Pickett's Charge—the balding Armistead, his black felt hat on his sword, leading a small band of Rebels over the low stone wall on Cemetery Ridge, breaking through a gap in the Union line. He did not make it far into the famous "Angle," maybe one hundred feet, before a hail of bullets from the Philadelphia Brigade brought him down. Exactly where he fell, and how many wounds he received, remain a matter of dispute, but modern-day visitors can see a small stone tablet inscribed with "Lewis A. Armistead Fell Here" at the approximate spot on the ridge. Significantly, it is the only marker to a Confederate soldier on the Union side of the battlefield.[570]

An ambulance carried Armistead to a Union Army field hospital at the George Spangler farm, where doctors treated non-life-threatening wounds to his arm and leg. Those same doctors were astonished, however, when he died two days later. (Most likely, modern physicians say, of a blood clot that developed in his leg and traveled to his lung.)[571] The Confederate general was buried in a shallow grave on the Spangler property, and the story might have ended there had it not been for an enterprising Gettysburg doctor, Cyrus N. Chamberlain, who thought Armistead's relatives might pay if they could receive the body. Cold-hearted as Chamberlain seemed, he turned out to be correct.

One of the doctor's associates, a former Baltimore resident named John O'Neal, exchanged a series of letters over the next several weeks with Lewis's first cousin in Baltimore, Christopher Hughes Armistead—who, by quirk of fate, was the son of the hero of Fort McHenry. Indeed, Christopher wrote, the family wanted the body.

In a message dated October 3, three months to the day after Pickett's Charge, he asked O'Neal to make "the best arrangement you can with a Dr. Chamberlain, who disinterred the remains of General Armistead, for their delivery to me here, encased so they may be put into a vault." For a total price of $150, Chamberlain also offered the body of another fallen Confederate general, William Barksdale, prompting Christopher to tell him, "Under these circumstances, I want to take charge of both."[572]

Less than two weeks later, however, with the remains still not delivered, Lewis's cousin backed away from the larger deal, writing, "I am only particularly interested in those of my relative, and have but little money to spare."[573] Negotiations continued until Tuesday, October 27, when a certificate of deposit for one hundred dollars made its way to O'Neal in Gettysburg. "My thanks for your many kindnesses," Christopher wrote. "I notice particularly your instructions to receive on Thursday evening at Calvert Depot [in Baltimore] the remains of my cousin, the gallant General Armistead."[574]

Without any fanfare—in fact, under a cloak of secrecy—Lewis Armistead's body was carried to Old St. Paul's Cemetery in Baltimore and placed in the Hughes family vault alongside his uncle, George Armistead, who, almost fifty years earlier, on the edge of the nearby harbor, had defended Fort McHenry for the United States in the War of 1812.[575]

George Armistead and his nephew, Lewis, are buried in the same vault at Old St. Paul's Cemetery in Baltimore with nameplates side by side. *(Author photo)*

It was in the spirit of reconciliation that veterans of the Philadelphia Brigade invited their counterparts from Pickett's Division to return to Gettysburg on the twenty-fourth anniversary of the battle in July 1887.

The idea was to swap war stories and honor the gallantry of "a charge not surpassed in its grandeur and unfaltering courage in the annals of war since time began," but negotiations grew heated that spring when Pickett's men asked to place a monument to their division inside Union lines, at the spot where Armistead fell.[576]

Angry Northerners rejected the request, salty Southerners threatened to pull out of the event, and only private correspondence from a quick-thinking Philadelphia officer saved the first major reunion of Civil War veterans at the Gettysburg battlefield. John W. Frazier, secretary of the Philadelphia group and a veteran of the Seventy-First Pennsylvania, which defended against Armistead, wrote of his support for "an imperishable monument" and encouraged the former Rebels to attend "the first [reunion] of the kind held since the war."[577]

In a second letter, Frazier added,

> *Writing as an individual member of the Brigade Association, I do not hesitate to say that I am sure every member of our Association would gladly and earnestly co-operate with your Association in securing the location of a monument on the spot where the brave General Armistead fell, and I believe that your Association will yet determine to place one there to mark the spot not only where General Armistead laid down his life, but to indicate for all time to come on the historic grounds of Gettysburg the position reached by Pickett's Division in the face of a hail of musket balls, solid shot, and shell, more terrible, perhaps, than was hurled against any body of men on either side during the late war.*[578]

The outreach worked. About three hundred veterans from Pickett's Division flocked to Gettysburg on July 1, 1887 and were greeted by five hundred Pennsylvanians who had fought them and repelled the famous charge. They spent three days together, extending hands and taking part in several formal ceremonies while touting a new motto: "One Country and one flag."[579]

William Aylett, colonel of the Fifty-Third Virginia in Armistead's brigade at the time of the battle, and a great-grandson of the Revolutionary patriot Patrick Henry, spoke at one event on behalf of the ex-Confederates, as U.S. flags fluttered all around him:

> *We come as the survivors of a great battle, which illustrated the greatness and glory of the American people... We have come forth from the baptism of blood and fire*

in which we were consumed, as the representatives of
a New South, and…Above the ashes left by the War
and over the tomb of secession and African slavery we
have created a new empire, and have built a temple to
American liberty, in which you and I can worship, and
over it we have run up the Star-Spangled banner.[580]

Northern veterans still refused to allow a monument to a Confederate division on the Union side of the battlefield, but feelings had softened enough that they approved a small marker to Armistead at the site where he was wounded. Meeting only a few days after the reunion, the Gettysburg Battlefield Memorial Association authorized the battlefield's historian "to mark with a suitable tablet the spot where General L.A. Armistead of the Confederate army fell mortally wounded." A four-foot, six-inch stone scroll was placed about one hundred feet inside the Angle in February 1888, inscribed "Brigadier General Lewis Armistead Fell Here July 3, 1863."[581] It remains one of the most visited monuments on the field and marks the deepest penetration by any Rebel general during the failed charge.[582]

Armistead's memory was feted again at Gettysburg in 1906, when Pickett's Division and the Philadelphia Brigade met as organized units for the final time. Sergeant Michael Specht of the Seventy-Second Pennsylvania had captured Armistead's sword during the climax of the battle, but now, feeling pangs of guilt on the forty-third anniversary, wanted to turn it back to his former enemies. "When it has come to pass that the bitterness is gone," a spokesman said, "it seems right and fitting to Sergeant Specht that he should return this sword to those who followed General Armistead…surely no time more fitting than this, which perhaps will be the last time we shall meet as representative bodies."[583] Pickett's survivors promptly announced the sword would be donated to a museum of Confederate relics in Richmond.[584]

Word soon reached newspapers in Baltimore, where a new generation of Armistead descendants was eager for more details. "We tried again and again to recover the sword of General Armistead after the battle of Gettysburg, but could find no trace of it," wrote a relative named George Armistead, grandson of the hero of Fort McHenry.

"We are indeed glad to know of it after all these years." He began a correspondence with John Frazier of the Philadelphia Brigade and noted the ancestral connection between Lewis Armstead of Pickett's Charge and George Armistead of Fort McHenry, highlighting the unique roles they played in two of the epic military events of the nineteenth century.

In a letter to Frazier that was also published in the *Baltimore Sun*, Armistead wrote:

> *General Armistead's remains repose in Old St. Paul's Churchyard of this city, and it may interest the Philadelphia Brigade to hear that their one-time enemy, but now dearest foe, sleeps by the side of Col. George Armistead, and that it was the latter's gallant defense of Fort McHenry against the British in 1814 that made possible and inspired the poet, Francis Scott Key, to write our national anthem, 'The Star-Spangled Banner.'*

> *That same old flag that Key strained his eyes "in the morn's early light" to see "streaming so gallantly o'er the ramparts" remains to this day in the custody and possession of our family. Thus you will observe that the survivors of the Philadelphia Brigade and of Pickett's Division are linked together by legend and tradition with hooks of steel.*[585]

There are now five markers to Lewis Armistead at Gettysburg National Military Park, more than any other Confederate soldier, including Robert E. Lee, but his fame in the late twentieth century was due largely to two popular works of historical fiction.[586]

The novel *Killer Angels*, which won the Pulitzer Prize for fiction in 1975, and its companion movie, *Gettysburg*, released in 1993, turned a romanticized version of the Armistead-Hancock friendship into one of the major narratives of the war's most famous battle. The "Armistead" character had several emotional speaking roles that made indelible impressions on an entire generation of Civil War students and battlefield visitors.

In one of the movie's climactic scenes, he is approached by a British military observer just before the start of Pickett's Charge.

"I'm told you're descended from an illustrious military family," the man says.

"Who told you that?" grunts Armistead.

"He tells me it was your uncle who defended Fort McHenry during the War of 1812…and that he was therefore the guardian of the original Star-Spangled Banner."

The British officer pauses to look across at U.S. flags waving on Cemetery Ridge.

"I must say I do appreciate the irony of it all."[587]

CHAPTER ELEVEN
"There is Our Flag!"

The original Star-Spangled Banner was kept from public view and largely forgotten for more than five years after the end of the Civil War, seemingly fading from history and memory. Apparently, it was not even mentioned again in print until 1872, when a U.S. Navy officer named George Henry Preble addressed it briefly in a book titled *Our Flag: Origin and Progress of the Flag of the United States of America.*

Commodore George Preble, author of a history of the U.S. flag who played such a key role in publicizing the Star-Spangled Banner in the late nineteenth century. *(Wikimedia Commons)*

Preble's key role in the story of the flag's survival was another quirk of historic fate. Born into a family of sailors in 1816, he followed ancestral tradition by joining the Navy as a teenager, serving on a heart-pounding cruise around the world and fighting with distinction in the Second Seminole, Mexican, and Civil Wars. His career almost ended when he allowed a speedy Confederate cruiser to escape in Mobile Bay—the Navy dismissed him in September 1862—but President Lincoln restored his rank and command five months later, and Preble went on to support William T. Sherman during the Union Army's March to the Sea. After the war he was named inspector general of the Boston Navy Yard and embarked on parallel ventures as a historian and author.[588]

From the time he was a boy, Preble had been intrigued by national flags and the roles they played in identifying ships on the high seas. After writing two books about personal war experiences, he spent years digging into the history of flags from around the world, with particular focus on the U.S. version. In the introduction to his 1872 edition of *Our Flag*, Preble wrote that "history has, in general, failed to appreciate the value of these symbols, which have often given ascendancy to party, and led armies on to victory with more certainty and dispatch than the combinations of tactics and the most disinterested valor." To emphasize that point, he quoted the U.S. statesman Daniel Webster on the book's second page: "There is but one other emblem so significant as a flag—the cross."[589]

Preble's research was so deep and detailed that he spent 143 pages on the ancient history of flags before getting around to his main topic, the evolution of America's stars and stripes. He claimed that the "earliest instance" of a thirteen-stripe design was for a banner presented to a Philadelphia horse militia in 1775 and wrote that the first U.S. ship to fly the flag in English waters after the Revolution was the *Bedford* of Nantucket, Massachusetts, which arrived off the coast of Kent in February 1783. A London periodical decried it as "the first vessel which has displayed the thirteen rebellious stripes of America in any British port!" Preble then described the debate to add two more stripes in 1794, noting that a congressional bill to that effect was passed with less-than-unanimous approval.[590]

One mystery that he could not solve, however, was the location of the flag that flew over Fort McHenry in September 1814, the original Star-Spangled Banner. Preble sorted through several disparate rumors that it might be in the possession of George Armistead's descendants before curiously settling on a second-hand report from an American history periodical in 1868:

> *A correspondent of the Historical Magazine says that visiting [Fort McHenry] in 1859, his attention was called while in the garret of the barracks, to an American flag, which was rolled up in a piece of dirty muslin and lay thrown into a corner covered with dust, and which Captain [Otis] Tillinghast informed him was the identical flag that floated over McHenry during the bombardment.*"[591]

It is possible that the reporter saw the smaller "storm flag," which flew over the fort during the heat of battle (and which since has been lost to history), but the implication that it might have been Armistead's vaunted garrison flag caused a firestorm of national attention. Rolled up in a piece of dirty muslin? Thrown in a corner and covered with dust?

When news of Preble's report began to circulate and found its way to Georgiana Armistead Appleton, she was beside herself with anger.

Georgiana had never heard of George Preble and had no idea how to reach him, but it is likely that her husband's family, with deep roots in Boston, tracked him down at that city's naval yard. It was, in retrospect, a crucial connection in U.S. history, because it brought the Star-Spangled Banner out of hiding and into the mainstream of American life.

In the first of more than ten letters to Preble, establishing ownership of the flag and addressing its chain of custody in detail, Georgiana wrote on February 18, 1873:

> *My father, Col. George Armistead, defended Fort McHenry during the bombardment of the British*

in 1814, and the veritable flag was in his possession at the time of his death in 1818. It then passed into the hands of his widow, my mother, and she in turn bequeathed it to me. This venerated flag is connected with my earliest recollections…

Had the flag been at Fort McHenry during the rebellion, would not have the government produced it, as the watchword for Union and Liberty? Even then it was mine, and a jealous and perhaps selfish love made me guard my treasure with watchful care, lest this trophy of our gallant father should meet with some untoward accident.[592]

In the same letter, pouring out feelings that had evolved over ten-plus years of ownership, she also pondered the idea of donating the flag to a museum or historical society, as opposed to having it wither away in a private home:

Now I have come to look at the matter in a different light and I think this time-honored relic should not remain in private hands, but that it should be in some public place, where our sons and daughters might be taught to look at and love this labarum of our country.[593]

She was not yet ready to do that, however, and such a decision would not be made for more than thirty years. But Georgiana and Preble began a robust correspondence that brought them together as dual marketing managers of the Star-Spangled Banner, ensuring that it would become far more than a regional treasure in Baltimore.

Preble dashed off a response to her first letter in a matter of days. Delivered on February 26, 1873, it offered "many thanks for your note about the 'Old Flag,'" which inspired the words of our National Song," and promised the proper corrections in the next edition of his book. In the meantime, Preble's work had led him to other famous flags, including one from the 1779 ship *Bon Homme Richard*, commanded by John Paul Jones and described by the *New York Times* as "the first flag…ever hoisted over an American vessel of war." He believed that such valuable relics should not remain for long in private hands.[594]

"I have suggested [that we should] deposit the flag of the *Bon Homme Richard* with the trophies of our naval success at the Naval Academy in Annapolis," Preble wrote, "and in the same spirit I suggest that your flag should be deposited at the Military Academy at West Point, with the trophies they have there—unless you prefer the Academy at Annapolis, as being nearer the scene that has given is such historic interest."[595] There was no immediate movement on either matter, and, in fact, the *Bon Homme Richard* flag was discovered to be a replica, but this was the first time that someone outside the extended Armistead family had thought of a permanent home for the Star-Spangled Banner.[596]

Preble could not believe his good fortune in these early months of 1873. The commodore wrote a series of letters to Georgiana, posing questions about the flag, her family, Fort McHenry, and their overlapping connections in history. He wondered if she could supply him with a photo of the flag, advising that "it should be stretched on a board to straighten its [wrinkles], and all that the damage that time and bullets had done to it." He then fairly begged for a portrait of her father ("whose memory is historical") and told her, "I shall be glad to have under your own hand as complete a history of the Old Flag as you can give."[597]

She was overwhelmed by the interest in her flag and its legacy, especially from a military officer based outside of Baltimore. It convinced her that the story should extend beyond hometown boundaries, and she eagerly responded to as many of his requests as possible, while confessing with some embarrassment that the flag had never been photographed. Georgiana provided contemporary newspaper accounts of the battle at Fort McHenry, along with her father's portrait and his official 1814 battle report to the U.S. secretary of war. Any lingering doubts about the national scope of the story were dispelled when Charles B. Norton of the United States Centennial Commission in Philadelphia reached out in late March 1873, writing that "this commission has been advised that you have in your possession the original of the Star-Spangled Banner…please advise us as to your wishes in reference to its connection with our Centennial celebration of 1876."[598] The timing of the request makes it almost certain that Preble had tipped off the commission.

His primary goal during this period was to persuade Georgiana to lend him the flag—and then, once it was in his possession, to have it spread out and photographed for the first time. After working incessantly since February to earn her trust, Preble made the formal request on May 15, 1873, writing that "if you express the Old Flag to the address of this letter, my home in Boston, after or about the 1st of June, I will have it photographed…[and] if it can be hoisted on the Naval Yard Flag Staff, I will have it done."[599] Any anxiety she may have had over parting with the flag was counteracted by the chance to see Preble's photograph displayed in newspapers across the country, and, perhaps, the world. On May 27, she alerted him that "I expect to leave for New York tomorrow and will send you The Banner in the early part of next week—I am glad that you kept the paper with my father's [battle] report as I feel sure that in your hands it is in safe keeping."[600]

Commodore George Preble collaborated with Georgiana Armistead Appleton to take the first photo of the Fort McHenry flag in 1873. Preble posted a soldier in front of the flag at the Boston Naval Yard to give context to its massive size. *(Courtesy of the American Antiquarian Society)*

With that, the most famous flag in U.S. history was placed in a crate and sent by railway express to a man from Boston whom she had never met in person.

Thankfully, it arrived.

George Preble's next letter confirmed that the Star-Spangled Banner had entered a new phase of publicity and promotion. Up until that time, few Americans would have known that the "Old Flag" from the War of 1812 still existed as an icon of history, and news of its sudden presence in Boston was as unexpected as it was thrilling.

"The flag of Fort McHenry came safely by express yesterday morning," he told Georgiana in a dispatch dated June 12, 1873.

> *...it is now spread on the floor of the Sail Loft at the Naval Yard, where it has attracted much attention. I am having some of the seams that are ripped re-stitched together, and hope to soon have it photographed, by having it hung [out of the wind] against the wall of one of the Naval Yard buildings. It is altogether too frail and tender to be hoisted on the flag staff as I wished. After it is photographed, and I have exhibited it at the New England Historical Genealogical Society, I will have it placed in the fire-proof room of the society to await your orders. I also have had a scale drawing made of it."[601]*

Preble then rattled off another long list of questions for Georgiana, in an effort to make the flag's full story part of the public record. These included:

- "Do you know whether any of the flag or the ends have been cut off?"

- "Was the star that is obliterated cut out by a shot?"

- "What is the meaning of the new piece of old cloth shaped like an 'A' which is sewed on one of the white stripes?"

- "Is this bag, in which it came to me, the original bag in which it was kept at Fort McHenry?"[602]

She answered in less than a week, revealing for the first time in writing that, yes, many pieces of the flag had been snipped as souvenirs; that the star was apparently given to "some official person" (possibly, it was speculated, to the Marquis de Lafayette on his 1824 visit); that the red letter shaped like an "A" was sewn on by her mother; and that the bag was probably the same one used to store it at Fort McHenry after the bombardment.[603] In another letter written several days later, Preble asked, "Am I at liberty to state what you told me, your father was ordered by General Smith to surrender the fort, but he chose to fight at the risk of being court-martialed?"[604] Though the story sounded enticing, and was apparently believed by Georgiana and other relatives, this was one of many rumors about the Battle of Baltimore that simply was not true.

The historic first photo of the sixty-year-old Star-Spangled Banner was taken at the Boston Naval Yard on June 21, 1873. Surprised at its ragged appearance and delicate condition, Preble had it stitched to a rigid canvas backing before putting it on display for the camera lens. "I have had the Glorious Old Flag quilted to a sail so it could be hung from the 2nd story of one of the buildings at the Naval Yard," he told Georgiana in a letter the next day, assuring her that it had been "successfully photographed" for posterity. To offer perspective of the flag's massive size, Preble commandeered a Marine private in full dress uniform to stand beside it as an unofficial honor guard, and he looked like a miniature toy soldier against the backdrop of red-and-white stripes.[605]

From that day forward, Preble became the unofficial public relations director of the Star-Spangled Banner, eager to share the narrative of what he considered the most consequential flag in U.S. history. A few weeks later, he gave a speech at the New England Historic Genealogical Society, titled "Three Historic Flags and Three September Victories," which was published as a pamphlet and distributed widely.

The two other banners on display were remnants of U.S. naval battles on the high seas, but Preble considered the Fort McHenry flag, "which is canopied over you," the undisputed star of the show. "After the lapse of sixty years, its colors, as you see them, are so bright it would seem as if, in the words of another of our songs, 'all its hues were born in heaven.'"[606]

Expanding on the story, based on talks with Georgiana and other sources, the commodore added, "there can be no doubt as to the authenticity of this flag. It was preserved by Colonel Armistead and bears upon one of its stripes his autograph, his name and the date of the bombardment. It has always remained in his family, and his widow, in 1861, bequeathed it to their youngest daughter, Mrs. William Stuart Appleton…She was named Georgiana Armistead, for her father."[607] He then introduced her as his special guest to thunderous applause.

The July 1873 event made national news, including a New York account that described the flag as "covering part of the ceiling and held up at the sides by cannon balls and chains," drawing periodic gasps from the crowd. The grand finale was a solo of "The Star-Spangled Banner," with a standing ovation that included "the immense audience joining in the last stanza."[608] It was likely the first time that Francis Scott Key's song had been performed in a public forum in the presence of the Fort McHenry flag.

Preble now was basking in the glory of his connection to the Star-Spangled Banner, feted by the New England society with a proclamation noting his success in obtaining such "relics of national value." With Georgiana's permission, he even contributed to the desecration of the flag by taking some fragments for personal use to display with his pamphlets and photos. Seemingly oblivious to the damage this caused, he convinced himself that the few "snippings…will not be missed." Preble also obtained a copy of Key's hand-written lyrics and developed a unique design by placing it in a frame, flanked by small red, white, and blue pieces of the flag that inspired the song. He advised Georgiana to do the same.[609]

Preble continued in his role as primary custodian of the Star-Spangled Banner for the next three years, delighted that it still existed "in a tolerable state of preservation" but growing increasingly concerned about the long-term future.[610] He advised Georgiana that she should not loan the flag to the centennial in Philadelphia unless they would "give a full guarantee of its safety in every respect" and agree to insure it for its value as a historic relic, up to $10,000.[611]

Georgiana had several years to make her decision, but the unintended consequence was that more offers to display the flag arrived almost weekly from across the country. One came from an old Baltimore acquaintance, Alice C. Etting, who wrote that she and her husband had founded a new national museum at Independence Hall in Philadelphia and were "very anxious to have the original Flag deposited for a while." The opportunity was intriguing because, if an agreement could be reached, the daughter of George Armistead would be loaning the Star-Spangled Banner to the niece of Francis Scott Key. The history of their families beckoned again.

In a letter dated December 29, 1873, Mrs. Etting wrote that she would be presenting one of Key's letters at the museum and thought the flag would be a perfect companion:

> *The building has been made as safe as possible, so there will be no risk in regard to it. We will undertake to hang it in such a manner as so it is out of harm's way. It could be boxed up and sent to us at Independence Hall (the charges to be paid here), and a certificate of deposit will be formally made out and sent to you.*[612]

Etting's letter affected Georgiana more than any other because of the deep Baltimore connection—"that dear old home around which clusters our fondest memories"—but she was being inundated during this time with a dizzying series of proposals from multiple sources. Preble's photo had been circulated, copies of his speech had been re-printed, and stacks of letters soon arrived with requests for small pieces of the flag, as well as images of her father and other mementos related to the story. A businessman named James Lick from San Francisco asked for several photographs to be placed in the cornerstone of a monument he planned to erect to Key on the west coast. It soon became too much for her to handle.[613]

In the draft of a letter written in mid-January 1874, Georgiana told "my dear Mrs. Etting" that the old flag was no longer strong enough for repeated public viewing.

> *I regret to say that by the advice of friends, both civil and military, I am warned that so precious a relic must be carefully handled and secured, not only from fire but from mutilation. The Banner, notwithstanding its wonderful preservation, shows that time has laid on it a heavy hand, and it required the gentlest care to preserve its integrity.*[614]

Almost eight feet had already been cut away by that point, and the topic of its continued "mutilation" was clearly on their minds. In April 1874, after snipping off yet another piece for an honored guest, Preble wrote, "I would advise that there be no further mutilations of the flag, for as much has been taken from it as can be without destroying it as a whole."[615] Sometime the next summer, he convinced the Appletons that if the flag were to be displayed at all for the upcoming national centennial, it should at the sprawling Centennial Exposition in Philadelphia, where it would be protected in an exhibit sponsored by the U.S. Navy. The plan, he said, was "to have it exhibited in the Government building, displayed in full, out of reach of the destruction of relic hunters."

In October 1875, after moving his own headquarters from Boston to Philadelphia, Preble took the lead in negotiations with Admiral Thornton Jenkins.[616]

The flag and its canvas backing were so heavy that nine men had to lift it onto the USS *Tallapoosa*, a Civil War–era ship that was now a training vessel for the U.S. Navy. The trip along the coast toward Pennsylvania required a stop in Portsmouth, Rhode Island, where an officer "had it unrolled to be dried as it smelled musty, but it was under guard all the time and not a shred was taken from it." It was back in Preble's possession at the navy yard in Philadelphia by November 10, 1875, when he began to finalize arrangements with Admiral Jenkins for the banner's most extensive display since Lafayette's visit more than forty years earlier. He emphasized that it "is very ragged and unless looked after and placed so it cannot be reached will suffer at the hands of relic hunters"—a common refrain over the next six months.[617]

Preble saw another chance for publicity and leaked word of the impending exhibition to local and national newspapers, setting off another surge of coverage. Shortly after headlines appeared in the *Baltimore Sun*, Georgiana heard from a woman whose late father had served under George Armistead at the Battle of Fort McHenry. "He often said that your father's gallant defense of Fort McHenry had not been fully appreciated, that your father was the only man in the fort who knew it was not bombproof," Susan Warfield wrote. "Had he communicated the fact to the garrison, not a man would have remained in the fort; and the anxiety he suffered produced the heart disease of which he died." Enclosed with the letter were a few verses of a poem she composed years earlier, which had never been published or seen by anyone outside her family.

> To the shells bursting wide, and the cannons' loud roar.
> Our brave gallant Armistead as an adamant rock;
> Tho' vengeance propelled by the sale and the oar,
> The thunder of Britain to him was no shock.
> Their midnight assault he with vigilance met,
> Oh! The gloom of that night we shall never forge
> And lovely the morn that beheld them retiring,
> For vanquished were Britons, and Ross was expiring.[618]

As it turned out, however—and for reasons that were never fully explained—neither the Star-Spangled Banner nor the tribute to George Armistead ever became part of the Centennial Exhibition in Philadelphia. Jenkins made several promises to Preble that the flag would be displayed overhead and out of reach of the public, with "a printed card in three languages describing it as a relic," but there are no indications that any of it ever happened. Preble was "very annoyed" at this missed PR opportunity on the country's one hundredth birthday—it would have been the largest audience ever to see the flag—and an even angrier Georgiana lashed out at the handlers, demanding that both Jenkins and Preble return it to her possession.[619] "I now intend to have my banner again in my own keeping," she wrote in September 1876. "Had I known it could not have been shown at the Exhibition I should have loaned to Mr. Etting (at Independence Hall)."[620]

Long before the flag was back in Georgiana's possession, her husband's cousin, Nathan Appleton, Jr. of Boston, had written to ask about her plans for its long-term future. As the Armistead and Appleton descendants all got along in years, momentum was building to donate the flag to a museum for permanent preservation and display.

The following letter was sent from Nathan to Georgiana in November 1875:

> *I write now to ask you what are your plans for the Star-Spangled Banner, of which you know we have often talked, that is whether you still think of presenting it to the people of the United States, and allowing me to be the medium of presentation, at some great national fete day as for instance the Fourth of July next and at Philadelphia [July 4, 1876]...It would like as I have told you to have the orating part of the programme.*[621]

Nathan Appleton would, indeed, have his chance to speak on a nationally historic date, but it would not come until June 14, 1877, the one hundredth anniversary of the Flag Act (now known as Flag Day). Georgiana was still not ready to make a permanent donation, but she agreed to loan it for Nathan's celebration at Old South Church in Boston. The master of ceremonies called attention to the original Star-Spangled Banner, "exhibited on one side of the platform...by the kind permission of the owner, Mrs. William Stuart Appleton," and an ebullient Nathan began his lengthy remarks by blurting out, "Ladies and gentlemen, *there is our flag!*" He gave an account of the battle at Fort McHenry and detailed Key's emotions in writing the national song. Acknowledging former Confederates who were now back in the Union, he also referenced "a war in which many of our brothers, who had been born under the guardianship of this flag, felt that it was their duty to fight against it." But the banner, he said, was now a symbol of reconciliation, showing "to mankind, as has never been done before, that social, political and religious liberty can go hand in hand together…I wish that every citizen of our great republic could gaze upon this very flag we are so fortunate as to have here to-night!"[622]

The *Boston Daily Advertiser* reported that "the most stirring feature" of the evening was a rendition of "The Star-Spangled Banner" by soprano Julia Houston West, which brought the event to a closing crescendo. "The audience rose to their feet and joined most heartily in the chorus," the paper said, "and the interludes were filled with storms of applause."[623] It was another rare nineteenth-century coupling of Key's song and the flag it so proudly hailed.

The Star-Spangled Banner returned with Georgiana to her new home in New York City, where, suffering from the ravages of rheumatism and gout at age sixty, she lived out the final year of her life in relative misery. It would never again make a public appearance under her stewardship. The family's financial situation declined significantly over the years, but she rejected repeated overtures to put the flag up for sale, telling Preble, "In heavy reverses of fortune, when friends have suggested that I might perhaps sell it for a high price…I have felt that I would rather beg than part with my treasure."[624] Georgiana died in New York on July 25, 1878 and was buried at Old St. Paul's Cemetery in Baltimore, in the same family vault as her father. Custody of her "precious relic" passed by the terms of her will to her son, Eben, a no-nonsense New York stockbroker who was uncomfortable in the public eye.[625]

CHAPTER TWELVE
A Home for All Time

Ebenezer Stuart Appleton was only thirty-two years old when he inherited the Star-Spangled Banner following his mother's death in 1878.

With all due respect to George Armistead's grandson, seldom has anyone been less prepared to care for a revered national treasure.

Ebenezer "Eben" Stuart Appleton, Armistead's grandson and the final private owner of the flag who loaned it to the Smithsonian in 1907. He made the gift permanent in 1912. *(Courtesy of Christopher Hughes Morton and Karen Morton)*

One of his first acts as owner was to contact Commodore Preble and ask about storage of the new possession. "I received some days since in the settlement of my mother's estate a box weighing about two hundred pounds, six feet long, and I should say twenty inches thick and about the same width," Eben wrote. "My object in writing is to ask you to let me know details of how the flag is packed." He winced a bit when telling Preble that he had already received a request to loan the flag for Baltimore's sesquicentennial celebration in 1880, which would include the placement of a cornerstone for a new monument to his grandfather on Eutaw Street. He was agreeable, he said, but only because of the generous civic tribute to his family: "I presume at the unveiling I will have to take it to Baltimore and exhibit it on that interesting occasion."[626]

Indeed, the 1880 event promised to be one of the grandest in the city's history. The schedule called for a formal military parade featuring nine veterans of the 1814 battle at Fort McHenry—heralded locally as the "Old Defenders"—along with modern-day sailors, marines, and infantry units. Organizers were thrilled that the notoriously private Eben consented to bring the flag from New York and carry it in a carriage with his friend William W. Carter, a Baltimore historian and fierce "proponent of the George Armistead monument." Fort McHenry's twenty-two-piece band would help lead the way, followed by flower-strewn carriages escorted by Union Civil War veterans, local militia companies, and volunteer firemen, many of them decked out in red, white, and blue.[627]

Extensive advance coverage by the *Baltimore American* lowered expectations by informing attendees that they would see only a small portion of the Star-Spangled Banner, however. "When the flag was taken from its box at City Hall, it was found to weigh nearly 200 pounds, the great weight being largely due to a backing of canvas, carefully made by Admiral Preble," the paper reported. "In its infirm condition, and owing to its very large size, it will of course be impossible to completely show the flag, but the people may rely upon at least a glimpse of this precious relic."[628]

Word of the event soon spread to other descendants of Fort McHenry royalty, and at least two of them reached out to inquire about taking part. Friends of Mary Briscoe, said to be the oldest living relative of Francis Scott Key, wrote a letter to the *American* asking that "the old banner should be allowed to pass her house, and to play the national song."[629] Margaret Young Sanderson, who helped sew the flag as a teenager with her aunt, Mary Pickersgill, traveled to Baltimore from New York City for one last look at her handiwork. According to the *Baltimore Sun*, "Mrs. Sanderson gave a history of the construction of the flag…[she] remembered perfectly well that her portion of the labor was to baste the stars on the blue field."[630]

The parade and accompanying ceremonies more than lived up to their spectacular buildup. Tears flowed freely along the parade route as ninety-year-old battle veterans made their final public appearances, dressed nattily in black suits and top hats, and William Carter accompanied the big flag the entire way, with Eben beside him, riding shotgun, seeming to enjoy the moment despite his reclusive personality. "As the tattered old relic was seen by the crowds," a newsman wrote, "the enthusiasm [in the streets] was unbounded."[631] The laying of the cornerstone for the future Armistead monument capped a remarkable chapter in the city's history. At the conclusion of the ceremony, Eben cut three small pieces from the flag—red, white, and blue—and presented them to Carter as a thank-you for his efforts.[632]

Little did anyone know that it was the last time the Star-Spangled Banner would ever appear in Baltimore—and the last anyone but Eben would see it for twenty-seven years. Inherently disdainful of civic ceremonies and determined more than ever to avoid publicity, he rejected numerous requests to loan it to cities and veterans' groups, feeling "much annoyed on account of his heirloom."[633] He locked it in a vault near his home in New York and refused to divulge its location. Such obstinance was largely unknown to the public, however, until a new group of Maryland civic leaders approached him about displaying it at the seventy-fifth anniversary of the Battle of Baltimore in 1889. Unfortunately for Eben, that developed into a widely reported public spat.

The Maryland men seemed at first to be more interested in celebrating the state's diverse economy than focusing on the battle anniversary. News reports of the upcoming "Industrial and Agricultural Exposition Fair" from September 6–14 at the Pimlico racetrack infuriated Eben, who declined to participate, deeming it disrespectful to the memory of his grandfather. "Do you think I should be called to account for refusing to loan the flag over a prize sheep pen?" he seethed.[634] That, in turn, drew a vehement response from the Exposition Association, which, contrary to his knowledge, had planned a concurrent ceremony at Fort McHenry.

Not content with a war of words, the association sent a delegation to Washington, D.C. to meet with General Robert MacFeely, the acting U.S. secretary of war. After describing how carefully the Star-Spangled Banner had been handled on its previous trip to Baltimore in 1880, they made the bold assertion that the flag no longer belonged in private hands and *was actually the property of the U.S. government.* "Since Mr. Appleton was showing a disposition to stand on alleged rights," the *Baltimore American* reported on August 29, "the committee…was beginning to think the city had some rights, too. The flag had never been given to Col. Armistead, Mr. Appleton's respected ancestor, but to the garrison." Following such a theory, they said, "the flag belonged to the government."[635]

MacFeely heard them out and promised to send a letter to Eben, although he took a much more diplomatic approach than the committee members would have liked:

> *I desire to say, without at all undertaking to settle any right whatever of yourself or the government in this matter, that as the celebration at Baltimore is commemorative of the seventy-fifth anniversary of the Battle of Baltimore…and as the citizens of Baltimore will at the same time hold a grand exposition of the agricultural and mechanical resources and industries of the state, with civic parades, the dedication of the new post office, etc.…I am of the opinion you should be pleased to comply with the reasonable request…upon just and proper agreement between you, looking to the safety and security of this valuable relic…and, therefore, advise you to permit its use as desired.*[636]

The acting secretary reminded Armistead's grandson that all flags of United States troops and garrisons "belong to the government," but he advised the committee that inasmuch as "possession is nine points of the law," any effort to re-take the flag as permanent property "would probably result in long and tedious lawsuits."[637]

Eben, hearing of the challenge to ownership for the first time—and considering it an affront to family legacy—could barely contain his fury.

He stepped out of his comfort zone to meet with a reporter from the *American*, countering the committee, and making his case in detail to the public.

> *Mr. Appleton said to-day that the action was an outrage. He had refused to loan the flag because the occasion was not of national importance. Regarding his legal title to the flag, Mr. Appleton said that it had been in possession of his family for seventy-five years, and he had no doubt that his grandfather, Lieutenant Colonel Armistead, who was in command of Fort McHenry during its bombardment, had obtained it by honest and upright means… [Appleton also said], "The flag is in no condition to be toted around to every agricultural fair, and certainly should not be floated from the ramparts of Fort McHenry, as the committee desires. I think it shows a lack of patriotism on the part of those asking for the flag. I have tried to prove a faithful custodian of the flag, and think it belongs to me by right of possession."[638]*

Several days later, a still-aggrieved Eben spoke with another reporter, and, while pointing to a photograph of his grandfather, exclaimed "Does that look like the face of a man who would claim property not his own?"[639]

He added, with chutzpah, "The government does not own the flag, and their demanding it, I think would equal any despotic notion displayed by the Czar of Russia….I will loan it where and to whom I please…I will protect it as long as I live and leave it in good hands when I die."[640]

The controversy led to widespread newspaper coverage in the northeast, including a searing headline in the *New York Times* that demanded to know "Who Owns The Flag?" Each of the news accounts mentioned Eben's name in the first sentence, highlighting his refusal to loan the flag and often mocking him while debating the issue of proper ownership.[641] Hoping to use this public pressure as a wedge, the Baltimore committee sent a representative to New York to speak with him directly and make a final, impassioned plea on behalf of the city—but, like all previous efforts in this regard, it failed miserably.

"I went up to see Mr. Eben Appleton, 71 East Fifty-Fourth Street," the envoy reported, in a letter that was published in local papers. "I had a long talk with him about the flag [and] I find the is very determined about not lending it…He says he is just as determined not to loan it as you are to have it, so I think you'd better give up the idea of trying further to change his mind."[642]

The public challenge to his ownership of the Star-Spangled Banner, and the personal attacks that followed from many Marylanders, had destroyed any chance of a last-minute change of heart before the seventy-fifth anniversary. A massive replica flag was sewn in haste by the ladies of Baltimore for the event, but it lacked the historic grandeur of the original icon, and harsh feelings on both sides endured.[643] Eben went back under cover, fading from public life, and would not even discuss the flag or reveal its location for the next eighteen years.

"Oh, it is in a safe place," he told a reporter at the height of the 1889 Baltimore controversy, "quite free from moths, destruction by fire or appropriation by thieves. In other words, I do not care to tell where it is. I do not see it very often, as it has grown very frail and there is no telling what might befall it."[644]

It was only in the early 1900s, as he was turning sixty years old, that he began to ponder his own succession plan.

As often happened with Armistead descendants during the Star-Spangled Banner saga, Eben's next move was influenced by a relative—although this time it was a distant cousin from Virginia named James B. Baylor.

The ancestral ties were intriguing, if not downright eerie: George Armistead's mother was a Baylor; James was a direct descendant of George's uncle, John Baylor, who was part of the Revolutionary generation; and James now owned the historic home in Caroline County, Virginia, where George was born and raised in the late 1700s. (Another line of descendants moved west and helped to found Baylor University in Waco, Texas.)[645]

Family histories tell us that James Baylor attended the Virginia Military Institute during the Civil War, fought as a fifteen-year-old Confederate cadet at the Battle of New Market, and went on to earn a degree in civil engineering from the University of Virginia in 1872. That led to a career with the United States Coast and Geodetic Survey Department, where his duties as a field agent ranged from studying elements of the earth's magnetism to surveying natural oyster grounds in Virginia and Louisiana. In 1900, he was appointed by the U.S. Supreme Court to settle a long-standing border line dispute between Virginia and Tennessee, and some years later to define the boundary between the U.S. and Canada.[646] By the early 1900s, his work in the Washington, D.C. region brought him into contact with leaders of a new national museum that was established by a gift from British scientist James Smithson.

The "Smithsonian Institution" had opened in 1846 as a scientific research organization, designed to "expand scientific knowledge in the United States and advance the nation's reputation as a scientific power." Following the success of the 1876 Centennial Exposition in Philadelphia, however, Smithsonian leaders sought to expand their focus, with a new emphasis on documenting the country's past. In 1881, they opened a second building, the United States National Museum (which still stands today as the iconic Arts and Industries Building on the Smithsonian campus), and within twenty years it had already established itself as the preeminent cathedral of early American history.[647]

When the flag arrived at the Smithsonian in 1907, excited museum officials draped it from the outside of a building known as "The Castle." This photograph was published in local papers, leading to a surge of visitation. *(Library of Congress, Prints & Photographs Division, LC-DIG-npcc-19637)*

It was here that the journey of the Star-Spangled Banner took its final, remarkable turn in the spring of 1907. Baylor learned that Eben was considering two options to loan the flag—to the Baltimore City Hall or Maryland State House—and wanted to suggest the Smithsonian as a better and more prestigious site. He reached out to his cousin in mid-May, learned that a final decision had not been reached, and scribbled a hasty note to Smithsonian Secretary Charles Walcott, saying, "My motivation in writing to you is to get you to second my efforts to induce Mr. Appleton (grandson of Colonel George Armistead) to either loan or give the flag to the

National Museum…It certainly should go on exhibition somewhere in Washington and with some short account of its history."

With a playful nudge, Baylor added, "If you handle him in a tactful manner, I believe he will do this."[648]

Walcott was stunned by the stroke of luck. Relics from the estates of George Washington, Abraham Lincoln, and Ulysses S. Grant had given the Smithsonian instant credibility, but this sudden opportunity to acquire the original Star-Spangled Banner from a direct Armistead descendant was an unexpected bonus. "The addition of this notable object to the historical collections of the national museum would be very deeply appreciated and attract widespread attention," Walcott wrote back, assuring him that it would be "given a conspicuous position such as it deserves."[649] Baylor responded by providing Eben's New York City address, putting the two principles in touch, and stepping back from his role as middleman of one of the colossal transactions in museum history.

Eben had already warmed to the idea of the Smithsonian as a destination, so there was no need for a major sales push. Regarding the flag's "final disposition…the National Museum appeals to me more than any other place," he said.[650] In a series of letters with Walcott over the next few weeks, he nonetheless posed a number of questions: could the secretary send more information on the Smithsonian? How would the flag be placed for public viewing? Could he request that it be returned to his private possession at any time?

When the information and answers were satisfactory, the two men came to an astonishingly quick agreement.

"I have decided to act on your suggestion and shall be glad to send on the Star-Spangled Banner as a loan to the National Museum," Eben wrote on June 25, 1907 (underlined in the original). He said he would "gladly conform to the condition requiring an exhibit to remain on view for two years," but, as a continuing sign of concern for the flag's future, and defense against others hoping to poach it for their own use, noted, "I presume you would not loan it to any person or State without first consulting me."[651]

Eben planned to escape the New York City bustle for the summer but waited a few days to personally oversee the shipment by Adams Express Co. on July 5. In a letter alerting the Smithsonian that the prized cargo was on its way, he said he regretted "not being able to open the box & have the flag cleaned and dusted, but the weight of the package and the difficulty of handling made it impossible." He reiterated that he trusted the museum staff to display it in the best way possible, "leaving it all to your good judgement," while adding a final stipulation that "I would like it to remain attached to the canvas."[652] Then he held his breath, hoping that Commodore Preble's old wooden crate would survive the trip to Washington undamaged.

It was one of the remarkable missed opportunities of history that Secretary Walcott was out of town when the Star-Spangled Banner arrived in Washington on July 6. Filling in for his boss at this crucial moment, assistant secretary Richard Rathbun signed an official museum document that "the very flag which floated over Fort McHenry, Baltimore" had been formally "received."[653] This was not the first time that Rathbun found himself by chance at the intersection of historic events. In 1899, a little-known citizen of Dayton, Ohio named Wilbur Wright wrote to the Smithsonian to request books and other published papers on the subject of aviation, and Rathbun's response helped put the Wright brothers on the path to the first powered flight in human history at Kitty Hawk, North Carolina in 1903.[654] Now, he was on the receiving end of a flag that would become the crown jewel of the museum's collection.

Rathbun's presence that day was fortuitous, because he recognized the once-in-a-lifetime marketing opportunity. He noticed with some trepidation that the "much too heavy" canvas backing had "done much harm to the flag" over the years, but any concern over its fragile condition would not prevent him from taking an iconic publicity photo. On July 10, Rathbun had the massive Star-Spangled Banner draped on an exterior wall of the Smithsonian's primary building, known as "The Castle," providing what he thought was an ideal background setting for posterity. Writing to Eben the next day, he reported proudly that "we hung the flag in such a way as to secure a most excellent picture."[655] By design, the museum's own camera expert was the only photographer on the scene.

It was the first photo taken of the flag since Preble's historic effort thirty-four years earlier, but this one generated much more hoopla among the public. Though it was intended only for use in Smithsonian marketing materials, word spread quickly through the city and found its way to several newspaper editors, who reached out immediately to Rathbun. "The newspaper men are after me," he told

Eben in a July 11 letter, "and they all want a photograph to publish in various local papers." Eben gave permission for several outlets to publish the official photo on Sunday, July 14, barely a week after the flag's arrival, touching off a huge spurt of visitation at the Smithsonian. By that time, the flag had already been placed in a large case in the Arts and Industries Building's "Hall of History," next to artifacts that once belonged to Washington and Grant. "Its presence in the Museum has caused a wave of patriotism," Rathbun wrote, "which it is very good to see."[656]

Beyond assurance that the Star-Spangled Banner would never be loaned to unapproved third parties, Eben's biggest concerns were that the story of the flag's creation and the role played by his grandfather were still largely unknown by the general public. He wondered if the Smithsonian staff might undertake research to assemble all the facts in an official publication. "Do not pay any attention to newspaper accounts concerning the history of the Flag," he told Rathbun with a snarl. "There is scarcely a word of truth in such articles as I can see." He was promised that research was already underway and pronounced himself pleased with the arrangement.[657]

The relationship with the Smithsonian went so well over the next five years that Eben decided to convert the loan into a permanent gift, ensuring that the Fort McHenry flag would be preserved far into the future. He made it official in a letter to Walcott on December 12, 1912—one of the most important dates in the museum's history. "It has always been my intention to present the flag during my lifetime to that institution in the country where it could be conveniently seen by the public, and where it would be well cared for," Eben wrote, "and the advantages and appropriateness of the National Museum are so obvious as to render consideration of any other place unnecessary."[658] Had the fifty-seven-year-old Walcott been capable of a backflip, he would have done one that very moment at the entrance to the Hall of History. His ecstatic acceptance letter, written two days later, noted that "your public-spirited action is worthy of admiration, and will, I hope, serve as an inspiration to others."[659]

As with all matters involving Eben, however, this one had a stipulation. He continued to fret that the American public knew the phrase "Star-Spangled Banner" only as it related to Key's song, fearing that the Armistead angle was being lost to history. (As far back as 1874, one of Georgiana Appleton's nephews had written, "My dear Aunt…shall we allow Key and the anthem to swallow up the few recollections left us?")[660] Eben had written his own suggested text for the flag's new display at the Smithsonian, and he included it with a strong hint in his formal donation letter to Walcott:

> *Whilst realizing that the poem of Mr. Key is the one thing which renders this flag of more than ordinary interest, it is only right to appreciate the fact that there was a cause for his inspiration. Being detained temporarily on board a British Man of War, he witnessed the bombardment of Fort McHenry, and was inspired by that dramatic scene to give to the Nation his beautiful lines. I must ask therefore, as a condition of this gift, and in justice to the Commandant of the Fort, and the brave men under him, that their share in the inspiration of this poem be embodied in the inscription to be placed in the case containing this flag. I have had forwarded to me copies of the inscriptions contained in the case at present, and do not think they could be improved upon, but as I desire now to make a specific choice, will say that the following is the one which I prefer, and should like to be assured by you will be the official marking –*

> ### The Star-Spangled Banner

> **Garrison flag of Fort McHenry, Baltimore, during the bombardment of the Fort by the British Sept. 13-14, 1814, when it was gallantly defended by colonel George Armistead, and the brave men under him. Francis Scott Key, detained with the British Fleet, had eagerly watched for the Flag during the fight, and as he saw it still waving over the fort on**

the morning of September 14th he was inspired to write the verses of the "Star Spangled Banner."

Presented to the National Museum, Washington, D.C., by Mr. Eben Appleton of New York, Grandson of Col. George Armistead [emphasis added].

The fact of my preferring the above as the official inscription does not imply that I would like the others removed from the case. Thanking you for the good care you have taken of the flag during the past few years, and for the beautiful manner in which it has been displayed, and awaiting the pleasure of your reply, I beg to remain.

Very truly yours,
Eben Appleton [661]

It was hardly a deal-breaker. Walcott and Rathbun did not object to the request, and, in fact, both men thought it most helpful in framing the story for future generations of visitors. Walcott deemed it "entirely appropriate" and said, "the new inscription [would be] placed in the case as soon as it can be printed," which it was.[662] Much as everyone wanted to close this chapter of the story, however, the drama did not end there, because the Smithsonian received *two* inquiries about lending the flag to sites in Ohio and Maryland within the next year. Eben's anxiety grew with each notification.

The first arrived in January 1913, only one month after the gift had become permanent. It came from the Toledo Museum of Art, where the director, George Stevens, was compiling a centennial celebration of Commodore Oliver Perry's victory at the Battle of Lake Erie in the War of 1812. Rathbun turned it down without Eben's direct involvement, talking of the flag's deep meaning to the Smithsonian and explaining the details of its feeble condition, which made travel an unacceptable risk. "We have nothing else in the Museum quite so precious, quite so delicate or so near annihilation as to make its preservation a question of constant care and attention," he told Stevens. The issue passed quietly, much to Eben's relief.[663]

A more tense and dramatic exchange began late in 1913, when Arthur B. Bibbins, chairman of the National Star-Spangled Banner Centennial Commission in Baltimore, contacted Smithsonian officials to request the flag for the September 1914 battle commemoration at Fort McHenry. "The flag could never be restored to a condition that would permit it to be carried about," Walcott responded, and "if taken away, it would mostly fall to pieces."[664] Frustrated by that answer, Bibbins tried to circumvent the process by contacting Eben directly.

With that, Eben's anger boiled over. He sensed that lending the flag to the Bibbins event, even on a "temporary" basis, might mean that it would never *return* to the Smithsonian, and told Walcott in a letter that he firmly rejected the request. But he added, "it has naturally raised in my mind the question [as to] whether the Authorities of the Museum would at this time or any future time, entertain a proposition looking to the temporary or permanent transfer of this flag to any other home than the National Museum where I placed it, with the intention of having it remain there forever."[665]

Such an outrageous transfer would never happen, the Smithsonian leaders assured him. But Bibbins would not relent, pressing his case to the U.S. secretary of war and the House Committee on Military Affairs, at one point writing that Baltimore officials "never contemplated the removal of the flag from the city that preserved it...it remained here until after the Civil War, when its inheritance by heirs living away from Baltimore carried it from our midst."[666] Eben took this as a personal insult, and it became his breaking point on the matter.

He had bequeathed the flag to the Smithsonian, he said, "with the firm and settled intention of having it remain there forever," and he told Walcott he "could not for one moment consent to its transfer to any other place, even temporarily." A January 10, 1914 letter spelled out in clear terms an unwavering condition that it was never to leave the Smithsonian, regardless of the request or proposed celebration.[667]

"Therefore," Eben wrote in August of the same year, only a few weeks before the battle's centennial, "let us all stand firm at *this time* and at *all* times, and under *all* circumstances, and let any American citizen who visits the museum with the expectation of seeing the flag be sure of finding it in its accustomed place."[668]

The journey was over.

The Star-Spangled Banner was almost one hundred years old by the time it found a permanent home at the Smithsonian Institution, and it was very much starting to show its age.

Folded inside a glass case at the museum's main entrance, open to viewing by the public for the first time in decades, it was now "a frail piece of bunting, worn, frayed, pierced and largely in tatters," very much in need of repair.[669]

Walcott reached out to colleagues and learned that the nation's premier flag preservation expert was Amelia Bold Fowler, a teacher of embroidery in Boston with a sterling resume. Fowler previously advised the state of Massachusetts on the restoration of Civil War flags and had been retained by the U.S. Naval Academy to preserve its collection of 172 historic banners.[670] Accordingly, one of the museum's curators, Theodore Belote, traveled to Annapolis in February 1914 to meet with academy officials and observe the quality of Fowler's work. "She appears to have been very successful in her work on the Naval Academy's flags," Belote reported, "and she has certainly exhibited great ingenuity in arranging the designs of flags which were formerly reduced to a more or less fragmentary condition." It was especially noteworthy that two of the flags were remnants from the War of 1812, including Perry's banner from the Battle of Lake Erie and another captured from a British ship.[671]

This led to an exhausting series of twenty-eight letters between the Smithsonian and Fowler's representatives, the two sides debating cost and parameters before eventually ironing out details. Fowler's proposal to preserve the flag was accepted in late May at a cost of $1,243 (with no one mentioning at the time that it was more than three times what Mary Pickersgill charged to create the flag in 1813). Belote and others knew the cost was steep, but they convinced themselves that there was no better option, given that she was "about the only person in the United States who does work of this exact character." Fowler was tasked with providing all materials and labor, including a team of skilled "needlewomen" to assist in the process, although it was noted that she would handle the most "delicate and difficult" parts of the work herself.[672]

Flag preservation expert Amelia Fowler and her crew worked diligently on the Star-Spangled Banner at the Smithsonian in 1914. *(Wikimedia Commons)*

The embroidery teacher had patented a system for preserving fragile flags by attaching a thin backing of Irish linen for support. In the case of the Star-Spangled Banner, that meant removing the heavy, bulkier canvas sail that George Preble and his sailors applied in 1873. Once the flag was freed of the canvas for the first time in more than thirty years, Fowler and her team stretched it across a makeshift series of tables in the Smithsonian's chapel and spent eight weeks attaching the linen with an astounding 1.7 million stitches, each about one-half inch in length, interlocked horizontally and vertically.[673] In the aftermath of the painstaking needle work, an emotional Fowler wrote of her experience and placed the impact of the Fort McHenry flag in context with previous preservation efforts.

> *Perhaps this is the most impressive flag in the posses-*
> *sion of the Nation. Its mute testimony to the cause of*
> *freedom, the fact that bullets cannot destroy principle,*
> *what the flag stood for in the day of trial it stands for*
> *still, and always will, are the dominating thoughts of*

all who behold it today. No veneration is too great for the flag whose power is in its zenith at this time and constantly increasing. It might well be enshrined in a building of its own where every inch of its surface could be displayed in the fullest light, where the greatest concourse of people might proclaim this to be the land of freedom and kindness with all race hatreds left behind.[674]

The newly-preserved relic was displayed in a glass case in the Smithsonian's Arts and Industries Building, in a prominent location just to the right of the main entrance. However, because the specially-built case was only sixteen feet and ten inches high, it was far too small to allow the entire massive flag (of thirty feet high) to be viewed by the public. Only eight of the stripes were visible, while seven were folded under. Visitors also noted that the flag's blue union (with stars) was located on the right side, instead of the traditional left. That was because Fowler and her team had attached the linen on the same side as Preble's canvas backing, making a proper display impossible.[675]

The position of the blue union was soon in violation of the Flag Code, passed by the National Flag Conference in 1923, but the museum dealt with visitor complaints by explaining that the Star-Spangled Banner had been preserved and mounted almost ten years before the code went into effect. There was a happier publicity issue in the 1920s, when George Armistead's great-grandson, Alexander Gordon, donated the commemorative silver service George had received from the citizens of Baltimore in 1816 for his gallant stand at Fort McHenry.[676] It added more history and luster to what was already the most popular exhibit at the Smithsonian in the early twentieth century.

CHAPTER THIRTEEN
Becoming the Anthem

As for Francis Scott Key's song?

It took more than one hundred years from the time of the Battle of Baltimore before "The Star-Spangled Banner" was declared the national anthem by an act of Congress, and there were significant obstacles almost every step of the way.

Several other patriotic airs vied for attention in the first half of the nineteenth century, "Hail Columbia," "Yankee Doodle," and "My Country 'Tis of Thee" among them—and there was no immediate pressure from the public to choose a single unifying tune. "The Star-Spangled Banner" was not rushed to the front of our national songs until the Civil War," wrote the legendary anthem historian, Oscar George Sonneck, chief of the division of music at the Library of Congress. "Before that time its progress…had been steady but comparatively slow." Key's lyrics did not even appear in every popular songbook in the 1820s and 1830s.[677]

But Americans knew that anthems in other countries inspired reverence among the citizenry—notably "God Save the King" (or Queen) in England and "La Marseillaise" in France—and, starting as far back as 1806, there were several clumsy attempts to choose a standard-bearing song for the United States. Renowned showman P.T. Barnum tried to organize a contest to declare an official anthem in the 1850s, but he quickly shut it down because the entries were so bland. It was not until the start of the Civil War in 1861, when a group of New York businessmen offered a five-hundred-dollar prize for music and lyrics to a new national song, that the public accepted the challenge with an unprecedented surge of musical fervor.[678]

The group's spokesman, Richard Grant White, gained attention by taking aim at "The Star-Spangled Banner," deeming it "almost useless" as a patriotic song and calling Key's words "altogether unfitted for a national hymn." Fresh thinking was needed, he said, because most of the other favorites were bygones of the revolutionary era, no longer worthy of serious consideration. "'Yankee Doodle' has the claim on long association," White wrote, "…but no sane person would ever dream of regarding it as a national hymn." As for "Hail Columbia?" It was "really worse than 'Yankee Doodle.' Both the words and music…are common-place vulgar and pretentious, and the people themselves have found all this out."[679]

The New Yorkers received more than 1,200 entries, including from as far away as England and Italy, but excitement over the volume of submissions was substantially degraded by the quality of their work. White's cohorts were stunned and appalled, rejecting 1,170 almost immediately. The remaining thirty were then reduced to fifteen, and then just a handful, until all were eventually discarded. "A vast washing-basket was made the temporary tomb of these extinguished hopes," White said, "and this receptacle was filled five times." A large portion of the entries focused far too heavily on religion or the current war, with titles ranging from "God Save Our Fatherland" to a most-uninspiring "Hymn of Our Union." "Not one of them was deemed to satisfy all the requirements of the need for a hymn," it was reported, "and so the prize was not awarded."[680]

White had tried to help contestants by outlining the standards in advance. The ideal national song would "proclaim, assert and exult in the freedom of those who are to sing it." Aside from that, he said, "Let it be brimful of loyalty to the flag, which is our only national symbol, and for that all the dearer…let its allusions to our fathers' struggle for national existence, and its spirit be that of our nationality." It never dawned on him that he had unwittingly described "The Star-Spangled Banner," which, in retrospect—and quite remarkably—seemed to fit his criteria more than any of the contemporary entries. Instead, he and the committee were left with "the merest common-place, brief effusions of decent dullness, or fantastic folly."[681]

There was a hard lesson, repeated over and over in the nineteenth century, that public competitions could never produce an acceptable anthem on demand. No less an authority than the great composer John Phillip Sousa mocked the concept, saying "it would be as easy to make a stream run uphill as to secure a new National anthem as the result of a contest."[682] Sousa had once entered such a contest himself, being pressured to do so because he was director of the U.S. Marine band, but the effort he produced was half-hearted, and he failed almost by design. Once again, nothing came of it.

"Nations will seldom obtain good national anthems by offering prizes for them," Sousa said. "The man and the occasion must meet."[683]

"The Star-Spangled Banner" continued its ascendancy after the Union Army defeated the Confederates in 1865, reuniting the country and clearing the way for a new national identity. Key's song had been a favorite of Union soldiers, who played it triumphantly as they entered Savannah, Richmond, and New Orleans to reclaim land and free slaves on behalf of the United States.[684] For many years afterward, Union veterans "continued to associate the tune with the excitement and emotion of their wartime experiences," and a general desire for unity under the flag gave it a fresh appeal among the populace.[685]

As early as 1869, a Union Army chaplain named George Armistead Leakin considered approaching Congress to seek official sanction for the song, but, for reasons that were never explained, did not go through with his proposal (George was not an Armistead relative but had been named in honor of the hero of Fort McHenry.)[686] On July 4, 1876, at the centennial celebration in Philadelphia, a pipe organ played "The Star-Spangled Banner" as one of three popular patriotic numbers in a regular rotation throughout the festive day. Seventeen years later, at the 1893 World's Columbian Exposition in Chicago, supporters of Key's song from Maryland built an extensive exhibit hall and provided patrons with a fact book prepared by the *Baltimore Sun*, touting its virtues. As an aside, a local band also feted special guests with a rare composition known as "Col. George Armistead's Grand March."[687]

The first significant step toward national anthem status took place in 1889, when Benjamin F. Tracy, the secretary of the U.S. Navy, ordered all naval bands to play "The Star-Spangled Banner" at flag-raising ceremonies each morning.[688] The army soon followed suit, and for the next two decades it seemed as though the competing service branches were trying to outdo one another. In 1890, the U. S. Marine Band started to play the song to close all public performances; in 1895, the army made it a mandatory part of evening colors; in 1903, the navy required each sailor to stand at attention from "O say can you see" through the "home of the brave;" in 1904, army soldiers also rose in unison.[689]

The military's influence in determining the fate of Key's song was both understandable and profound. It had been written during a battle of the War of 1812, gained stature with the Union Army's victory in the Civil War, and continued to inspire U.S. troops on foreign soil during the Spanish-American War in 1898. Veterans had a natural affinity for the music and lyrics that carried far beyond their "band of brothers" days on the battlefield. Beyond the military, however, other groups played crucial roles in the "The Star-Spangled Banner" campaign, including the Daughters of the American Revolution (D.A.R.) and the United States Daughters of 1812. At an 1895 D.A.R. conference in Atlanta, Janet E. Hosmer Richards was the first to publicly suggest a petition calling for Congress to designate Key's song "from among all rivals" to be "the American National hymn."[690]

Her reasoning was simple and straightforward: it talked about the flag.

"In this soul-stirring hymn we have embodied a sentiment which will serve all true Americans for all occasions," Richards said. "In times of peace, dear flag, we hail thee! In times of danger, inspired by this anthem, we will gladly rally to thy defense and she our life's blood, if necessary, in order that we may proclaim, after the heat and hardship of the struggle, 'Our flag is still there!'"[691]

The D.A.R. took no formal action at the time, but her speech roused the Colonial Dames of America to propose that "The Star-Spangled Banner" be played "at all theatrical performances, in order thus to encourage patriotism and loyalty." In 1898, the Philadelphia chapter of the D.A.R. passed a similar resolution and challenged other chapters to form "Star-Spangled Banner Committees," with the goal of lobbying Congress.[692]

The next major step came in 1907—the same year that Eben Appleton loaned the flag to the Smithsonian—when the Library of Congress tasked Oscar Sonneck to conduct a scholarly study of four of the most popular patriotic songs in the country: "The Star-Spangled Banner," "Hail Columbia," "Yankee Doodle," and "America (My Country 'Tis of Thee)."[693] His report, originally published in 1909 and updated in 1914, tried not to favor one over the others but clearly showed a fondness for "The Star-Spangled Banner." Although acknowledging concerns over the music's English origins, Sonneck firmly brushed them aside, asserting that "We took the air and we kept it. Transplanted on American soil, it thrived." Each song under consideration had its selling points, he said, "but Key's work stirs the blood of every American."[694]

Sonneck's words sparked a series of Congressional actions that helped clear a path toward recognition, slowly but inexorably. In 1910, U.S. Representative William Griest of Pennsylvania introduced legislation to fund the printing and distribution of ten thousand copies of Sonneck's book to schools, libraries, and patriotic groups around the country. In 1912, Representative Edmund Foss of Illinois offered a bill to make "The Star-Spangled Banner" the "national air for the United States of America"—the first of thirty-five similar bills over the next decade and a half. It was not long before Representative J. Charles Linthicum of Maryland stepped forward to take leadership of the anthem movement, with support from Ella Virginia Houck Holloway, a flamboyant member of the Maryland chapter of the D.A.R. and the United States Daughters of 1812.[695]

Their efforts received a significant boost in 1916, when, on the verge of America's entry into World War I, President Woodrow Wilson designated "The Star-Spangled Banner" as the official song of the U.S. military.[696] Wider public recognition continued to elude them, however, as Congress faced far more pressing matters than the designation of a national anthem. The song still had its detractors, the competition still had support, and the first few bills died in committee without ever making it to a vote.

Criticism of "The Star-Spangled Banner" early in the twentieth century often centered on charges that it was too militaristic and glorified war. Many argued that the song's roots traced to a single battle in a long-forgotten conflict and didn't seem appropriate for a national hymn. Some seethed that the original music to "Anacreon in Heaven" had been composed by a "foreigner," an Englishman named John Stafford Smith; a different group was offended that Key's third verse taunted England, now a trusted ally; others claimed it was based on a bawdy "drinking" ballad, stirring up anti-alcohol zealots in the prohibition movement. If there was any agreement among the wide-ranging anti-Banner forces, it was that the song was simply too difficult to sing. (The fact that Key was a slaveholder and mentioned the word "slave" in his third verse, a focus of modern-day criticism, was rarely mentioned at this time.)[697]

Some of the opposing voices were particularly loud and damaging. Catherine Smiley "Kitty" Cheatham, a New York City singer and Christian Scientist, assailed "The Star-Spangled Banner" as "insidious mental poison," claiming that its war-like language and anti-British sentiments from a long-ago battle were unacceptable in the song of a Christian nation. "It behooves the people of America not to 'linger in an age that is dead and gone,'" she wrote. "The 'bombs bursting in air and rocket's red glare' of a dead past can no longer disrupt Anglo-Saxon unity, nor continue its schismatic influence against ultimate world-wide unity."

Cheatham produced a pamphlet in 1918 titled "Words and Music of 'The Star-Spangled Banner' Oppose the Spirit of Democracy Which the Declaration of Independence Embodies." Elements of her essay were carried in the February 10, 1918 edition of the *New York Times* and, almost overnight, turned into impassioned talking points for foes of Key's lyrics. Cheatham became a powerful advocate for her cause on the national stage, but she often rambled uncontrollably while attempting to identify more reasons to dismiss the song. At one point she wrote that loyal Americans should "indignantly protest...the perpetuation of 'The Star-Spangled Banner' because it is *not* American, because it is of Bacchanalian origin, and because, metaphysically, it can never be separated from the *mental* influence which it exhales and by which those who sing it are more or less mentally inoculated."[698] Many read that final passage and rolled their eyes.

Another Christian Scientist, Angela E. Stetson, supported the anti-Banner rhetoric but used a different platform to get the message across. In 1922, just before a Flag Day celebration at Fort McHenry in Baltimore, Stetson purchased a series of newspaper ads across the northeast to declare in the strongest terms that Key's song "can never become our National Anthem." After claiming that the lyrics had an "evil influence" on youngsters because they exalted war, sowed hatred of England, and were born of a "foul drinking song." She asked, "Shall we shout, in violent, unsingable cadences, of the 'rockets' red glare, the bombs bursting in air' and refer today to our democratic partner in Anglo-Saxondom—Great Britain—as the 'foe's haughty host' which 'in dead silence reposes?' Shall such seeds be planted in the budding minds of America's schoolchildren? God forbid!

"Every American worthy of the name…will forever repudiate it."[699]

Individual dissenters from across the country shared these concerns but often hammered home a more fundamental theme: the song was too difficult to sing. Indeed, when the music was composed in England more than a century earlier, the goal of the Anacreontic Society was to challenge a singer's vocal capacity; the range is an octave and a half, which meant that regular folks without professional training could not the high notes without screeching. A 1917 story from the *Detroit Free Press* noted that "'The Star-Spangled Banner' is distinctly difficult of successful negotiation by an untutored singer. Some professional vocalists confess to trepidation when called upon to interpret it."[700] An editorial in the *Imperial Valley Press* of El Centro, California agreed: "There is the lack of a good national song characteristic of the American temperament. 'The Star-Spangled Banner' is difficult, as its notes run both high and low with wide intervals. The average person drops out when the verse reaches the more squealy parts."[701]

Both newspapers were joined by a substantial group of supporters in endorsing "My Country 'Tis of Thee" as a better choice, but the fact that its music was the same as England's national anthem, "God Save The King," made their movement a non-starter. By the early twentieth century, however, a new and unexpected entry in the debate had become the biggest challenger to Key's composition.

It was early in 1893 when an English professor from Wellesley College named Katherine Lee Bates set off on a cross-country trip to Colorado, ostensibly to take a summer teaching job.

The trip became historic because of her literary inspiration—and it still resonates to this day.

Eager to experience "the fertile and almost inexhaustible" frontier, Bates traveled on a train west from Boston to Chicago, site of the spectacular World's Columbian Exposition; through vast, rambling prairies in Missouri and sun-splashed wheat fields in Kansas, gaining "a quickened and deepened sense of America;" and, finally, to a temporary summer home at Colorado College in Colorado Springs, where, on one adventurous Saturday in late July, she rode a mule-drawn covered wagon to the 14,110-foot summit of Pike's Peak.[702]

The views were breathtaking. Bates and her companions stayed for less than an hour in thin mountain air, in part because a male professor fainted, but the impact of that visit shaped her legacy for future generations. "Gazing in wordless rapture," she took in scenes that could not have been imagined by a native of the Cape Cod seashore—from skies that seemed expansive and endless to flowing waves of grain on the edge of the Great Plains. "The purple range of the Rockies" went off in a long, unbroken line toward Canada. Moved to put pencil to paper in a record for her diary, Bates composed a poem that she titled, simply, "America"—the precursor of the song we know today as "America the Beautiful."[703]

Initially unhappy with the work, feeling it did not fully capture her vision, Bates re-worked the text twice over the next eighteen years, leaving us with three distinct versions.[704] But the first one, conceived during her Pike's Peak jaunt in July 1893, formed the foundation of a long-standing classic in American poetry:

> *O beautiful for halcyon skies,*
> *For amber waves of grain,*

For purple mountain majesties
Above the enameled plain!
America! America!
God shed his grace on thee
Till souls wax fair as earth and air
And music-hearted sea![705]

Bates hesitated to make her poem public but finally relented after two years, in 1895. The original version was published for the first time in a weekly New England church publication called *The Congregationalist*, and reaction from the religious community exceeded her wildest expectations. As news of the poem spread beyond the small church audience, and then beyond New England to other regions of the country, "America" became a national sensation. Unlike Francis Scott Key—who wrote "The Star-Spangled Banner" with a specific tune in mind—Bates had opted for a work of pure poetry, but musicians soon recognized a blend of grandeur and style that had wondrous rhythmic potential. "Americans embraced her lines and started setting them to music—all kinds of music," a Bates biographer wrote.[706]

Dumbfounded at first—"no one was more amazed than I," Bates said—she warmed to the task and "rewrote it in some respects to make it a bit more musical." In her second version in 1904, she changed "halcyon skies" to "spacious skies" and "enameled plain" to "fruited plain," while completely reworking the last two lines of the first verse. "And crown thy good with brotherhood/From sea to shining sea" became a more fitting conclusion. Bates also made tweaks to the second, third, and fourth verses, underscoring her sense of optimism but calling on the country to live up to its founding values (The second verse now ended with "America! America!/God mend thine every flaw/Confirm they soul in self-control/Thy liberty in law.")[707]

The updated version was published in the November 19, 1904 edition of the *Boston Evening Transcript*, which introduced it as a "thoroughly American production well-nigh perfect as poetry... America has only to live up to its aspirations here breathed to realize its Golden Age."[708] A New York clergyman felt it merited recognition as a national "hymn," and, while looking for music that matched the cadence of the lyrics, settled on "Materna"—a familiar song printed in many church hymnals since 1882. Bates's poem had already been paired with several other tunes, including "Auld Lang Syne" and an Irish favorite, "The Harp That Once Through Tara's Halls," which tended to confuse the public, but "Materna" soon became the most commonly-heard melody. Bates made her final revisions to the lyrics in 1911 and, in a book published later that year, gave the song its long-accepted formal name, "America the Beautiful."[709]

Anthem historian Marc Ferris notes that "pacifists, educators, aesthetic objectors and anti-alcohol advocates publicly endorsed 'America the Beautiful' instead of 'The Star-Spangled Banner' as the national anthem." Several organizations, including the National Federation of Women's Clubs and the National Association of Organists, hailed it for expressing "the highest and deepest emotions of patriotism, not in any spirit of militant aggression and world-conquering imperialism, but with a profound gratitude for the country, the government and the traditions that have made us what we are." The Hymn Society of America even tried to push a bill for recognition before Congress.[710] But, as supporters of "The Star-Spangled Banner" had learned the hard way, legislators were in no mood to take up an anthem issue during, or even immediately after, World War I.

Critics of Bates's song as an anthem candidate groused that there was nothing uniquely American about spacious skies, purple mountains, or amber waves of grain (Canada and other countries had those, too). The Baltimore firebrand, Ella Holloway, dubbed it "namby pamby" and said it was useful only as "fairly good Harvest Home Song."[711] A modern-day activist might even question whether a segment of the second verse is properly sensitive to indigenous people who had their land confiscated during America's western expansion ("O beautiful for pilgrim feet/Whose stern, impassioned stress/A thoroughfare for freedom beat/Across the wilderness!") Any entry that dared to join the debate, it seemed, would stir up opposition.

The song's biggest weakness, however, was that it was a late-arriving outsider to the anthem competition. Key's words had been around for more than one hundred years and claimed historic connections to several successful wars; other songs had roots that dug even deeper, some of them back to the Revolution. "*America the*

Beautiful suffered from a limited historical legacy," Ferris wrote, "and its backers remained disorganized and outnumbered. In addition, experiments with musical pairings continued to cause confusion." It did not help that Bates, who lived until 1928, and would have been the best possible advocate for their cause, declined to become personally involved.

"As to making it the national anthem," she wrote, "I am personally more than content with the heart-warming reception to the song…has already had. I am glad to have it go as far as popular goodwill carries it. As for 'pushing' it or 'urging' it or striving to have it 'supplant' something else, nothing could be more at variance with my constant attitude toward it nor more adverse to my temperament."[712]

As it turned out, "America the Beautiful" never had a chance.

Supporters of "The Star-Spangled Banner" were more numerous and more organized, had much deeper history on their side, boasted the backing of both major branches of the military, and—perhaps most importantly—were willing to play the long game to gain Congressional recognition.

All of that was necessary—and yet it still wasn't easy.

Between 1912–1917, eleven U.S. Congressmen from nine states introduced fourteen separate bills nominating "The Star-Spangled Banner" as the national anthem, but none gained enough support to reach the House floor. There simply was "not enough public sentiment," one legislator said, "for Congress to act."[713] Frustrated by this lack of progress, Ella Holloway and the Maryland Society of the U.S. Daughters of 1812 enlisted Representative Linthicum to champion their efforts and lead a more robust legislative charge. It was the beginning of a magical pairing that, over the next decade, changed the dynamic of the anthem debate and cleared a path for Key's song.

Linthicum confirmed to Holloway in a March 30, 1918 letter that he would "introduce such a bill within a few days, after which the fight must be waged until a successful conclusion."[714] He knew that anthem legislation was "not classed with the vital matters of Congress" but felt that a well-organized, concerted effort with several other legislators could build momentum in their favor.[715] There were nineteen bills put forth between April 1918 and April 1929—six of them by Linthicum himself—and, despite their lack of progress in forcing a Congressional vote, the sheer volume of documents on the same topic began to have an impact.[716]

Among those who took notice were two groups of military veterans: The Veterans of Foreign Wars (VFW), started after the Spanish-American War in 1899, and the American Legion, founded by World War I vets in 1919. Both pushed patriotism "100 percent Americanism."[717] In the immediate aftermath of the first great world war, when U.S. troops had fought and died on overseas battlefields, respect for the flag and its symbolism became more of a focus than at any time since the end of the Civil War.

By the mid-1920s, when Captain Walter Joyce, a Spanish-American war veteran, became chairman of the VFW's Americanization Committee, the anthem campaign reached a new level of enthusiasm and commitment. He flooded the country with petitions urging the adoption of "The Star-Spangled Banner," sought testimonials from patriotic groups in every state, and dispatched a "caravan" of red, white, and blue cars up and down the East coast to generate unprecedented news coverage. "I believe that this will be the greatest piece of patriotic publicity that the organization has ever obtained," he said, "and its value cannot be counted in dollars and cents."[718]

Continuing to believe that the "fight must be waged until a successful conclusion," Representative Linthicum introduced his sixth and final bill on April 15, 1929—designated as House Bill H.R. 14 (because September 14, 1814 was the day Major Armistead's forces held off the British at Fort McHenry).[719] His confidence grew when he learned of Joyce's effort with the VFW to promote Key's song across the country.[720] They could all feel the momentum building. It reached a crescendo on January 30, 1930 when the House Subcommittee on the Judiciary finally opened hearings on "Legislation to Make 'The Star-Spangled Banner' the National Anthem," with a full roster of thirty-four speakers, led by the omnipresent Linthicum and Joyce.[721]

Supporters knew it was a good sign that the subcommittee was chaired by Representative Leonidas C. Dyer of Missouri, who, back in 1916, had introduced his own bill about in support of "The

Star-Spangled Banner." The event began in a distinctly atypical atmosphere, as noted local soprano Elsie Jorss-Reilley performed Key's song with musical support from the U.S. Navy band. The audience even stood at attention. "When you hear the music, when you hear this lady sing it, or when it is sung anywhere, there seems to be an inspiration about us," Linthicum said in his powerful opening statement. "This anthem, written by Francis Scotty Key, united us into one great nation."

Ella Holloway, scheduled to be the second speaker, was unable to attend because of an illness, but she sent along a letter that hailed "our beloved Star-Spangled Banner" and declared, "Behold the flag!"[722]

The floor then belonged to Captain Joyce, who, in a spectacular display of showmanship, produced a massive petition with more than 5 million signatures from patriotic citizens across the country, including one from the Minnesota Star-Spangled Banner Campaign that was "upwards of twenty feet in length." It was the product, he said, of nineteen months of determined outreach by the sixty-plus members of his VFW committee. He also brought along signatures from twenty-five governors and one hundred and fifty organizations—"patriotic, civic, professional, fraternal and others"—ranging from teachers and housewives in Boone, Iowa to the American War Mothers in Tucson, Arizona; from the chamber of commerce in Buffalo, New York to the William and Mary Alumni Club, including Francis Scott Key's grandson; and from the warden and state prison employees in Jefferson City, Missouri to the mayor and the board of alderman in Charleston, South Carolina, with additional stated support by the "prominent businessmen" of that city.[723]

"Songs, like poetry, have to be created at inspired moments by competent minds or they are not of great value," Joyce said near the end of his lengthy prepared remarks. "The strain of watching from Baltimore Harbor a night battle which might strike forever from the face of this earth the flag of his country was the impelling and compelling background of Francis Scott Key when he wrote his immortal song. He was not asked to write it, not ordered to do so. He wrote it because he could not help doing so.

"No other song has ever meant anywhere near as much to our people. No composer working for pay or personal fame has ever achieved anything which could be considered worthy to take its place. It is the national anthem of the United States of America."[724]

The only person to speak against the anthem bill was a familiar opposition figure, Kitty Cheatham, charging that the song "was a shameful thing...un-American...un-Christian," but her voice was drowned out by the cacophony of all the others.[725]

Sufficiently impressed, the subcommittee forwarded the bill to the full House, where it was passed unanimously on April 21, 1930. Full recognition did not happen immediately, however, because the Senate put off a vote and seemed to forget about the anthem for almost a year. Only persistent pressure from Linthicum, Holloway, Joyce, and Maryland Senator Millard E. Tydings got it back on the agenda at the end of the legislative session on March 3, 1931, and it took relentless work by Tydings to coax a "symbolic unanimous vote" from the Senate just before the noon deadline.[726] President Herbert Hoover closed the loop by signing the bill that afternoon, confirming that "the composition consisting of the words and music known as 'The Star-Spangled Banner' is designated the national anthem of the United States of America."[727]

Remarkably, from the time Key saw the final bomb bursting in air over Fort McHenry, it had taken 117 years.

CHAPTER FOURTEEN
National Treasure

The official recognition of "The Star-Spangled Banner" as the U.S. national anthem in 1931 sparked renewed interest in the historic flag at the Smithsonian Institution, and staffers did their best to prepare for a surge of visitation.

"The passage of the bill…will, of course, attract even greater attention in the future than has in the past been given to the original flag of this name in the care of this Division," curator Theodore Belote wrote within days to museum executives.[728] He included the first of several proposals to build a new case and display for the flag, which, for financial reasons—and given other priorities—could not be accepted immediately. What *did* happen, however, was an increased series of inquiries to loan the Star-Spangled Banner to patriotic celebrations in other cities and regions.

The Smithsonian had conditioned itself to reject all requests over the years, mindful of Eben Appleton's 1914 edict that the old flag could never be moved. One pre-dated the anthem's recognition, when a military veteran from New York City wrote to Eben's son, William Sumner Appleton, asking if it could be "transported to New York on a flat bottom car, under appropriate Army, Navy and Marine guard, to be saluted along the journey by all the school children singing patriotic songs." Channeling the spirit of his father, Appleton exploded. "It seems to me that the flag of Fort McHenry is far too precious to be exposed to the risks of transportation all over the country whenever wanted as a feature of any local celebration," he wrote. "If New York may have it, then why not San Francisco, and it wouldn't take many trips across the continent…to finish what is left of it."[729] The Smithsonian agreed and turned down the request, noting "the fragile condition of the flag, and the fact that, if by any accident it was destroyed, it could not be replaced."[730]

A later inquiry was much more problematic, however. On November 13, 1957, U.S. Senator John Marshall Butler of Maryland wrote to Smithsonian Secretary Leonard Carmichael, asking that "the flag that flew over Fort McHenry" be returned, *permanently*, "to its proper place of honor at the Fort." This was followed by a missive from Maryland's other senator, J. Glenn Beall, who wrote, under the imposing letterhead of the Senate's Banking and Commerce Committee, that he had been "requested by a group of constituents" to look into the matter. A third salvo of governmental pressure came when John Rogers of the Library of Congress called to ask for "the exact wording of the contract" signed by Eben Appleton when he donated the flag.[731]

Museum staffers were understandably unnerved. Not only was this a concerted effort from powerful figures in the legislative branch of the U.S. government, but the makeup of the museum's management had changed completely in the forty-five years since Armistead's grandson signed his document. None of the current executives had worked with Eben directly, and, as a result, most were only vaguely aware of his precise criteria for stewardship of the flag. They quickly dug into their own archives to obtain, review, and distribute copies of Eben's 1914 declaration: "Therefore, let us all stand firm at *this time* and at *all* times, and under *all* circumstances, and let any American citizen who visits the museum with the expectation of seeing the flag be sure of finding it in its accustomed place."[732]

The Smithsonian folks took a brief break for Christmas, but otherwise responded promptly, denying the requests. Adding practical logic to what they thought was a water-tight argument, they reminded the legislators that "Congress has appropriated funds for the construction of a new building for the National Museum, and designs have been completed to exhibit the flag in an inspiring setting in the great central hall of the new building." Carmichael wrote letters to both senators, arguing that, even beyond the condi-

TOM McMILLAN

tions of Eben's donation, "the flag has such great national significance that it requires to be displayed permanently in the National Capital." Visitation in Washington, D.C. would surely trump anything in Baltimore.[733]

Butler read the letters, fumed, and fired back.

There was irony to his involvement, inasmuch as Butler was elected to the senate in 1950 by defeating Millard Tydings, who had pushed through the final anthem legislation in 1931.[734] But it was clear that Maryland officials, regardless of seniority or party affiliation, felt that Baltimore and Fort McHenry were more natural homes for the flag. Butler wrote a pointed response, insisting that the Smithsonian was not "under any legal limitation" to keep the flag at the museum and noting that "substantial questions exist as far as Mr. Eben Appleton's title to the flag, as against the Federal Government's, is concerned." (In that regard, he raised the same argument Baltimore officials had made against Eben years earlier.) Adding to the political pressure, the Library of Congress prepared a legal memorandum to challenge the donor's conditions. As a final thumb-in-the-eye to Smithsonian officials, Butler wrote, "the Institution has so many cases of exhibits that, to a certain degree, the significance of the 'Star Spangled Banner' is lost among them, irrespective of how it may be displayed."[735]

It took all of Carmichael's patience and management skill over the next six months for the Smithsonian to prevail and retain possession of the flag. He wrote a respectful note to Butler in February, thanking the senator for his interest and promising to take up the matter with the museum's board of regents at its next meeting.[736] In the meantime, Carmichael uncovered evidence that the U.S. Army's deputy commissary of purchases, James Calhoun, had paid Baltimore seamstress Mary Pickersgill directly for her services in August 1813, and that "consequently the flag became Federal property." Eben Appleton's feelings on the matter were so well documented that the secretary considered them legally and morally unbreakable. Moreover, when he learned that Smithsonian visitation topped 2.1 million in 1957, compared to just 650,000 for Fort McHenry, he thought "preventing such a large segment of the public from seeing the flag and honoring this symbol of the democratic heritage of our country would certainly be neither fitting nor proper."[737]

The Smithsonian's Board of Regents issued a formal resolution in June 1958, asserting that, because of ironclad conditions attached to the original donation, "it is impossible to consider the request for the transfer of the Star-Spangled Banner to the National Park Service for display at Fort McHenry."[738]

The case, at long last, was closed.

It should be noted, however, that there *was* one instance when Eben Appleton's mandate to the Smithsonian was broken—a by-product of the unforeseen chaos of World War II.

Fearful of foreign incursion after German bombing raids in London and the Japanese attack on Pearl Harbor, harried Smithsonian officials discussed ways to protect their historic collections, including the possibility of building a bomb-resistant shelter near Washington, D.C. When that proved impractical, they decided to move the most precious objects and documents to an 86,000-square-foot warehouse complex that the National Park Service owned near Luray, Virginia. "If any part of these collections should be lost, then something would be gone from this nation that could not be replaced," Assistant Secretary Alexander Wetmore explained in a letter.[739]

In early 1942, only a few months after Pearl Harbor, the Smithsonian transported sixty tons of material to the series of nondescript buildings in Shenandoah National Park. The 129-year-old Star-Spangled Banner was folded and tucked into a specially constructed, fifteen-foot box before being sent to the secret location along with George Washington's uniform and sword, Benjamin Franklin's walking stick, Abraham Lincoln's plaster death mask and the desk used by Thomas Jefferson to draft the Declaration of Independence. They remained off-site for two years until November 1944, when officials determined the bombing threat had ended.[740]

It was not long after the artifacts were returned that the Smithsonian began considering options for different ways to display its growing collection. Secretary Carmichael wrote about a "press of objects" and "crowded exhibits" that led, ultimately, to a "confused impression of our history and technology." The space in the Arts and

Industries building was no longer sufficient, especially with more than 2 million visitors pouring through the doors each year.[741] In particular, the Fort McHenry flag seemed overshadowed—folded in half in an undersized glass case and crowded out, almost hidden at times, by other less substantial items. Even more alarming from a preservation standpoint was the fact that the floor of the case was found to be "several inches deep in moth crystals."[742]

The proposed solution was to construct a new museum building that "would enable the Smithsonian to fulfill its obligation to disseminate knowledge and meet the educational needs of the public." Named the Museum of History and Technology, its center-piece would be a three-story "Flag Hall," large enough to display the Star-Spangled Banner in its full thirty by thirty-four foot majesty for the first time since 1907. Workers even designed a way to fill in the missing star in the middle while extending the stripes at the end, creating a "false fly end" that artificially extended its massive size to the original thirty by forty-two feet.[743] Modern ingenuity trumped pure history in this case, allowing the flag to look much as it had when Pickersgill delivered it to Fort McHenry early in the nineteenth century.

The Star-Spangled Banner was displayed vertically in the Smithsonian's "Flag Hall" from 1964 through the late 1990s. Note that the museum artificially filled in the missing pieces, including the star, to give the old, tattered flag a full appearance. *(Division of Political and Military History, National Museum of American History, Smithsonian Institution)*

Ground was broken in 1958 and the new museum (later re-named the National Museum of American History) was opened to the public in January 1964. The centerpiece hall was built specifically so that the flag could be hung vertically with its blue union in the upper left corner. It was mounted on a forty-foot framework and hung from the second floor near the National Mall entrance, suspended fifty feet in the air. In addition to enchanting millions of visitors for the next thirty-plus years, it served as a stunning backdrop for special private ceremonies and other events, often involving significant visitors to the nation's capital.[744] One of the most iconic photographs from this period is of the Star-Spangled Banner hovering over President Richard Nixon's first inaugural ball in 1969.[745]

By 1982, however when the flag had turned 169 years old, Smithsonian staffers began to fret again about its deteriorating condition. It was now apparent that years of exposure to varying light, humidity, and temperature levels, along with a steady increase in public visitation, had led to even more subtle damage. The museum announced in a news release that "continuing conservation studies have documented the need for more modern protective measures," noting that dust found on the flag's surfaced contained "particles of grass, tree leaves, soil, and blue cotton fibers, possibly from denim jeans."[746] A story in the *Washington Post*, headlined, "the Dust-Strangled Banner," may have been only slightly exaggerating when it said "the flag has become so filthy...that it's in danger of wasting away to rags."[747]

Armed with new technology in the treatment and preservation of textiles, the Smithsonian embarked on a two-year preservation project in 1981 that included carefully vacuuming the flag and its linen backing, adjusting light levels and providing a new air-handling system. "We used a vacuum with very low suction, so as not to remove any of the original fiber," said chief conservator Suzanne Thomassen-Krauss, the museum's textile authority. "It just took off the same light dust you'd find on your furniture."[748] The most profound change was the installation of an opaque screen to protect it from the elements, including airborne matter, which was designed by a theatrical curtain-maker in New York City; it was lowered once every hour to give visitors a clear view, while different renditions of "The Star-Spangled Banner" played in the background.

But a mechanical mishap that took place in 1994, when the screen fell and dangled in front of the flag—causing no damage, thankfully—led to an even deeper reassessment of preservation policy. The challenge of continuing to display a frail and damaged textile that was almost two hundred years old clearly required innovative thinking. Accordingly, in 1996, Smithsonian officials convened a two-day strategic planning session, bringing together some of the best conservators, curators, historians, and scientists in the country to discuss and debate options. The result was the Star-Spangled Banner Preservation Project, a massive undertaking designed to extend the Fort McHenry flag's life far into the future.[749]

"The conference acknowledged that this flag was no longer a 'simple piece of military history,'" curator Lonn Taylor wrote in *The Star-Spangled Banner: The Making of an Icon*, a book he co-authored with Smithsonian colleagues Kathleen Kendrick and Jeffrey Brodie. "Given its role in the War of 1812 and its status as the inspiration for and the subject of the national anthem, the flag is a significant part of the country's national heritage."[750]

Staffers knew that massive amounts of funding would be required to sustain and complete the renovation project. What they could not have expected was that their efforts would be bolstered by a public shout-out from the president of the United States.

At his State of the Union Address in January 1998, President Bill Clinton offered a tantalizing glimpse of his new "Save America's Treasures" program, a joint effort of the White House, the National Park Service, and the National Trust for Historic Preservation. Near the end of his televised speech, Clinton reminded tens of millions of viewers that "nearly 200 years ago a tattered flag, its broad stripes and bright stars still gleaming through the smoke of a fierce battle moved Francis Scott Key to scribble a few words on the back of an envelope, the words that became our national anthem…. Today that Star-Spangled Banner, along with the Declaration of Independence, the Constitution and the Bill of Rights are on display just a short walk from here. They are America's treasures and we must also save them for the ages. I ask all Americans to support our project to restore all our treasures so that the generations of the 21st century can see for themselves the images and the words that are the old and continuing glory of America."[751]

Intervention by the president in his annual address to the nation made this one of the great fundraising launches in American history. Among the first to answer Clinton's call was the billionaire fashion designer Ralph Lauren, whose famed line of Polo shirts and jeans had often featured the American flag and patriotic color schemes. Lauren joined the president and First Lady Hillary Clinton at a Flag Day press conference on June 14, 1998, when he announced he was making a $13 million gift, the largest in the history of the Smithsonian—with $10 million targeted specifically to conservation of the Star-Spangled Banner. "I am a product of the American dream, and the flag is its symbol," Lauren said. "It's been an inspiration for me, and I want it to be an inspiration for future generations." The donation accounted for more than half of the anticipated $18 million to complete the restoration project.[752]

Corporate groups and individual citizens followed the lead with significant contributions, ensuring that a public-private partnership was at the foundation of the new Star-Spangled Banner display. Additional funds then poured in to renovate the National Museum of American History and provide a new permanent home to ensure the flag's longevity.[753] In his next State of the Union Address in January 1999, Clinton noted that the public and corporate response had been nothing short of astonishing. "Just one example," he said. "Because of you, the Star-Spangled Banner will be preserved for the ages. In ways large and small, as we look to the new millennium, we are keeping alive what George Washington called 'the sacred fire of liberty.'"[754]

The unprecedented preservation effort began on December 1, 1998, when the Star-Spangled Banner was carefully removed from its display in Flag Hall and spread out on a platform for a thorough examination. This was as close as anyone had been to the aging textile in decades, and its condition startled the assembled experts.[755] "My stomach fell to the floor," said Marilyn Zoidis, one of the new curators assigned to the project. "To see it up close, to see the amount of damage and how fragile it was…I remember asking the [chief conservator], 'can this really be saved?' She said, 'I think we can do it.'"[756]

Thomassen-Krauss, the chief conservator, made it clear that the aim was to stabilize the flag in its historic state and not try to make it look like new. To do otherwise would have detracted from the grandeur of a relic so resilient that it was about to survive into its third century. "Our goal was to extend its usable lifetime," Thomassen-Krauss said, noting that it was already 185 years old when the project started. "All textiles undergo an aging process when they are exposed to years of ultraviolet light, pollution and changes in humidity and temperature…[but] we didn't want to change any of the history written on the artifact by stains and soil. Those marks tell the flag's story."[757] That includes the gaping hole for the missing star in the blue union, which remains one of history's great mysteries. As far back as 1873, Georgiana Armistead Appleton offered only a vague, unhelpful hint that "the star was cut out for some official person."[758]

In February 1999, the preservation team gingerly moved the flag into a specially designed "conservation research and treatment laboratory" on the second floor of the museum. It was placed on a series of portable stage platforms behind a large plate glass wall, allowing visitors a rare opportunity to view conservation work as it happened.[759] "We were mindful of the responsibility we had," Zoidis said. "We were committed to giving public tours by team members every week. We rotated through, talking with the public and sharing what we were learning, getting their feedback."[760]

The first major task was to remove approximately 1.7 million stitches that Amelia Fowler and her team had used in 1914 to attach the linen backing; the linen was weathered and soiled and had to be detached. Although, Fowler's stitching process was on the cutting edge of flag preservation in the early twentieth century: what she "did was put in, oh God, a million holes into many of the fibers of the flag itself," said Jennifer Jones, curator of military history at the Smithsonian.[761] It was overkill. To solve the problem, conservators had to cut each stitch by hand, using clippers and tweezers—and microscopes and headlamps—often while lying on their stomachs for up to six hours a day. That tedious, painstaking effort alone took ten months.[762]

Smithsonian workers were suspended over the flag, lying prone on their stomachs, to protect the fragile textile during the modern preservation work. *(Division of Political and Military History, National Museum of American History, Smithsonian Institution)*

"This was a truly unique experience because it was on public view the whole time," Thomassen-Krauss said. Despite the seemingly endless pressure of the work, there were numerous "heartwarming" moments along the way. "One day a family of three generations came in," she said. "The older gentleman looked to be of a World War II generation age, and, as we were working, we all looked up, and he saluted us! Those are the kinds of things, when your back is aching and your knees are aching and you think you can't remove one more stitch…that is when you know you can still do it, because of the appreciation of the American public for the work that you do."[763]

The result of almost a year of snipping and tweaking was spectacular enough to be worth every second. Freed after almost one hundred years from its restrictive stitches and unnatural backing, the Star-Spangled Banner somehow seemed stronger, more powerful, now able, in a sense, to finally breathe. "It began to relax," Jones told the Smithsonian's website, "and that made the threads and the weave of the flag start to come back together, which made it start to pucker and 'move' like it was meant to do." In addition to removing faded stitches, the clipping of the linen also exposed a side of the Fort McHenry flag that had not been seen by the public since George Preble attached an original canvas backing in 1873. Neither visitors to the museum nor conservators ever imagined such vibrant colors in the aging broad stripes and bright stars.[764]

It was breathtaking.

The next step was a careful examination of the newly visible front side of the flag, followed by a meticulous cleaning process before it could be displayed in full to the public. Workers poring over the textile found sixteen previously undocumented patches to repair tears and other damage and evidence of possible cursive writing that could have been faded signatures from George Armistead and his daughter, Georgiana.[765] "They found all these signatures and all these tell-tale signs of use as well as souveniring, and where things were cut out and how they were stitched," Jones said. "And they were actually able to date many of the patches that were put on the flag. All of that gets documented, and we've probably got 30 linear feet of documentation of different reports of every inch of that flag."[766] Thomassen-Krauss said she and Jones discovered 165 areas where the Star-Spangled Banner had been mended over the years; "and we can tell they were done by different people, because of the different skill levels." They found thirty-seven patches in all—some of which appeared to repurpose other snipped remnants from the flag.

"One of the things that we like to point out is that the family understood and valued this flag so much—even though they souvenired it, they cared for it greatly." Jones said. "Without the family valuing it so dearly, it may not exist today."[767]

Distressingly, however, the flag was found to be virtually "embedded" with dust and debris, following ninety years of private possession by the Armisteads and almost one hundred years of public display at the Smithsonian. Conservators reacted by using non-abrasive cosmetic sponges to gently dab the surface and remove harmful particles, sometimes working inch by inch along the thirty-four-foot length, mindful of avoiding further damage. They then brushed it with an approved cleansing mixture of acetone and water to wipe away soil, dirt, and other debris. The final stage was attaching a sheer material known as Stabiltex to support the flag with a minimum amount of stitching—although museum officials knew it would never again be strong enough to hang vertically.[768]

Cleaning and cosmetic snipping aside, Thomassen-Krauss was determined that the flag would now be displayed as it appeared, with no effort to cover the gashes and other damage of the past two hundred years. Back in the Flag Hall era of the 1960s, the Star-Spangled Banner "was made to look whole and restored, and there was a whole bottom section that was reconstructed," she said. "But there was a deliberate decision by the curators not to do that again. What we wanted was that the flag becomes a metaphor for the country. It's tattered, it's torn, but it still survives, and the message is really the survival of both the country and the flag. We're not trying to make it look pretty. We're trying to make it look like it's endured its history, and it can still celebrate its history."[769]

Completed by 2006, the conservation treatment rescued the Star-Spangled Banner for future generations, by cleaning and supporting the fibers, exposing its historic colors, and slowing continued deterioration.

Beyond that, however, and an equally important part of the process, was a major renovation of the flag's home at the National Museum of American History, which opened to the public in November 2008.[770]

An environmentally friendly new chamber for the Fort McHenry flag was built on the second floor of the updated museum and designed to be the focal point of the twenty-first century visitor experience.[771]

The remodeling project also gave curators a chance to magnify the story and provide historic context in ways that had been unavailable in previous Smithsonian displays.

There is a strong sense of solemnity when patrons enter a darkened hallway after passing a shimmering abstract version of the flag on the outside wall. Curators determined that the best approach was to teach a bit of history from the start, mindful that most modern-day Americans lack even a vague knowledge of the War of 1812—including that the British burned the nation's capital in Washington, D.C. less than a month before the Battle of Baltimore. The exhibit opens by explaining why U.S. and British soldiers were converging in anger at Baltimore's harbor in September 1814, and why Key, of all people, was observing on a ship from a distance.[772]

"We sort of set the stage," project manager Jeffrey Brodie said in a behind-the-scenes video the Smithsonian released just before the display's debut. With elements of audio and video that a visitor may not expect, "you'll hear the sounds of Washington burning and sort of the panic of that night. You'll hear from the Battle of Baltimore the sounds of rockets and bombs bursting in air. And on that quiet morning, there are ambient sounds of water lapping against the ship that Key would have been on…so it really puts you in that moment. Visitors can learn from it very quickly before going to see the flag."[773]

Artifacts on display include a burned chunk of timber from President Madison's White House in 1814, a piece of a British bombshell, a British rocket, and the kind of spyglass Key might have used to watch the onslaught. The struggle for national survival comes alive in the space of twenty feet. Eyes have now adjusted to the darkness, but a quick left turn into a large and dimly-lit chamber transforms everything and startles the senses. Through what seems eerily like the dawn's early light, the Fort McHenry flag comes into view.[774]

"Dramatic," Brodie says.[775]

Mesmerizing.

Protected behind a wall of glass, mounted on a platform and displayed horizontally at a ten-degree angle to reduce stress, the original Star-Spangled Banner seems more vital and vibrant than ever. Though it will never again be exposed to the elements or natural light, visitors can lean close enough to the glass to see all of its tattered edges, imperfections, patches, and holes from just a few feet away. Remarkably thin and frail, the flag's bright colors nonetheless stand in contrast to its age, in part because the side now shown to the public was covered by canvas or linen for more than one hundred years, from 1873 to 1999. Visitors often are starstruck, and more than a few—especially military veterans—can be seen dabbing at tears.[776]

The self-guided tour continues into the next walkway of the chamber, known as the exit corridor, where more context is provided.

There is a section about the Armistead family, including a portrait of George drawn shortly after the battle at Fort McHenry, photos of his daughter and grandson, and the engraved silver punch bowl and serving set he received in 1816 from the thankful citizens of Baltimore. The emergence of Key's lyrics and the evolution of his song are also explored, with wide-ranging musical interpretations by various artists over the years. Lonn Taylor wrote that visitors to the exhibit will "share a moment of the past with Francis Scott Key, Lieutenant Colonel George Armistead, Georgiana Armistead Appleton, Eben Appleton, and all of the people in the succeeding generations who have treasured this great flag and helped to preserve it."[777]

A final element before departure dwells on a much broader perspective, on the legacy of the U.S. flag and different views of its symbolism throughout the country's history. In addition to celebrating patriotic moments and great achievements—Iwo Jima and the moon landing are two iconic photos—the flag, and, by extension, the anthem, have long been used to challenge prevailing norms and to protest U.S. involvement in numerous wars, social injustice, racial inequality, women's suffrage, and immigrant rights. Activists on all sides of critical public issues have always known it is a powerful attention-grabber. A Smithsonian slideshow offers a series of images, some of them jarring by design, to underscore that point.

"The Star-Spangled Banner is a national treasure," the presentation concludes. "It inspired the song that became the national anthem and established the American flag as the country's most significant symbol. In times of celebration and crisis, pride and protest, people have raised the flag to express their ideas about what it means to be an American."[778]

From the more personal perspective of someone who put her heart and soul into the project, Jones talked of how the display on the second floor of the history museum embodies the same basic concepts as the Smithsonian itself. "This is the beauty of it, and this is how I believe all exhibitions are, not just exhibitions about the Star-Spangled Banner," she said. "That is, every person brings to every object their own personal understandings and beliefs. The visitor just wants to think about what *they* want to think about, and we're not here to tell them it's right or wrong. We're just to present it, and surround the object with the history that it's a part of."[779]

This all comes against the backdrop of one of the most unique and revered heirlooms of U.S. history, the flag that flew over Fort McHenry on September 14, 1814, a two-hundred-year-old symbol of resilience and survival. Now just a thin remnant of its former self, shorter and more ragged than ever, ravaged by the elements and passage of time, it has somehow endured through triumph and tragedy, unity and chaos, lengthy periods of national strife, including the Civil War—at one point hidden from public view and locked in a vault—while always finding new ways to adapt.

It is, and hopefully always will be, still there.

CHAPTER FIFTEEN
Modern-Day Unrest

Colin Kaepernick, of the National Football League's San Francisco 49ers, wasn't the first athlete of color to invoke the flag and national anthem as platforms for social protest.

He was, however, the most impactful.

As far back as the Mexico City Olympics in 1968, U.S. track standouts Tommie Smith and John Carlos wore black gloves and raised their fists in Black Power salutes on the medal stand as "The Star-Spangled Banner" played. In 1972, Jackie Robinson, who broke baseball's color barrier twenty-five years earlier, wrote that "I cannot stand and sing the anthem. I cannot salute the flag. I know that I am a black man in a white world." In 1995, Mahmoud Abdul-Rauf of the NBA's Denver Nuggets sparked a national uproar and drew league reprimands when he refused to stand for the anthem, calling the flag "a symbol of oppression, of tyranny."[780]

But no form of dissent in the history of American athletics could match the uproar over Kaepernick's decision to kneel for the anthem in 2016. Playing for a marquee franchise in the country's most popular sports league, his act of quiet defiance caught fire on social media, rumbled across the internet and become one of the dominant news stories of the year, debated in bars, on op-ed pages, and in the relentlessly vitriolic atmosphere of partisan cable channels. Some fans bought his jerseys. Other fans burned them.

Kaepernick said from the start that his was an issue-based protest, intended to call attention to injustice against Blacks and other people of color—in particular, the recent spate of shooting deaths of unarmed Black and Brown men. "I am not going to stand up and show pride in a flag for a country that oppresses Black people and people of color," he said following a preseason game on August 26, 2016. "To me, this is bigger than football and it would be selfish on my part to look the other way. There are bodies in the street and people getting paid leave and getting away with murder."[781]

He explained his reasoning in a few brief interviews, but the storyline took on a life of its own and careened out of control over the next two years. Fans booed, NFL sponsors recoiled in horror, and an anti-Kaepernick narrative accused him of disrespecting the country and its military veterans. T-shirts and bumper stickers appeared with declarations that shouted "Real Americans Stand For The Flag to Honor Those Who Died For It" and "I Stand For The Flag, I Kneel For The Cross." But Kaepernick refused to back down, even at great risk to his football career (which he lost). "This is not something that I am going to run by anybody," he declared. "I am not looking for approval. I have to stand up for people that are oppressed…If they take football away, my endorsements from me, I know that I stood up for what is right."[782]

It is important to note that Kaepernick did not mention Francis Scott Key or criticize the anthem's lyrics. But that didn't dissuade others, especially in the media, from expanding the protest to excoriate the slave-owning Key and his little-known third stanza, which rhymes the phrase "hireling and slave" with "gloom of the grave." Jason Johnson was at the forefront of this effort, writing in *The Root* on July 4, 2016—more than a full month before Kaepernick's first protest—that "The Star-Spangled Banner" was "one of the most racist, pro-slavery, anti-black songs in the American lexicon, and you would be wise to cut it from your Fourth of July playlist." Johnson's piece was headlined "Star-Spangled Bigotry: The Hidden Racist History of the National Anthem," and, combined with Kaepernick's protest, it clearly touched a nerve in a time of racial reckoning.[783]

In the month after Kaepernick went public with his comments on August 26, the following stories and op-eds appeared on various media platforms:

- "Colin Kaepernick is Righter Than You Know: The National Anthem is a Celebration of Slavery," *The Intercept*, August 28, 2016 (with the sub-head, "No one seems to be aware that our national anthem literally celebrates the murder of African-Americans")

- "Colin Kaepernick and the Radical Uses of 'The Star-Spangled Banner,'" *The New Yorker*, August 29, 2016

- "Let's take the national anthem literally, and the songwriter at his word," *The Undefeated*, August 30, 2016

- "Is the National Anthem Racist? Beyond the Debate over Colin Kaepernick," *New York Times*, September 2, 2016

- "How 'The Star-Spangled Banner,' Racist or Not, Became Our National Anthem," *Los Angeles Times*, September 6, 2016

- "More Proof The U.S. National Anthem Has Always Been Tainted With Racism," *The Intercept*, September 13, 2016.

The temperature rose even higher the following September when U.S. President Donald Trump, in the first year of his raucous four-year term, told an audience in Alabama, "Wouldn't you love to see one of these NFL owners, when someone disrespects our flag, to say, 'Get that son of a bitch off the field right now? Out! He's fired.'"[784] That led to more furor, more protests, more kneeling by more players (with the media, at one point, keeping a weekly scorecard of the kneelers, team by team)—and some soul-searching conversations on both sides of the issue.

By 2021, anthem protests before NFL games had essentially run their course, but the controversy bubbled to the surface in other settings. At the Olympic track and field trials, Gwen Berry, who finished third in the hammer throw to qualify for the U.S. team, turned away from the flag during the playing of "The Star-Spangled Banner" and held a t-shirt over her head that said "Activist Athlete." In an interview with Black News Channel, Berry—who also raised a fist on the podium at the 2019 Pan American Games—was asked to explain why she had done it.

"History," Berry said. "If you know your history, you know the full song of the national anthem. The third paragraph speaks to slaves in America, our blood being slain…all over the floor. It's disrespectful, and it does not speak for Black Americans. It's obvious. There's no question."

Responding to critics who questioned whether she should even represent the U.S. team, Berry added, "I never said that I hated the country. All I said was I respect my people enough to not stand or acknowledging something that disrespects them."[785]

Stepping back from the headlines and emotion of the debate, however, some of the most strident anti-anthem sentiments seem to be based on the belief that Key's entire third verse was about slaves and slavery—which is plausible if one reads it as a stand-alone verse, as many have.

But there are other interpretations. To read it in context with the first and second verses is to sense that he was writing a sequential narrative of the 1814 battle he had watched two days earlier, and likely was following a declaration of victory by taunting the losing side—the *British*—in the third verse. It is important to understand that Key was not attempting to write a "national anthem" and was merely describing what he saw and felt in the aftermath of the unexpected U.S. victory at Fort McHenry (see a reconstruction of his song-writing efforts in Chapter 6). Key's use of the word "slave" in the fifth line is, indeed, disturbing and controversial, but it also can be viewed as part his attack on every aspect of the British military, including "hirelings" (paid soldiers and mercenaries) and about two hundred escaped slaves in the Colonial Marines.

The Colonial Marines were undoubtedly brave and skilled fighters, but they made up only a tiny fraction of the attacking force at Baltimore. What's more, they took part in the British Army's ground attack at North Point, which Key did not witness—he was miles away, on a ship in the Patapsco River.[786] In any analysis of the lyrics, it is fair to ask whether Key would have committed an entire verse—25 percent of his composition—to a small group that wasn't even part of the epic naval bombardment of Fort McHenry.

In the first verse, Key was uncertain about the bombardment's outcome that morning, desperate to know which flag flew over the fort (*O say does that star-spangled banner yet wave/ O'er the land of the free and the home of the brave?*).

In the second verse, he peered through the early-morning mist to make out the U.S. flag and proclaimed victory (*'Tis the star-spangled banner—O long may it wave/O'er the land of the free and the home of the brave!*).

The traditional view is that the third verse targeted British invaders who had just ransacked towns along the Chesapeake, stormed the nation's capital, set fire to the abandoned White House, and unleashed the Royal Navy's lethal bomb ships on Fort McHenry—a frightful tour-de-force that struck fear in every American heart. Keep in mind that the War of 1812 was the second war between the two countries in thirty-six years, and a serious affront to U.S. sovereignty. In that context, it is the marauding British military that fits Key's description of the "band who so vauntingly swore...a home and a country would leave us no more." It is even possible that Key heard such taunts from British soldiers guarding his ship during the battle, while bombs rattled Fort McHenry; they would have been fresh in his mind when he completed the song two days later.

As for the line about blood washing out "their foul footstep's pollution," Pulitzer Prize-winning historian Alan Taylor told CNN, "This part isn't meant as pro-slavery language. It's referring to the British-poisoned ground—their polluting presence on American soil" during the war.[787]

American musicians removed Key's third verse from most song sheets early in the twentieth century after England and the U.S. came together as world war allies, which explains why it is so little-known today. "So bitter is this stanza," one analyst explained in the 1970s, "that, in view of the subsequent close relationship between Britain and the United States, it often has been deleted" from printed copies.[788] Even at the Fort McHenry National Shrine and Historic Site, one of the formal displays notes that "the third verse is an angry tirade against the British. Key mocks their failure to crush America and destroy 'a home and a country.' Instead, the British have suffered terribly in the 'terror of flight.' Here, Key's words express pride in his nation as well as rage against the enemy."[789]

For context, casualty figures for the Colonial Marines at Baltimore were reported as two killed, two missing, and "several" wounded, while overall British casualties were forty-six killed and three hundred wounded.[790] One theory is that Key was exulting over the defeat of all enemy soldiers in the battle, both white and Black.

Here, again, are the lyrics to the third verse:

And where is that band who so vauntingly swore,
That the havoc of war and the battle's confusion.
A home and a country shall leave us no more?
Their blood has wash'd out their foul footstep's pollution.
No refuge could save, the hireling and slave,
From the terror of flight or the gloom of the grave,
And the star-spangled banner in triumph doth wave,
Oe'r the land of the free and the home of the brave.[791]

Mark Clague, an associate professor of musicology and American culture at the University of Michigan, and the country's foremost expert on the anthem, wrote a piece for cnn.com at the height of the controversy in 2016, headlined, "'Star-Spangled Banner' Critics Miss the Point." In it, he praised Kaepernick for his very public protest against racism, calling it "a potent attack that will add a vibrant chapter to the fascinating history of the U.S. national anthem." He said he was "grateful" to Kaepernick for inspiring a national conversation on race, describing it as "a productive call for Americans to make this 'land of the free' serve all its people."

But Clague also wrote:

...related claims about the song and its author as especially racist have been distorted and exaggerated. "The Star-Spangled Banner" in no way glorifies or celebrates slavery. The middle two verses of Key's lyric vilify the British enemy in the War of 1812, what Key refers to in Verse 3 as "hirelings and slaves." This enemy included both whites and blacks, largely professional soldiers (hirelings) but also the Corps of Colonial Marines (slaves)...

The graphic language of Key's denunciation of this British enemy led to the removal of Verse 3 in sheet music editions of the song in World War I, when the United States and Britain became staunch allies. Yet in 1814 Key's lyric honored American soldiers both black and white. "The Star-Spangled Banner" celebrates the heroes who defended Fort McHenry in the face of almost certain defeat against the most powerful gunships of the era. America's soldiers included many whites, but also free and escaped blacks. Escaped slave William Williams served in the U.S. infantry at Fort McHenry and was killed by a fragment of a British bomb. Another escaped slave, Charles Ball, writes in his memoirs of being among the American soldiers in the Chesapeake Bay Flotilla who courageously repelled a night attack and saved the city. "The Star-Spangled Banner" thus honors American military heroes, black and white, without regard to race.[792]

It is rarely mentioned today that free Blacks, as well as slaves, contributed to the defense of Baltimore during this period, in large part by helping to build fortifications on Hampstead Hill and around the city. By 1810, free Blacks outnumbered slaves in Baltimore (although they did not have full rights as citizens, could not vote and could not serve in the infantry militia). On August 30, 1814, about two weeks before the battle, a U.S. militia private wrote that "all hearts and hands have cordially united in the common cause...at least a mile of entrenchments with suitable batteries were raised, as if by magic, at which are now working all sorts of people, old and young, white and black."[793] Free Black sailors helped to man batteries at Forts Covington, Babcock, and Lazaretto, on the approaches to Fort McHenry, and "other black sailors stood ready to work both ship-borne cannons and land batteries for the defense of the city, should the Royal Navy force a way past the star fort."[794] One published estimate held that "between 10% and 20% of the naval contingent manning the city's fortifications were black sailors."[795]

Yet another viewpoint comes from Marc Ferris, author of *Star-Spangled Banner: The Unlikely Story of America's National Anthem,* who wrote a 2018 column for the Minneapolis *Star-Tribune* that specifically addressed the "troublesome" third verse. Referring to the phrase "hireling and slave," Ferris said, "Though tempting, a literal reading of this long-ignored line is facile and erroneous. No evidence supports the contention that the reference to 'slave' means African Americans in bondage."

Ferris continued:

> *Key's third verse sticks a finger in the eye of the British writ large. The song gloats over the American victory after years of warfare. So why would he even consider the Colonial Marines at all?*
>
> *Taken in context, the term, "hireling" likely refers to mercenaries who bolstered a British fighting force decimated by the Napoleonic Wars. Many are aware of the Hessians, German troops who augment British armies during the Revolutionary War.*
>
> *And rather than referring to a particular handful of fighters, the term "slave" describes all of the monarch's loyal subjects, including British troops—as contrasted with free patriot Americans. Key also has been criticized for being a poor poet, and this stilted third verse supports this contention: "save," "slave" and "grave" may merely have offered simplistic rhymes.*[796]

The issue can never be adjudicated properly, because Key addressed the song only once in a public setting, and, other than praising the defenders of Fort McHenry in that speech, never explained his composition verse-by-verse. More than two hundred years later, in a completely different and much more complex time for the country, we can only speculate as to what he meant by each phrase and each line.

Perhaps it is best left to Clague, the musicologist who has studied the anthem in detail for so many years, and served as board president of the Star-Spangled Music Foundation, to put it in proper perspective for a twenty-first century audience.

"The history of 'The Star Spangled-Banner,' like the United States as a whole, is convoluted," he wrote in his 2016 column for cnn.com. "The lines between justice and injustice are crisscrossed by crippling social blindness that each era must own and overcome.

"Colin Kaepernick's protest draws our attention to the unvarnished fact that today many Americans feel that the 'home of the brave' is not necessarily their 'land of the free.' Yet America's history and thus American's anthem can be powerful tools to achieve a better understanding to learn about ourselves and to imagine a better collective national future."[797]

The modern controversy shone a new light on Key's personal history with slavery, much of which was unknown to the American public.

Two books that were released just before the two hundredth anniversary of his song delved into much of the disturbing detail about Key's past: Jefferson Morley's *Snow-Storm in August; The Struggle for America's Freedom and Washington's Race Riot of 1835*, and Marc Leepson's *What So Proudly We Hailed: Francis Scott Key, A Life*. Leepson's book was the first full-length biography about Key in more than seventy-five years and corrected some of the misconceptions in Key's mythology.

But even while unpacking (and, in many cases, revealing) Key's slave-owning history in print, both authors acknowledged that he was a product of his troubling, early-nineteenth-century times. Morley wrote that "in his relations with enslaved people, Key was decent by the standards of his day…[he] abhorred the mistreatment of bondsmen and the sundering of families by slave dealers. A prim man, he was incapable of brutality. Condescension came more easily."[798] Leepson observed that "Key believed that blacks were inferior to whites, the accepted view of nearly all Americans at the time, including Abraham Lincoln. However, he also was a persuasive and important voice for ameliorating the worst aspects of slavery."[799]

According to U.S. Census records, Key owned five slaves in 1820, six in 1830, and eight in 1840.[800] Whether those figures grew or fell in the intervening years is uncertain, as is the total number of slaves he owned in his lifetime, but Key is known to have freed at least four of his slaves during the 1830s. One of them, a long-time servant named Clem Johnson, received his manumission papers in

Gettysburg, Pennsylvania in 1831, setting him "free to go wherever he may please." But Johnson returned with Key to Maryland and continued to work for him as a free man, apparently with a salary, for the rest of his life.[801]

"Full of contradictions," Key opposed slavery on moral grounds but was not sure how to bring it to an end on a national scale. He opposed full abolition, believing that a sudden emancipation of all slaves would create economic and social chaos (and calling freedmen, in one outrageous letter, "a distinct and inferior race of people"). A possible solution, Key thought, was to relocate free Blacks to their own new country in Africa, named Liberia, and he became one of the early proponents of the American Colonization Society in the 1820s, helping to write its constitution. The flag of Liberia was modeled after the U.S. flag, with red and white stripes and a blue canton, and the capital city was named Monrovia, after U.S. President James Monroe. "The idea never amounted to much," Steve Vogel wrote in *Through the Perilous Fight*, "but Key, with utopian fervor, never abandoned it."[802]

Throughout his career as an attorney, Key argued cases on both sides of the slavery issue, sometimes winning freedom for slaves in his district; he even earned a new nickname, "the Blacks' lawyer." In 1825 he appeared before the Supreme Court to oppose slave trafficking in the case of the *Antelope*, a ship carrying captured slaves that docked in Savannah, Georgia. Although the verdict went against him, Key made strong and impassioned arguments on behalf of the bondsmen, at one point claiming that "by the law of nature, all men are free. The presumption that...black men and Africans are slaves is not a universal presumption." And yet he owned slaves himself for the entirety of his adult life, an act of inexplicable hypocrisy.[803]

Key became involved in politics in the late 1820s, when he supported the presidency of Andrew Jackson, one of the legendary heroes of the War of 1812 (who reportedly told Key that the "The Star-Spangled Banner" inspired his troops at the Battle of New Orleans). Jackson named him U.S. attorney for the District of Columbia in 1833, and it was during this period that Key took on several controversial cases that came to define his post-anthem career.[804] He mounted what Leepson called a "steadfast and wrong-headed" prosecution of Dr. Reuben Crandall for circulating abolitionist papers in Washington, D.C. in 1835; court documents, listing Key as the lead attorney, charged Crandall with "publishing malicious and wicked libels, with the intent to excite sedition and insurrection among the slaves and free colored people of this District."[805] At about the same time, Key sought the death penalty for a nineteen-year-old slave, Arthur Bowen, who had allegedly threatened his owner with an axe in her bedroom. It was said that "Key did so apparently out of animus toward both men after their arrests led to the first race riots in the nation's capital." Crandall was found not guilty of all charges; Bowen was convicted but later received a pardon from President Jackson, following a request for leniency from his owner.[806] Both cases blemished Key's legacy. (For a deep dive into the details of the Crandall and Bowen stories, and the 1835 race riot, see Morley's *Snow-Storm in August*.)

As modern-day historians pore over more details of his life and career, Key also suffers from guilt by association with his friend and brother-in-law, Roger Taney. The two men became fast friends while reading law together at Annapolis in the 1790s, and Taney joined the family by marrying Key's younger sister, Anne, in 1806. When Taney was nominated as U.S. attorney general by President Jackson in 1831, it was Key who convinced him to take the job, saying, "you will find yourself…acting with men who know and value you & with whom you will have the influence you ought to have." In 1856, however, while serving as chief justice of the U.S. Supreme Court, Taney authored the despicable Dred Scott decision, denying citizenship to Black Americans and hastening the start of the Civil War. Taney's ruling came thirteen years after Key's death, but it is nonetheless an essential entry in any Key biography.[807]

This all has led to a twenty-first century re-examination of Key, his legacy and his role in writing the anthem. Shortly after the Morley and Leepson books appeared in 2014, the *Baltimore Sun* posted a piece headlined, "'Star-Spangled Banner' writer had complex record on race," probing the issue at the birthplace of the song.[808] Much more material appeared in the summer and fall of 2016, fueled in part by Kaepernick's protest and the accompanying media coverage. Even at the Smithsonian Institution, caretaker of the iconic flag that inspired the anthem, a lengthy story was published in *Smithsonian Magazine*, written by Christopher Wilson, director of experience design at the National Museum of American History. Balanced and thought-provoking, it ran under the headline, "Where's the Debate on Francis Scott Key's Slave-Holding Legacy?" [809]

Not all reactions were confined to the published word, however. In September 2017, a statue to Key on North Eutaw Street in Baltimore was defaced by vandals, who splattered it with red paint and scrawled "Racist Anthem" in black letters.[810] In June 2020, protestors tore down a statue to Key in San Francisco, along with several other monuments (including, curiously, one to U.S. Civil War hero Ulysses S. Grant), in the midst of a national uproar over racial injustice.[811]

Key's song came under attack as well, in periodic outbursts. In November 2017, the California NAACP called for it to be removed as the national anthem. "It's racist," said Alice Huffman, the organization's president. "It doesn't represent our community. It's anti-black people." In July 2020, as reported in the *Los Angeles Times*, a change.org petition charged that the anthem contained "'racism, elitism…even sexism" and demanded that it be replaced by "America the Beautiful." Neither effort gained legislative momentum, and the petition garnered less than five thousand signatures in a country of 300 million, but occasional media mentions gave the story an enduring, ghost-like presence.[812]

U.S. Representative James Clyburn, one of the country's most powerful politicians, tried to offer a moderating voice with his own middle-ground proposal in January 2021. The fifteen-term Black congressman from South Carolina introduced House Bill H.R. 301, calling for "Lift Every Voice and Sing"—long revered as the "Black national anthem"—to receive a new designation as the U.S. national *hymn*. Clyburn's hope was to give it a place alongside the national anthem and national march (John Philip Sousa's "Stars and Stripes Forever") in a triumvirate of formally recognized American patriotic tunes.

According to one media account, "Supporters argue that the bill elevates the song to an official status without taking away from Francis Scott Key's anthem."[813]

"To make it a national hymn, I think, would be an act of bringing the country together," Clyburn said. "It would say to people, 'You aren't singing a separate national anthem, you are signing the country's national hymn.' The gesture itself would be an act of healing."

The eighty-one-year-old congressman told *USA Today* he had always been "skittish" about the label "Black national anthem" and thought a new approach might help to foster unity in divisive times. "We should have one national anthem, irrespective of whether you're Black or White," Clyburn said. "So to give due honor and respect to the song, we ought to name it the national hymn."[814]

Here is the first verse from "Lift Every Voice and Sing," written as a three-verse poem by James Weldon Johnson in 1900:

> *Lift every voice and sing,*
> *'Til earth and heaven ring,*
> *Ring with the harmonies of Liberty.*
> *Let our rejoicing rise*
> *High as the listening skies,*
> *Let it resound loud as the rolling sea.*
> *Sing a song full of the faith that the dark past has taught us,*
> *Sing a song full of hope that the present has brought us;*
> *Facing the rising sun of our new day begun*
> *Let us march on 'til victory is won.*[815]

Clyburn's bill had forty-four congressional co-sponsors, including Representatives Cori Bush, Hakeem Jeffries, Sheila Jackson Lee, Ted Lieu, Debbie Wasserman Schultz, and Rashida Tlaib. Originally assigned to the Committee on the Judiciary, it was referred to the House Subcommittee on the Constitution, Civil Rights, and Civil Liberties on March 5, 2021, but no additional action was taken before the end of the legislative session, and, like most bills related to the anthem or other national songs, it has yet to come to a vote on the House floor.[816]

The bill underscored the notion that no other country has faced more angst about its anthem than the United States, particularly in recent years. A new focus on Key's slaveholding past has emboldened critics, but the music remains immensely popular in large swaths of the country, inspiring patriotism and silent reverence, bringing thousands to their feet whenever it is played, including the huge crowds at professional and collegiate sporting events. And it has historical bona fides. Few modern-day citizens know the history of the War of 1812, or what happened on that fateful night at Baltimore harbor in

1814—which, it can be argued, is part of the problem—but the song, at its very essence, speaks to the wonderment of the nation's survival during an attack from a foreign power more than two centuries ago. Through the "mist of the deep" at Fort McHenry, Key asked a simple question: *O say does that star spangled banner yet wave?*

The answer, then and now, is an emphatic "yes," leading many to believe that the words Key scribbled while standing on the deck of a ship, describing in real time what he witnessed during a seismic battle that changed the world, will continue to arouse the American spirit far into the future.

Consider what Christopher Wilson wrote at the conclusion of his piece on Key's legacy:

> *Though we should remember the flaws and failings that often animate our history, to me, at least, they do not need to define it. We should remember that if, 200 years after it was declared so by a slaveholder and an enemy of free speech, the United States is the "land of the free," that is because of "the brave" who have called it home since the dawn's early light in September 1814.*[817]

The gigantic remnant of the original Star-Spangled Banner, placed gently today in an environmentally-friendly chamber at the Smithsonian Institution—tattered, torn, pierced, snipped, and faded over time—is, indeed, a majestic sight.

It is a two-hundred-year-old testament to the country's survival, and, in the core of those stubborn threads, a quintessential symbol of American resilience.

Regardless of what happens to Key's song in the future, whether it be retained forever, modified in part or replaced as the anthem by some new generation—any outcome is possible—the flag that flew over Fort McHenry in 1814 will endure as a revered vestige of one of the most impactful chapters of early U.S. history.

The success of the brash American experiment in democracy was never guaranteed. It began in revolt against England's oppressive overreach in 1776; was confirmed, finally, by a clunky peace treaty in 1783; reached a new crescendo with the signing of the ground-breaking U.S. Constitution in 1787; and endured its first major challenge with the controversial Jay Treaty of 1794, to avoid (or at least delay by eighteen years) a second war with the British.

Imperial England was by far the more powerful country when naïve Americans brazenly declared war again in 1812. Reflecting in the hindsight of history, it is almost inconceivable that President Madison and his cohorts could have imagined a successful outcome. The U.S. barely had an army when the first shot was fired, suffered innumerable losses in the first two years, was repelled with ignominy from British forces in Canada, and watched in humiliation as enemy troops assailed the Maryland coast. But as time moved on—and as patience waned for the war-weary British—the underdog Americans found chances for success behind a new breed of military heroes, including George Armistead, the upstart defender of Fort McHenry.

Armistead wanted a massive U.S. flag for his new post, one the invading British would have no trouble seeing from a distance—but also a potent symbol to project confidence and pride in the face of overwhelming enemy power. Baltimore's Mary Pickersgill took on the assignment of a lifetime and delivered two flags, including a smaller storm flag, for what was then the astronomical price of $574.44. The big garrison flag itself cost $405.30.[818]

Armistead's men defended the flag in a perilous fight at Baltimore harbor, but its continued existence today is an astonishing story of passion, patriotism, foresight, defiance…and pure luck. The tens of millions of visitors who have seen it through the years therefore owe a debt of gratitude to George and Louisa Armistead, Georgiana Armistead Appleton, Christopher Hughes Armistead, Eben Appleton, George Preble, Nathan Appleton, John B. Baylor, Charles Walcott, Richard Rathbun, Amelia Fowler, Leonard Carmichael, Frank Taylor, Suzanne Thomassen-Krauss, Marilyn Zoidis, Ralph Lauren, Lonn Taylor, Kathleen Kendrick, Jeffrey Brodie, Scott Sheads, Jennifer Jones, and the countless others who have played roles in its unlikely preservation.

There are several other flags in U.S. history that proudly claim iconic status, led by "Old Glory," which flew in patriotic defiance at Nashville during the Civil War, and the flags planted by U.S.

Marines at Iwo Jima and by astronauts Neil Armstrong and Buzz Aldrin on the Moon. Twenty-first century Americans will never forget the unifying image of the banner raised by New York City fire fighters over the wreckage of Ground Zero at the World Trade Center on September 11, 2001, lifting the country's spirit in a time of despair. [819]

But the original "Star-Spangled Banner" that Key saw waving on the morning of September 14, 1814, the flag that inspired the national anthem, and remains on display at the National Museum of American History, inhabits a rare and distinguished place in the pantheon of American artifacts. Encased in its aged fibers is the genuine and multifarious story of the country—victories and defeats, achievements and failures, visions and aspirations, many still unrealized—dating back more than two hundred remarkable years.

APPENDIX A
Another Family Gift to the Nation

On a visit to the home of descendant Harry Armistead in Phila-delphia several years ago, I noticed three nondescript framed pieces hung along the stairway to the second floor.

From a distance, they looked like high school diplomas or community service certificates, tucked among traditional family portraits and youth sports photos, the kind you see on every stairway in every suburban home across the country.

But these were, uh, different.

They were three of George Armistead's original U.S. Army commissions from the early 1800s, signed, in descending chrono-logical order, by Presidents John Adams, Thomas Jefferson, and James Madison. One of them announced the promotion Armistead received from President Madison less than two weeks after defeating the British in the battle at Fort McHenry in 1814.

"You have these *in your house*," I asked incredulously.

"Well, yes," Harry said matter-of-factly. "Where else would I put them?"

Climbing the final few steps to the second floor, I then came across a handsomely-painted portrait of the hero of Fort McHenry, hanging between the bathroom and one of the bedrooms—which, especially after the presidential signatures, stopped me in my tracks. I naively assumed it was a replica of the famous image that had been published in numerous history books and displayed in local museums since Rembrandt Peale painted George's likeness in 1815, but that wasn't the case. Turns out it was one of the Peale originals, handed down gingerly through five generations of Armisteads for more than two hundred years—from George to his wife, Louisa, to their son, Christopher Hughes Armistead, and, eventually, to Harry.

"You have this *in your house?*" I asked again.

"Where else would I put it?" he asked matter-of-factly.

But history often takes twists and turns through unexpected personal connections. The great-great-grandson of Lieutenant Colonel George Armistead, was approaching eighty years old at the time of my visit, and told me that he and his wife, Liz, were looking to downsize their home. "But want to make sure these things are taken care of," he said. It gave me a long-shot idea.

"I wonder if the Smithsonian would be interested?"

My previous research had led me to the museum's curator of military history, Jennifer Jones, who was one of the guardians of the Star-Spangled Banner display, and had been so graciously helpful every step of the way. I was convinced that she *would* be interested, as long as the items could be properly authenticated, and offered to make an introduction.

Harry and Jennifer handled it from there.

The authentication process took longer than normal because of the restrictions of the Covid-19 pandemic, but those four historic items are now in the possession of the Smithsonian, with plans to place the portrait in the flag's exhibit on the second floor of the National Museum of American History (replacing a replica that has been there from the start). The commissions are held in the museum's archives and will be available to the public online.

"We are so grateful to Harry and his family for making this all available to us," Jennifer told me. "They are such important links in one of the great stories of American history."

Harry admitted a slight twinge of sadness when I spoke to him after the items were turned over—mostly "separation anxiety," because they had been on the walls of his various houses for the entirety of his life, over parts of nine decades. "Of course I miss the portrait and commissions," he said, "having lived with them at all times in my eighty-one years…but it's very gratifying to know that they will be well-curated and cared for at the Smithsonian Institution, and now available to the public as part of this great story. I know they're in the right place."

Harry's son, also named George Armistead, likely would have been the next private owner—and often dreamed of having those items in the future—but "given their value historically," he said, "keeping them felt riskier than donating to a place where they know how to take care of them.

"It's pretty mind-blowing that there was a portrait that was always at the top of our second-floor steps, and the next time I see it, it will be in the Smithsonian."

Direct descendants Harry Armistead (left) and George Armistead (right) pose with the author in front of the 1816 portrait of Lt. Col. George Armistead at their home in Philadelphia. The portrait has since been donated to the Smithsonian. *(Author photo)*

It goes without saying that Harry, his wife, Liz, and their three children revere their family's legacy, even if there was a matter-of-fact sense to seeing Thomas Jefferson's signature on their stairway all those years. Harry occasionally was irked that his great-great-grandfather was not as well known in U.S. history as another distant relative, General Lewis Armistead, who led a Confederate brigade in Pickett's Charge at Gettysburg, where he is remembered with multiple monuments and markers, thereby fixing the name in American memory. "Whenever I'm introduced and people learn my name is Armistead, I'm often asked if I'm related to *Lewis* Armistead. I'm always tempted to say 'Yes, I am' as a peremptory answer. But George Armistead deserves to be better-known because of what he did at Fort McHenry with the Star-Spangled Banner. I'm thinking your book will help that."

Great-great-great-grandson George Armistead (whose middle name, ironically, is Lewis) will never forget the surreal nature of learning his family's history from seemingly-mundane items on the walls. He recalls his earliest reading experiences with books titled *Meet George Washington* and *Meet Thomas Jefferson*, and coming to the realization that "Thomas Jefferson's signature is on a certificate in our house! It's pretty crazy, when you think of it. Those signatures were even crazier to me than the portrait when I was a kid, because, at first, I didn't understand the history of *that*."

When he was twelve years old, George visited Fort McHenry and was mesmerized to see a larger-than-life statue at the entrance "with my name on it." A National Park Service ranger announced to a nearby tour group that a direct descendant of Lieutenant Colonel Armistead was on-site, and a startled George remembered, "they even started taking pictures of me...I mean, I was twelve...talk about crazy...it let me know the story of what he did was pretty important to the people of our country."

George is in his late forties now, and he understands more than ever what the story means to the country. It is one of the many reasons he supported his parents' decision to donate their items to the Smithsonian, sharing them with generations of U.S. citizens who visit the museum in the future. From the standpoint of long-time preservation, he is satisfied that those "fading signatures" of legendary presidents from more than two hundred years ago now fall under the protection of professional curators at the national cathedral of American history.

"Knowing that those commissions and the portrait will now be the original Star-Spangled Banner," George Armistead said, "is something that stirs the soul."

APPENDIX B:
Where Is the Missing Star?

The fate of the Star-Spangled Banner's missing star remains one of history's mysteries. No one knows where it is.

The only clue we have is a vague line from Georgiana Armistead Appleton in an 1873 letter, explaining that "My impression is that the star was cut out for some official person."[820] The information came from her mother, Louisa, who was primary owner of the flag from 1818-1861, and began the process of clipping small souvenirs for battle veterans and other dignitaries.

Newspaper stories have mentioned many possibilities over the years, including that the star went to President Lincoln or his family, but they are based on little more than madcap speculation. The Lincoln theory is implausible because Georgiana owned the flag during most of his presidency and would have known about such a gift first-hand. Beyond that, she and other family members were Confederate sympathizers in the Civil War.[821]

The author's guess—and it is only a guess, based on thin but tantalizing circumstantial evidence—is that the star went to the Marquis de Lafayette on his celebratory tour of the United States in 1824.

The French aristocrat and Revolutionary War veteran remained one of the country's most popular figures in the 1820s. His contributions to the first war with England and close friendship with George Washington made him an icon of the American independence movement, leading President James Monroe to arrange for a national tour. Lafayette visited Washington's grave at Mount Vernon, met personally with three former presidents (Thomas Jefferson, John Adams, and James Madison) and became the first foreign citizen to address the U.S. House of Representatives. It was written that, "as a direct result of that tour and the patriotic enthusiasm it inspired, dozens of cities across the country were named in his honor."[822]

Receptions were held in Boston, Philadelphia, New York, Washington D.C., and many other cities, large and small. The tour brought him to Fort McHenry in October, when a sign declared, "WELCOME LAFAYETTE—to the land of the free and the home of the brave!" Washington's old campaign tent was set up on the grounds and attracted curious onlookers, but the signature moment came when Louisa Armistead brought the Star-Spangled Banner and allowed it to be hung from the flagpole—the first time it had appeared in public since her husband took it home after the battle. The *Baltimore American* wrote that "rising to its elevated station on the flag-staff of Fort M'Henry [was} the same 'STAR SPANGLED BANNER' which waved in triumph on that spot during the awful bombardment of 1814."[823]

Did she cut out a star that day and present it to Lafayette as a token of appreciation? Nothing was ever reported, but it could have been done privately and remains a possibility. The three principal figures—Lafayette, Louisa, and the flag itself—all were in the same place at the same time in a moment of great national celebration.

The Armisteads' daughter, Georgiana, was only seven years old at the time and would have been unaware of the specifics, perhaps explaining her vague statement many years later.

Had the star been given to a local dignitary—say, politician and battle hero Sam Smith—it likely would have been publicized by his family and cherished as a keepsake for all time. It was never mentioned in connection with Francis Scott Key or his descendants, and no other person seemed to rise to that level of prominence.

As for Lafayette? It is possible that he received so many mementoes over so many years that something as seemingly mundane as a star from an old flag may have been overlooked or even misunderstood by his family when he died in Paris in 1834.

There is certainly no hard evidence that Lafayette received the star. But the fact that he met with Louisa Armistead in the presence of the Star-Spangled Banner at a time when reverential Americans were presenting him with gifts makes it, at the very least, an option to consider.

There have been many theories through the years, but when I proposed this one to a curator at the Smithsonian, she did not dismiss it out of hand.

"Maybe this calls for a trip to France," she said with a smile.

APPENDIX C
Fort McHenry: Star-Spangled Icon

The Fort McHenry National Monument and Shrine is the gem of Baltimore's historic treasures, hailed as "the birthplace of the national anthem," but visitors are often surprised to learn that its rich military legacy spans centuries.

That includes the fort's debut as an earthen structure in the Revolutionary War era and service as a government-mandated support site during the Civil War, World War I, and World War II—long after its combat functions had become obsolete.

The need for a defensive presence at Whetstone Point was readily apparent once the British warship *Otter* sailed up the Patapsco River on March 5, 1776, sending the city into a panic. Though no shots were fired and an attack here was never contemplated, Baltimore's leaders scrambled to assemble a small earthen fort "from which red thunderbolts of war will be issued to meet our invading foes." By 1778 there were thirty-eight cannons manned by a company of artillery.

The British surrender at Yorktown in 1781 rendered the garrison unnecessary, but the Maryland General Assembly feared more invasions and passed a 1793 resolution to "erect a fort, arsenal or other military works on the said Point."[824] One year later, Congress agreed to build sixteen forts on the maritime frontier from Massachusetts to Georgia, and the new masonry structure in Baltimore was dedicated to U.S. Secretary of War James McHenry, who had hired engineers and raised funds for construction.[825]

The five-pointed star fort was "completed" by 1805, but work to upgrade its facilities went on for the next nine years. Water batteries were added, and local leaders constructed nearby redoubts (Fort Covington, Fort Babcock, and Lazaretto Battery) with an eye toward helping Fort McHenry fend off an attack. It was during this period that the fort's commander, Major George Armistead, ordered a garrison flag so large the British would have "no trouble seeing it from a distance."

Fort McHenry more than held its own in the 1814 battle (details may be found in Chapters Three through Six), but workers returned to the site almost immediately after the historic U.S. victory. That is because no one could be sure if or when the British would attack again. On September 18, only four days after cannons fell silent, a call went out for forty bricklayers and thousands of bricks to repair damage caused by the twenty-five-hour British bombardment. Six months later, a satisfied Armistead judged the fort to be in "a perfect state of repair."[826]

Fort McHenry never again saw battle after the War of 1812, but it remained an active military installation for almost one hundred years. The most divisive period came during the Civil War from 1861-1865, when the site became a federal prison, holding captured Confederate soldiers and other "traitorous" citizens, including grandsons of Armistead and Francis Scott Key (Chapter Nine).

Wary of Baltimore's significant pro-secession population, the army made clear that its artillery could and would be used to stifle insurrection. When Union Army General John A. Dix invited several "prominent Baltimore women with Southern sympathies" to visit the fort early in the war, he tactfully showed them a large cannon pointed toward Monument Square, site of the 1814 Battle Monument. "If there should be [an] uprising in Baltimore, I shall be compelled to try to put it down," Dix told them, "and that gun is the first that I shall fire." The jittery ladies spread the word and the message had the desired effect; Union artillery was never used.[827]

Sadly, by the early 1900s, Fort McHenry had ceased to be a combat-ready site and was no longer even useful for coastal garrison duty. Its "evening gun" was fired for the last time at 7:20 p.m. on July 21, 1912, after which the land and building were leased to the city as a municipal park. In September 1914, the one-hundredth anniversary of the battle was marked by a week-long celebration, which included picnics, parades, concerts, and the dedication of a bronze statue of George Armistead on the fort's grounds. But in 1917, shortly after the U.S. entered World War I, the government reclaimed the site for use as an army support facility by the Corps of Engineers and Medical Department.[828]

More than fifty acres surrounding the fort were co-opted and developed into U.S. Army General Hospital No. 2, which remained in operation for six years, until 1923. One hundred wood frame buildings were constructed, with three thousand beds and workspace for one thousand medical personnel. Despite this major transition, however, including rehabilitation and recreational facilities, the army vowed that it would not encroach on the original fort structure or its iconic features. "Should it ever be advisable to raze the present hospital buildings," a captain in the quartermaster department wrote in 1919, "Fort McHenry will remain intact as one of the landmarks of American history."[829]

There was at least a brief pause in hospital operations on June 14, 1922—Flag Day—to dedicate a statue to Francis Scott Key and the 1814 defenders. In a "more allegorical approach than other monuments," it was a forty-foot sculpted image of Orpheus, the ancient Greek hero of music and poetry. President Warren G. Harding was the keynote speaker and helped touch off a new era of historic commemoration in the city, praising Baltimore as "the one great American port over which no enemy flag has ever waved." Local leaders saw an immediate opportunity to capitalize on new-found fame.[830]

They were motivated in a different way by a critical column in the *Baltimore News American*, which noted the contrast between the sparkling new statue and some century-old buildings at the fort that had fallen into disrepair. "Deserted barracks and shacks gradually sink into ruin and weeds flourish where a great American victory of arms was won in the War of 1812," the paper wrote. "A movement is gaining headway to restore the ancient fort and transform it into a federal park worthy of its traditions and slightly to the tourists who come from distant places to visit the spot where a brilliant chapter of American history was written."[831]

A multi-layered restoration program being in earnest in 1925, after Congress passed legislation to make Fort McHenry a national park (albeit, still under the auspices of the war department). Over the next several years the fort was restored to is nineteenth century appearance, and local organizations funded the installation of historically accurate interpretive markers. Fundraising efforts got a significant boost in 1931 when "The Star-Spangled Banner" became the official national anthem of the United States, bringing increases in visitation and media coverage. Stewardship of the site was transferred to the National Park Service in 1933, and it was renamed the Fort McHenry National Monument and Historic Shrine in 1939—becoming the only place in the country with that dual designation.[832]

World War II brought yet another call to action. Although the fort itself remained open to visitors, the U.S. Coast Guard established a fire control and port security training facility on the nearby grounds, while also holding enlistment ceremonies and recruitment drives. Officials remembered that "the fort and its flag remained a beacon of inspiration" for the twenty-six thousand men and women who trained here, learning shipboard fighting, damage control, and fire safety techniques. But the most memorable event during those four years was a 1942 ceremony when the first captured Japanese battle flags were displayed as "war trophies."[833]

The end of World War II was an end to Fort McHenry's long history as a military installation, turning it back, in a sense, to the general public. Visitation soared again, topping 600,000 for five straight years from 1951–1955 (as opposed to just 299,000 in 1944).[834] An archeological excavation in the late 1950s led to the exciting discovery of an underground cross-brace for the original flagpole, confirming its location, as identified in an 1803 map.[835] Because of that, guests at the fort today can see a large flag flying from the same spot where Key saw it on the morning of September 14, 1814, inspiring him to write the national anthem.

As for other related sites for visitors to Baltimore? The Star-Spangled Banner Flag House on East Pratt Street is the site where Mary Pickersgill and her all-female crew began to sew the giant flag in 1813. The Maryland Center for History and Culture (formerly Maryland Historical Society) on Park Avenue contains documents, photos, and digital collections related to the Battle of Baltimore and the War of 1812. The Star-Spangled Banner National Historic Trail links various sites and events throughout Maryland,

Virginia, and the District of Columbia that impacted the story of the war and the song. The Battle Monument on North Calvert Street is a lasting tribute to George Armistead and stalwarts of the 1814 conflict, and its image is so central to local history that it is featured on Baltimore's city seal.

SELECTED BIBLIOGRAPHY

BOOKS

Altoff, Gerard T, *Amongst My Best Men: African-Americans and the War of 1812*, The Perry Group, Put-in-Bay, OH, 1996.

Appleton, Nathan, *The Star-Spangled Banner, An Address Delivered by Nathan Appleton at the Old South Meeting House, Boston Massachusetts, On June 14, 1977*, Lockwood, Brooks & Co., Boston, 1877.

Avirett, James B., *The Memoirs of General Turner Ashby and His Compeers*, Selby and Dulany, Baltimore, 1867.

Borneman, Walter R., *1812: The War That Forged A Nation*, Harper-Collins, New York, 2004.

Cate, Margaret Randolph and Wirt Armistead Cate, *The Armistead Family and Collaterals*, Reed Printing Company, Nashville, TN, 1971.

Cheatham, Kitty, *Words and Music of "The Star-Spangled Banner" Oppose the Spirit of Democracy Which the Declaration of Independence Embodies: A Protest*, New York, 1918 (reprinted by *Forgotten Books*).

Cocke, Clyde W., *Pass In Review: An Illustrated History of West Point Cadets, 1794-Present*, Osprey Publishing, Oxford, UK, 2012.

Cole, Merle T. and Scott S. Sheads, *Fort McHenry and Baltimore Harbor Defenses*, Arcadia Publishing, Charleston, SC, 2001.

Crawford, Michael J. (ed.), *The Naval War of 1812, A Documentary History, Volume III,* The Naval History Center, Department of the Navy, Washington, D.C., 2002.

Cruikshank, Ernest, *The Battle of Fort George*, Niagara Historical Society, Welland, Ontario, 1912.

Cruikshank, Ernest, *The Documentary History of the Campaign Upon the Niagara Frontier in the Year 1813, January to June, 1813*, Vol. 1., The Lundy's Lane Historical Society, Welland, Ontario, 1902 (reprinted by Forgotten Books).

Cullum, George W., *Biographical Register of the Officers and Graduates of the U.S. Military Academy at West Point, N.Y., Vol. 1, 1802-1840*, D. Van Nostrand, New York, 1868.

Cullum, George W., *Campaigns of the War of 1812-15 Against Britain, Sketched and Criticised (sic), With Brief Biographies of the American Engineers*, James Miller, New York, 1879.

Delaplaine, Edward S., *Francis Scott Key: Life and Times*, Biography Press, New York, 1937.

Delaplaine, Edward S., *John Philip Sousa and the National Anthem*, Willow Bend Books, Westminster, MD, 1983 and 2001.

du Bellet, Louise Pecquet, *Some Prominent Virginia Families*, Volumes 1–2, J.P. Bell Company, Lynchburg, VA, 1907.

Ezratty, Harry A., *Baltimore in the Civil War: The Pratt Street Riot and a City Occupied,* The History Press, Charleston, SC, 2010.

Frazier, John W., *Reunion of the Blue and Gray, Philadelphia brigade and Pickett's division, July 2, 3, 4, 1887 and September 15, 16, 17, 1906*, Ware Bros. Company Printers, Philadelphia, 1906 (reprinted from University of Michigan Library collection).

Ferris, Marc, *Star-Spangled Banner: The Unlikely Story of America's National Anthem*, Johns Hopkins University Press, Baltimore, 2014.

Filby, P.W. and Edward G. Howard, *Star-Spangled Books*, Maryland Historical Society, Baltimore, 1972.

Frederiksen, John C., *Green Coats and Glory: The United States Regiment of Riflemen, 1808-1821*, Old Fort Niagara Association, Youngstown, NY, 2000.

Frederiksen, John C., *The United States Army in the War of 1812, Concise Biographies of Commanders and Operational Histories of Regiments*, McFarland & Company, Jefferson, NC, 2009.

Fredriksen, John C. (ed.), *The War of 1812 U.S. War Department Correspondence, 1812-1815*, McFarland & Company, Inc., Jefferson, NC, 2016.

Garber, Virginia Armistead, *The Armistead Family 1635-1910*, Whittet and Shepherson Printers, Richmond, VA, 1910.

Gleig, George Robert, *A Subaltern in America: Comprising His Narrative of the Campaigns of the British Army at Baltimore (and) Washington During the Late War*, Carey, Hart & Co., Philadelphia and Baltimore, 1833 (reprinted by Forgotten Books).

Graves, Donald E., *And All Their Glory Past: Fort Erie, Plattsburgh and the Final Battles in the North, 1814*, Robin Brass Studio, Montreal, 2013.

Green, Bennett W., *Word-Book of Virginia Folk-Speech*, Wm. Ellis Jones' Sons, Inc., Richmond 1912.

Hall, Robert, *Register of Cadets Admitted into The United States Military Academy at West Point, N.Y., From Its Establishment Till 1880*, T.H.S. Hamersly, Washington, D.C., 1880.

Heitman, Francis B., *Historical Register and Dictionary of the U.S. Army, From Its Organization, September 29, 1789 to March 2, 1903*, Vol 1, Government Printing Office, Washington, D.C., 1903.

Hessler, James A. and Wayne E. Motts, *Pickett's Charge at Gettysburg: A Guide to the Most Famous Attack in American History*, Savas Beatie, El Dorado Hills, CA, 2015.

Hickey, Donald R. (ed.), *The War of 1812: Writings from America's Second War of Independence*, Library Classics of the United States, Inc., New York, 2013.

Howard, Frank Key, *Fourteen Months in American Bastiles*, Kelly, Hedian & Piet, Baltimore, 1863.

Howard, McHenry, *Recollections of a Maryland Confederate Soldier and Staff Officer Under Johnston, Jackson and Lee*, Williams & Williams Company, Baltimore, 1914.

Johnston, Sally and Pat Pilling, *Mary Young Pickersgill: Flag Maker of the Star-Spangled Banner*, AuthorHouse, Bloomington, IN, 2014.

Katheder, Thomas, *The Baylors of Newmarket: The Decline and Fall of a Virginia Planter Family*, iUniverse, Inc., Bloomington, IN, 2009.

Kennedy, Mary Selden, *Seldens of Virginia and Allied Families*, Volume 1, Frank Allaben Genealogical Company, New York, 1911.

Leepson, Marc, *Flag: An American Biography*, Thomas Dunne Books, St. Martin's Press, New York, 2005.

Leepson, Marc, *What So Proudly We Hailed: Francis Scott Key, A Life*, Palgrave MacMillan, New York, 2014.

Lessem, Harold I. and George C. Mackenzie, *Fort McHenry*, National Park Service Historic Handbook Series, No. 5, Washington, D.C., 1954.

Lord, Walter, *The Dawn's Early Light*, The Johns Hopkins University Press, Baltimore, 1972.

Lubar, Steven, and Kathleen M. Kendrick, *Legacies: Collecting America's History at the Smithsonian*, Smithsonian Institution Press, Washington, D.C., 2001.

Miles, Ellen G., *Saint-Memin and the Neoclassical Profile Portrait in America*, National Portrait Gallery and the Smithsonian Institution Press, Washington, D.C., 1994.

Moore, Robert J., Jr. and Michael Haynes, *Lewis & Clark, Tailor Made, Trail Worn: Army Life, Clothing & Weapons of the Corps of Discovery*, Farcountry Press, Helena, MT, 2003.

Molotsky, Irvin, *The Flag, The Poet & The Song: The Story of the Star-Spangled Banner*, Dutton and the Penguin Group, New York, 2001.

Morley, Jefferson, *Snow-Storm in August: The Struggle for American Freedom and Washington's Race Riot of 1835*, Anchor Books, New York, 2013.

Morrison, James L., *"The Best School," West Point, 1833-1866*, The Kent State University Press, Kent Oh. and London, 1986.

Motts, Wayne E., *"Trust In God And Fear Nothing," Gen. Lewis A. Armistead, CSA*, Farnsworth House Military Impressions, Gettysburg, PA, 1994.

Niles, Hezekiah (ed.), *Niles Weekly Register, From September 1814 to March 1815*, Vol. 7, Franklin Press, Baltimore (reprinted by Forgotten Books).

Norfleet, Filmore, *Saint-Memin in Virginia: Portraits and Biographies*, The Dietz Press, Richmond, VA, 1942.

O'Connell. Frank and Wilbur F. Coyle, *National Star-Spangled Banner Centennial, Baltimore, Maryland, September 6 to 13, 1914*, National Star-Spangled Banner Centennial Commission, Baltimore, 1914.

Pappas, George S., *To The Point: The United States Military Academy, 1802-1902*, Praeger Publishers, Westport, CT., 1993.

Ponder, Melinda M., *Katherine Lee Bates: From Sea to Shining Sea*, Windy City Publishers, Chicago, IL, 2017.

Preble, George Henry, *History of the Flag of the United States of America, and of the Naval Yacht-Club Signals, Seals and Arms, and Principal Songs of the United States*, Houghton, Mifflin and Company, Boston and New York, 1894.

Preble, George Henry, *Three Historic Flags and Three September Victories: A Paper Read Before The New-England Historic, Genealogical Society, July 9, 1873*, Boston, printed for private distribution, 1874.

Reardon, Carol, *Pickett's Charge in History and Memory*, University of North Carolina Press, Chapel Hill, NC and London, 1997.

Reilly, John F., *An Account of the Reunion of the Survivors of the Philadelphia Brigade and Pickett's Division of Confederate Soldiers* (with McDermott, Anthony W., *A Brief History of the 69th Regiment Pennsylvania Veteran Volunteers*), D.J. Gallagher & Co., Philadelphia, PA, 1889

Scharf, John Thomas, *History of Maryland: From the Earliest Period to the Present Day*, Vol. 3, Tradition Press, Hatboro, PA (reprint), 1967.

Sheads, Scott Sumpter and Daniel Carroll Toomey, *Baltimore During the Civil War*, Toomey Press, Baltimore, 1997.

Sheads, Scott Sumpter, *Guardian of The Star-Spangled Banner: Lt. Colonel George Armistead and The Fort McHenry Flag*, Toomey Press, Baltimore, 1999.

Sheads, Scott, *Fort McHenry*, The Nautical & Aviation Publishing Company, Baltimore, 1995.

Sheads, Scott S., *The Rockets' Red Glare: The Maritime Defense of Baltimore in 1814*, Tidewater Publishers, Centreville, MD, 1986.

Sherr, Lynn, *America the Beautiful: The Stirring Story Behind Our Nation's Favorite Song*, Public Affairs, New York, 2001.

Sonneck, Oscar George Theodore, *Report on "The Star-Spangled Banner," "Hail Columbia," "America," "Yankee Doodle,"* Government Printing Office, Washington, D.C., 1909.

Sonneck, Oscar George Theordore, *The Star-Spangled Banner*, Government Printing Office, Washington D.C., 1914.

Svejda, George J., *History of the Star-Spangled Banner from 1814 to the Present*, National Park Service, Washington, D.C., 1969 (reprinted by *Forgotten Books*).

Taylor, Lonn, *The Star-Spangled Banner: The Flag that Inspired the National Anthem*, Henry N. Abrams, Inc. Publishers, New York, 2000.

Taylor, Lonn, Kathleen M. Kendrick and Jeffrey L. Brodie, *The Star-Spangled Banner: The Making of an American Icon*, Smithsonian Books, HarperCollins, New York, 2008.

Thomas, Clarence, *General Turner Ashby: The Centaur of the South*, Eddy Press Corporation, Winchester, VA, 1907.

Tucker, Dr. Spencer D (ed.), *The Encyclopedia of the Wars of the Early American Republic, 1783-1812*, Vol. III, ABC-CLIO, Santa Barbara, CA, 2014.

United Sates War Department, *The War of the Rebellion: Official Records of the Union and Confederate Armies*, various volumes, Government Printing Office, Washington, D.C., 1887–1889.

Vanderslice, John Mitchell, *Gettysburg: A History of the Gettysburg Battle-field Memorial Association, With an Account of the Battle, Giving Movements, Positions, and Losses of the Commands Engaged*, Gettysburg Battlefield Memorial Association, Philadelphia, 1897.

Vile, John R., *America's National Anthem: "The Star-Spangled Banner" in U.S. History, Culture and Law*, ABC-CLIO, Santa Barbara, CA, 2021.

Vogel, Steve, *Through the Perilous Fight: From The Burning Of Washington To The Star-Spangled Banner, The Six Weeks That Saved The Nation*, Random House Trade Paperbacks, New York, 2014.

Wade, Arthur P., *Artillerists and Engineers: The Beginnings of American Seacoast Fortifications, 1794-1815*, CDSG Press, McLean, VA, 1977.

Weiss, John McNish, *The Merikens: Free Black American Settlers in Trinidad 1815-16*, McNish and Weiss, London, 2002.

White, Richard Grant, *National Hymns: How They Are Written and How They Are Not Written: A Lyric and National Study for the Times*, Rudd and Carleton, New York, 1861 (reprinted by *Forgotten Books*).

Whitehorne, Joseph W.A., *While Washington Burned: The Battle for Fort Erie, 1814*, The Nautical and Aviation Publishing Company of America, Charleston, SC, 1992.

Wilcox, Cadmus Marcellus, *History of the Mexican War*, The Church News Publishing Company, Washington, DC, 1892.

Wilkinson, James, *Memoirs of My Own Times*, Vol. 1, Abraham Small, Philadelphia, 1816.

Young, Maureen, *A Tapestry of Heroes: Appleton, Armistead, Baylor, Donnel, Faris, Hughes, Hunter, Kerr*, Create Space, Inc., Middletown, DE, 2011.

ESSAYS, PERIODICALS

"Armistead Family," *The William and Mary Quarterly*, Vol. 6, No. 3, January 1898.

Barrett, Robert J., "Naval Recollections of the Late American War," *The United Service Magazine*, Vol. 35, April 1841.

Clague, Mark and Jamie Vander Broek, "Banner Moments: The National Anthem in American Life," Special Collections, University of Michigan Library.

Fennell, Charles C., "A Battle From The Start: The Creation of the Memorial Landscape at the Bloody Angle in Gettysburg National Military Park," www.npshistory.com.

George, Christopher T., "Mirage of Freedom: African Americans and the War of 1812, *Maryland Historical Magazine*, Vo., 91, No 4, Winter 1996.

Hickey, Donald R, "The Quasi War: America's First Limited War," *Northern Mariner*, Vol. 18, Issue 3/4, July–October 2008.

Kyff, Robert S., "Whiskey Rebellion," *American History*, July/August 1994, Vol. 29, Issue 3.

Lineberry, Cate, "The Story Behind The Star-Spangled Banner: How the flag that flew proudly over Fort McHenry inspired an anthem and made its way to the Smithsonian," *Smithsonian Magazine*, www.smithsonianmag.com, March 1, 2007.

Poole, Robert M., "Star-Spangled Banner Back on Display: After a decade's conservation, the flag that inspired the National Anthem returns to its place of honor on the National Mall," *Smithsonian Magazine*, www.smithsonianmag.com, November 2008.

Reardon, Carol, "Pickett's Charge: The Convergence of History and Myth in the Southern Past," from *The Third Day at Gettysburg & Beyond* (ed. Gary Gallagher), The University of North Carolina Press, Chapel Hill, NC and London, 1994.

Robinson Ralph, "The Use of Rockets by the British in the War of 1812," *Maryland Historical Magazine*, Volume XL, No. 1, March 1945.

Schmitt, Emily Karcher, "The Keeping of the Star-Spangled Banner: A story of emblematic resilience," July 4, 2017, Smithsonian Insider, https://insider.si.edu.

Sheads, Scott S., "Lt. Colonel George Armistead Statue at Fort McHenry, Sept. 1914" (draft), Fort McHenry Library, Armistead file.

Wilson, Christopher, "Where's the Debate on Francis Scott Key's Slave-Holding Legacy?" *Smithsonian Magazine*, www.smithsonianmag.org, July 1, 2016.

Youmans, Harold W., "Hear Ye! Hear Ye! All Rise For His Honor The Judge – George Armistead And Civil Process In Arkansas, 1807-1808," found at Maryland Historical Society.

MILITARY SERVICE AND PENSION RECORDS
(National Archives and www.fold3.com)

George Armistead, War of 1812 Pension Application (submitted by Louisa Armistead)

Lewis A. Armistead, Compiled Service Records, CSA

Lewis A. Armistead, General and Staff Officers, CSA

ADDITIONAL NATIONAL ARCHIVES DOCUMENTS
(many copies also available at www.fold3.com and some
at www.ancestry.com)

Civil War Draft Records: Exemptions and Enrollments

Engineering Department Letters Relating to the USMA, 1812–1867, Military Academy Orders

Letters Received by the Office of the Adjutant General Main Series, 1822–1860

Registers of Enlistments in the United States Army, 1798–1914

U.S. Military Academy Cadet Applications, 1805–1866

U.S. Returns from Military Posts, 1806–1916

U.S. Returns of Killed and Wounded in Battles, 1790–1844

UNITED STATES MILITARY ACADEMY LIBRARY RECORDS

Engineering Department Letters Relating to the USMA, January 1833–December 1834

List of Orders Relating to Cadet Lewis A. Armistead, Extracted From "Post Orders/No. 6, 1832-1837, U.S. Military Academy"

Register of Merit, No. 1, 1817–1835 (academy academic and disciplinary records)

Special Collections, Lewis Armistead Commissions

U.S. Military Academy Cadet Application Papers, 1805–1866

LIBRARY OF CONGRESS

"Legislation to Make 'The Star-Spangled Banner' The National Anthem" – Hearings Before the Committee on the Judiciary, House of Representatives, Seventy-First Congress, Second Session, on H.R. 14, 1930

NATIONAL MUSEUM OF AMERICAN HISTORY (Smithsonian)

"Star-Spangled Banner Accession File No. 58476" (including all relevant documents relating to the donation, acceptance and preservation of the Fort McHenry flag at the Smithsonian)

DIGITAL SOURCES

https://americanhistory.si.edu, "Making the Museum: Part One," National Museum of American History

http://americanhistory.si.edu, "Original Star-Spangled Banner Debuts in New State-of-the-Art Gallery at the Heart of the National Museum of History," NMAH

http://americanhistory.si.edu, "Smithsonian Announces Preliminary Findings of Star-Spangled Banner Preservation," NMAH

http://americanhistory.si.edu, "Smithsonian Completes Star-Spangled Banner Conservation Treatment," NMAH

https://americanhistory.si.edu, "Smithsonian's Star-Spangled Banner To Undergo Three-Year Conservation."

http://americanhistory.si.edu, "Transforming the Museum: Part Two," NMAH

www.ancestry.com, *Colonial Families of the United States, 1607-1775*, Vol. 1, "Armistead," p. 14

www.baltimorecity.gov, "Battle Monument Conservation"

www.britannica.com, "Napoleon I," "Battle Of Leipzig"

www.britannica.com, "Mexican-American War"

www.c-span.org, "American Artifacts: The Star-Spangled Banner, May 15, 2014.

www.ead.lib.virginia.edu, "A Guide to the Baylor Family Papers," from the Special Collections of the University of Virginia Library, accession number 2257

www.encylopedia.com, "James Madison: Facts, Figures"

www.encyclopediavirginia.org, "John Baylor III"

www.explore.baltimoreheritage.org, "Battle Monument

www.friendsoffortgeorge.ca, "The History of Fort George"

www.fortmchenryguard.blogspot.com, "Rebuilding The Dry Moat"

www.founders.archives.gov, "Founders Online," George Washington letters, John Adams letters, Thomas Jefferson letters

https://history.army.mil, American Military History, "The War of 1812," Chapter 6

www.history.com, "Treaty of Ghent"

www.history.com, "8 Memorable Protests by American Athletes"

https://history.house.gov, "Star-Spangled Banner Telegram," U.S. House of Representatives

https://history.house.gov, "The Designation of the 'Star-Spangled Banner,'" U.S. House of Representatives

www.historynet.com, "British Amphibious Operations, War of 1812"

https://journals.psu.edu, Dr. D. G. Brinton, "From Chancellorsville to Gettysburg, A Doctor's Diary"

www.mdhistory.org, Maryland Center for History and Culture, "The Star-Spangled Banner (handwritten)"

https://maryland1812.wordpress.com, "Lt. Colonel George Armistead Monument, Federal Hill," and various other items

http://mht.maryland.gov, Maryland National Register Properties

www.militarymuseum.org, George C. Armistead, "California's Confederate Militia: The Los Angeles Mounted Rifles"

www.mountvernon.org, "George Baylor"

www.newworldencylopedia.org, "Gustavus Adolphus of Sweden"

www.nfl.com, Steve Wyche, "Colin Kaepernick why he sat during the national anthem," August 27, 2016

www.nps.gov, "Francis Scott Key"

www.nps.gov, "Liberty Island Chronology"

www.nps.gov, "Nest of Pirates"

www.nps.gov, "Summer 1814: American troops flee in humiliation, leaving Washington exposed"

www.nps.gov, "The Star Fort," Fort McHenry National Monument and Historic Shrine

www.nps.gov, "We have met the enemy and they are ours"

www.nyhistory.org, New York Historical Society Museum and Library, "Columbian Anacreontic Society Medal."

www.oldfortniagara.org, "History of Old Fort Niagara"

www.penelope.uchicago.edu, "Class of 1803, Cullum's Register"

www.starspangledmusic.org, Star-Spangled Music Foundation, *Poets & Patriots: A Tuneful History of "The Star-Spangled Banner,"* with "Complete Lyrics" transcribed by Mark Clague, Ph. D., American Music Institute, University of Michigan

www.stripes.com, "War of 1812: An American surprise at Craney Island," by Mark St, John Erickson

http://teaching.msa.maryland,gov, Mary Pickersgill: Maker of the Star-Spangled Banner, Teaching American History in Maryland, Documents for the Classrom

www.theroot.com, Jason Johnson, "Star-Spangled Bigotry: The Hidden Racist History of the National Anthem, July 4, 2016.

www.virginiaplaces.org, "Craney Island"

www.theundefeated.com, Jess Washington, "Still No Anthem, Still No Regrets for Mahmoud Abdul-Rauf," September 1, 2016

www.youtube.com, "Gwen Berry Talks Decision to Turn Back on American Flag," video taken from BNC Live on bnc.tv

www.youtube.com, PBS, "The War of 1812"

COUNTY COURTHOUSE DOCUMENTS

Fauquier County, Va. Deed Book 23, Walker K. Armistead

Prince William County, Va. Will Book H, 1792–1803, John Armistead

NEWSPAPERS

Baltimore American and Commercial Advertiser

Baltimore Sun

Charleston Mercury Extra (Charleston, SC)

Charleston Post and Courier (Charleston, SC)

Charleston Times (Charleston, SC)

Civilian & Telegraph (Cumberland, MD)

Daily Ardmoreite (Ardmore, OK)

Evening Sun (Baltimore)

Federal Gazette & *Baltimore Daily Advertiser*

Gettysburg Star and Sentinel

Gettysburg Times

Imperial Valley Press, (El Centro, CA)

London Times

Los Angeles Times

Maryland Gazette and Political Intelligencer (Annapolis, MD)

Minneapolis Star-Tribune

National Advocate (New York, NY)

National Intelligencer (Washington, D.C.)

New Bern Sun Journal (New Bern, NC)

New Orleans Daily Picayune

New York Herald

New York Times

Niles Weekly Register (Baltimore, MD)

Richmond Dispatch

Richmond Examiner

Savannah (G.) Republican

The Daily Exchange (Baltimore, MD)

The New York Times

The Times (Port Tobacco, MD)

USA Today

Virginia Gazette

Washington Post

ENDNOTES

1   Author visit to the National Museum of American History, Washington D.C.

2   According to anthem historian Mark Clague, Key wrote three songs and ten hymns during his lifetime. Clague, "Separating fact from fiction about 'The Star-Spangled Banner,'" September 14, 2016, https://constitutioncenter.org/blog/separating-fact-from-fiction-about-the-star-spangled-banner.

3   Original manuscript of the Star-Spangled Banner, Library of Congress, https://www.loc.gov/resource/hec.04309/.

4   Lonn Taylor, Kathleen M. Kendrick, and Jeffrey L. Brodie, *The Star-Spangled Banner: The Making of an American Icon* (Smithsonian, June 24, 2008), 43, 53.

5   Mark Clague and Jamie Vander Broek, "Banner Moments: The National Anthem in American Life," Special Collections, University of Michigan Library, 11.

6   "How a Drinker's Poem Became Our National Anthem," https://www.youtube.com/watch?v=lOtHjgpoqo4.

7   Walter Lord, *The Dawn's Early Light* (W.W. Norton & Co. Inc., January 1, 1972), 274.

8   Sally Johnston and Pat Pilling, *Mary Young Pickersgill: Flag Maker of the Star-Spangled Banner* (AuthorHouse, October 24, 2014), 18, 76; Lonn Taylor, *The Star-Spangled Banner: The Flag that Inspired the National Anthem* (Harry N. Abrams, June 1, 2000), 39–40.

9   Taylor, Kendrick, and Brodie, *The Star-Spangled Banner*, 86, 98, 103.

10 Author interview with Brent D. Glass, 2020.

11 1860 United States Federal Census for Baltimore, Md. for William S. Appleton and Georgiana Appleton; "Will of John Armistead of Caroline County," Prince William County, Va. Will Book H, 1792-1803, 478-480; "John Baylor III," https://encyclopediavirginia.org/entries/baylor-john-iii-1705-1772/. Baylor was George Armistead's great-grandfather.

12 Tom McMillan, *Armistead and Hancock: Behind the Gettysburg Legend of Two Friends at the Turning Point of the Civil War*, (Stackpole Books, July 15, 2021), 1, 10–14; McHenry Howard, *Recollections of a Maryland Confederate Soldier and Staff Officer Under Johnston, Jackson and Lee* (Andesite Press, August 20, 2017), XXX.

13 Interview with Suzanne Thomassen-Krauss, "American Artifacts: The Star-Spangled Banner," https://www.c-span.org/video/?319838-1/star-spangled-banner, video released May 15, 2014.

14 Scott S. Sheads, *Guardian of the Star-Spangled Banner: Lieutenant Colonel George Armistead and the Fort McHenry Flag* (Toomey Press, September 14, 1999), 7–8, 11–17; Walter Lord, *The Dawn's Early Light* (Open Road Media, March 6, 2012), 274.

15 Sheads, *Guardian of the Star-Spangled Banner*, 10.

16 Ibid., 4–5, 8.

17 Henry Dearborn to John Armstrong, June 8, 1813, Fort McHenry Library, Armistead file. Published in *Niles Weekly Register*, March 5, 1814.

18 *Federal Gazette & Baltimore Daily Advertiser*, July 12, 1813.

19 Steve Vogel, *Through the Perilous Fight: Six Weeks That Saved the Nation* (Random House, May 7, 2013), 121, 147–157, 170–174; Lord, *The Dawn's Early Light*, 145–148, 162–164. The contemporary phrase for the president's residence in 1813 was the President's House (it was not yet the "White House"), but the more familiar public term is used here, and throughout, for clarity.

20 George Armistead to Louisa Armistead, September 10, 1814, Maryland Historical Society (name now changed to Maryland Center for History and Culture).

21 Ibid.

22 Vogel, *Through the Perilous Fight*, 238.

23 Ibid., 50, 270, 282–283. Published contemporary estimates of the distance from North Point to Baltimore range from 10–15 miles.

24 George Armistead to Samuel Smith, September 12, 1814, Fort McHenry Library, Armistead file, from the Samuel Smith Papers, Library of Congress.

25 Vogel, *Through the Perilous Fight*, 317.

26 "Isaac Munroe to a Friend in Boston," September 17, 1814, from *The War of 1812: Writings from America's Second War of Independence,* Donald R. Hickey, ed., 541–543. Munroe was one of the volunteer defenders of Fort McHenry and editor of the *Baltimore Patriot.*

27 George Armistead to James Monroe, September 24, 1814, Records of the Office of the Secretary of War, National Archives, Record Group 107. Also published in *The Naval War of 1812, A Documentary History,* Vol. 111, 302–304.

28 Vogel, *Through the Perilous Fight*, 308, 338; "Isaac Monroe to a Friend in Boston;" Lord, *The Dawn's Early Light*, 293.

29 Letter from Chief Justice Roger Taney, published in *Poems of the Late Francis Scott Key*, 24–25.

30 Scott S. Sheads, *The Rockets' Red Glare: The Maritime Defense of Baltimore in 1814*, (Tidewater Pub, January 1, 1986), 104; Vogel, *Through the Perilous Fight*, 332.

31 "Isaac Monroe to a Friend in Boston."

32 Robert J. Barrett, "Naval Recollections of the Late American War," *The United Service Magazine,* Vol. 35, April 1841, 464. Barrett was a teenaged midshipman serving aboard the British frigate *Hebrus.*

33 Ibid., 12.

34 Edward S. Delaplaine, *Francis Scott Key: Life and Times* (Heritage Books, Inc., December 30, 2019), 378–380. Key's now-famous remarks were recorded third-hand. They came at a political dinner in Frederick, Md. to honor his brother-in-law, Roger Taney, on August 6, 1834. It was said to be the only time Key spoke publicly about the events at Fort McHenry; Marc Leepson, *What So Proudly We Hailed: Francis Scott Key, A Life* (St. Martin's Press, June 24, 2014), 55, 160–162.

35 Vogel, *Through the Perilous Fight*, 352–352, 376.

36 Sheads, *The Rockets' Red Glare*, 105; General Sam Smith Letter to the War Department, Smith Papers, LC; Vogel, *Through the Perilous Fight*, 350.

37 George Armistead to James Monroe, September 24, 1814, Records of the Office of the Secretary of War, NA.

38 George Armistead to Louisa Armistead, September 22, 1814, Fort McHenry Library, Armistead file.

39 War of 1812 Pension and Bounty Land Warrant Application Files, Pension Application filed by Louisa Armistead, May 15, 1856, NA. Louisa wrote that her husband "died on the 25th day of April 1818, at Baltimore, in consequence of disease contracted while in service in the line of duty."

40 The statue is a larger-than-life image of Armistead in uniform. A smaller statue is located on Federal Hill, and he is listed with other local commanders on the Battle Monument in downtown Baltimore.

41 Virginia Armistead Garber, *The Armistead Family* (August 3, 2021), 1635–1910, 19.

42 Wayne E. Motts and Lewis B. Armistead, *Trust In God And Fear Nothing* (Farnsworth House Military, January 1, 1994), 7–8.

43 Garber, *The Armistead Family*, 19, 29, 41, 45–48, 61–71, 231. President William Henry Harrison was the grandfather of President Benjamin Harrison; Mary Selden Kennedy, *Seldens of Virginia and Allied Families* (Andesite Press, August 8, 2015), 166–167. Author Kennedy notes that the family named was spelled "Armstead" in a 1651 patent; J. Jay Myers, "Who Will Follow Me? The story of Confederate Brigadier General Lewis Armistead, a hero of the Battle of Gettysburg," *Civil War Times*, July/August 1993, 29.

44 Garber, *The Armistead Family*, 29.

45 Ibid. 62.

46 George Washington to John Armistead, December 29, 1786, https://founders.archives.gov/documents/Washington/04-04-02-0413 (also see George Washington to John Armistead, April 17, 1786).

47 Thomas Katheder, *The Baylors of Newmarket: The Decline and Fall of a Virginia Planter Family* (iUniverse, June 8, 2009), 9, 75; "A Guide to the Baylor Family Papers," 4-5, www.ead.lib.virginia.edu; George Washington from Colonel George Baylor, September 26, 1788, https://founders.archives.gov/documents/Washington/03-17-02-0129.

48 Katheder, *The Baylors of Newmarket*, 1, 46–47, 49–50, 130; The *Virginia Gazette*, March 22, 1770 (John Baylor advertisement for Fearnought's services); "John Baylor III, https://encyclo-pediavirginia.org/entries/baylor-john-iii-1705-1772/;" George Washington from John Baylor, April 25, 1785, https://founders.archives.gov/documents/Washington/04-02-02-0374.

49 Garber, *The Armistead Family*; John B. Armistead to William Simmons, October 17, 1797, National Archives and Records Administration: Letterbook, War Dept Accountant, RG217; Armistead identifies himself as "late aid de camp to Major General Morgan, Virginia Militia" and refers to service "to suppress an insurrection in the western counties of Pennsylvania in the year 1794;" Robert S. Kyff, "Whiskey Rebellion," *American History*, July/August 1994, Vol. 29, Issue 3; Spencer C. Tucker (ed.), *The Encyclopedia of the Wars of the Early American Republic, 1783-1812* (ABC-CLIO, June 11, 2014), 997.

50 Donald R. Hickey, "The Quasi War: America's First Limited War" *Northern Mariner*, Volume 18, Issue 3/4, July–October 2008, 67–77; Francis B. Heitman, *Historical Register and Dictionary of the United States Army*, Vol. 1 (Forgotten Books, August 24, 2018), 169.

51 Robert K. Krick, *The Third Day at Gettysburg & Beyond* (The University of North Carolina Press, September 16, 1994), "Armistead and Garnett," 94 –95; Bennett W. Green, *Word Book of Virginia Folk Speech* (Kessinger Publishing, LLC, September 10, 2010), "Some Virginia Names Spelt One Way and Called Another," 13.

52 Candidates for Army Appointments from Virginia, November 1798, https://founders.archives.gov/documents/Washington/06-03-02-0161-0002, 2, 7–8; Heitman, *Historical Register and Dictionary of the United States Army*, Vol. 1, 169.

53 John Adams to United States Senate, April 17, 1800, https://founders.archives.gov/documents/Adams/99-02-02-4267, 9; Heitman, *Historical Register and Dictionary of the United States Army*, Vol. 1, 169; Sheads, *Guardian of the Star-Spangled Banner*, 54–55. The George Armistead commission is also available in the Armistead file at the Fort McHenry Library.

54 Heitman, *Historical Register and Dictionary of the United States Army*, Vol. 1, 169. The inscription on John's tombstone in

Upperville, Virginia indicates service in the War of 1812, but, if true, it was likely as an elderly member of the hometown militia. There is no record that he served in the U.S. Army during the War of 1812.

55   Ibid., 169; Arthur Wade, *Artillerists and Engineers: The Beginnings of American Seacoast Fortifications 1794-1815* (CDSG Press, January 31, 2011), 250.

56   Garber, *The Armistead Family*, 62–66; Maureen Young, *A Tapestry of Heroes: Appleton, Armistead, Baylor, Donnel, Faris, Hughes, Hunter, Kerr* (CreateSpace Independent Publishing Platform, June 22, 2011), 265; "Armistead Family," *The William and Mary Quarterly*, Vol. 6, No. 3, January 1898, 167–169; *Colonial Families of the United States*, 1607–1775, Vol. 1, "Armistead," 14, https://www.ancestry.com/discoveryui-content/view/222:61175?_phsrc=kdc361&_phstart=successSource&gs-fn=Addison&gsln=Armistead&ml_rpos=1&queryId=aed-35f7163a6675bf9887118e4a84059. It should be noted that, although the other brother, William, never served in the military, he was hired as a clerk in the office of the War Department's accountant in 1816, worked in a similar position in the Treasury Department from 1817-1818 and served as post sutler at Fort Monroe Virginia from 1820–1840. This information is found in notes to a letter from Wilson Cary Nicholas to Thomas Jefferson, September 30, 1816, https://founders.archives.gov/documents/Jefferson/03-10-02-0299. The letter to Jefferson described William Armistead as "the brother of Col. Armistead who defended the fort at Baltimore and one or two other officers of great merit who were lost in the service."

57   "Will of John Armistead of Caroline County," Prince William County, Va. Will Book H, 1792–1803, 478–480.

58   Register of Enlistments in the United States Army, 1798–1914, "Addison B. Armistead," www.fold3.com; Frederick County, Va. Marriages, 1771–1825, "Addison Bowles Armistead and Mary Howe Peyton," www.ancestry.com; Sheads, *Guardian of the Star-Spangled Banner*, 3. Author Sheads does not specifically say that George traveled to Dumfries to attend Addison's wedding, but the timing of his trip home "to visit his mother" could not have been a coincidence.

59 Heitman, *Historical Register and Dictionary of the U.S. Army*, Vol. 1, 169; Henry Dearborn to Thomas Jefferson, February, 24, 1807, www.founders.archives.org. Dates sometimes vary slightly from source to source. Addison's promotion is alternately listed as Oct. 1 and Sept. 30.

60 Wade, *Artillerists and Engineers*, 11.

61 "British Amphibious Operations, War of 1812," https://www.historynet.com/war-1812-british-amphibious-operations/, 2.

62 Wade, *Artillerists and Engineers*, 249–251.

63 Fillmore Norfleet, *Saint-Memin in Virginia: Portraits and Biographies* (The Dietz Press Inc., January 1, 1942), 137, 139; Ellen G. Miles, *Saint-Memin and the Neoclassical Profile Portrait in America* (National Portrait Gallery/Smithsonian, December 17, 1994), 14; Robert J. Moore Jr. and Michael Haynes, *Lewis & Clark, Tailor Made, Trail Worn: Army Life, Clothing & Weapons of the Corps of Discovery* (Farcountry Press, April 1, 2003), 134.

64 Addison Bowles Armistead to William Eustis, January 20, 1812; February 7, 1812; April 18, 1812; June 4, 1812; John C. Fredriksen (ed.), *The War of 1812 U.S. War Department Correspondence, 1812-1815*, 15.

65 U.S. Army Register of Enlistments, 1798–1914, "Addison B. Armistead," https://www.fold3.com/image/310978712?rec=300934993&terms=armistead,addison; "Died at Fort Moultrie," *Charleston Times*, February 20, 1813 (the same obituary also ran in the *Richmond Enquirer* on March 16, 1813).

66 James E. Poindexter, "General Armistead's Portrait Presented," *Southern Historical Society Papers*, Vol. 37, 144; Motts, *Trust In God And Fear Nothing*, 8.

67 "Gustavus Adolphus of Sweden," https://www.newworldencyclopedia.org/entry/Gustavus_Adolphus_of_Sweden; Richard Brzezinski and Richard Hook, *The Army of Gustavus Adolphus 2, Cavalry*, 1, 22–23, 42.

68 U.S. Army Register of Enlistments, 1798–1914, "Lewis G.A. Armistead," https://www.fold3.com/image/306346586?rec=283032907&terms=war,armistead,lewis,1812,of.

69 L.G.A. Armistead to Major Wm. Kirke, October 20, 1807, *Calendar of Virginia State Papers and Other Manuscripts, January 1, 1799 to December 31, 1807*, 607–608.

70   John Tayloe to Henry Dearborn, June 19, 1808, Letters Received by the Office of the Adjutant General, 1805–1899, https://catalog.archives.gov/id/56217469, filed under Lewis Armistead, 1812, Folder 665.

71   Thomas Jefferson to United States Senate, January 16, 1809, https://founders.archives.gov/documents/Jefferson/99-01-02-9557.

72   U.S. Army Register of Enlistments, 1798–1914, "Lewis G.A. Armistead," https://www.fold3.com/image/306346586?rec=283 032907&terms=war,armistead,lewis,1812,of; Heitman, *Historical Register and Dictionary of the U.S. Army, Vol. 1,* 169.

73   John C. Frederikson, "Regiment of Riflemen/1st Regiment of Rifles," *The United States Army in the War of 1812: Concise Biographies of Commanders and Operational Histories of Regiments, with Bibliographies of Published and Primary Sources* (McFarland & Company, May 13, 2009), 280.

74   L.G.A. Armistead to Richmond Court House ("Sir"), February 24, 1812, Letters Received by the Office of the Adjutant General, 1805–1899, NA, Lewis Armistead, Folder 665.

75   Frederiksen, "Regiment of Riflemen/1st Regiment of Rifles," *The United States Army in the War of 1812,* 282–283; John C. Frederiksen, *Green Coats and Glory: The United States Regiment of Riflemen, 1808-1821* (Old Fort Niagara, January 1, 2000), 43.

76   Heitman, *Historical Register and Dictionary of the U.S. Army, Vol. 1,* 169; John Grant and Ray Jones, *The War of 1812: A Guide to Battlefields and Historic Sites* (Turner, October 4, 2011), "Sackets Harbor," 99.

77   Joseph W.A. Whitehorne, *While Washington Burned: The Battle for Fort Erie, 1814* (Nautical & Aviation Pub. Co. of Amer., December 1, 1992), 29, 37–42, 47–48.

78   Ibid., 59, 109–110; Frederiksen, *Green Coats and Glory,* 60.

79   Frederiksen, *Green Coats and Glory,* 60, also located in the Armistead file at the Fort McHenry Library.

80   Donald E. Graves, *And All Their Glory Past: Fort Erie, Plattsburgh and the Final Battles in the North, 1814* (Robin Brass Studio, Inc., November 25, 2013), 251–252.

81   Ibid., 252–253.

82   Ibid., 256; U.S. Returns of Killed and Wounded in Battles, 1790–1844, "L.G.A. Armistead," https://www.ancestry.com/discoveryui-content/view/2664:3652?tid=&pid=&query-Id=5399cb786524cdafa670a1a7dacee693&_phsrc=kdc371&_phstart=successSource; Whitehorne, *While Washington Burned*, 123. In 2010, an auction house offered a "magnificent officer's dirk or dagger inscribed 'Lewis Adolphus Gustavus Armistead,'" apparently recovered at Fort Erie. The accompanying text at jamesdjulia.com said that "based on all the scabbard dents, dings and scratches, Armistead must have been wearing this when we he was killed and his captured trophy sent home as a memorial."

83   Graves, *And All Their Glory*, 260–261.

84   Whitehorne, *While Washington Burned*, 81.

85   George W. Cullum, *Biographical Register of the Officers and Graduates of the U.S. Military Academy at West Point, N.Y., Vol. 1, 1802-1840*, 91; https://www.fold3.com/image/312877810?rec=308347617&terms=walker,us,k,armistead,army.

86   Garber, *The Armistead Family*, 62-66; Maureen Young, *A Tapestry of Heroes*, 265; "Armistead Family," *The William and Mary Quarterly*, Vol. 6, No. 3, January 1898, 167-169; *Colonial Families of the United States, 1607–1775*, Vol. 1, "Armistead," p. 14, https://www.ancestry.com/discoveryui-content/view/222:61175?_phsrc=kdc361&_phstart=successSource&gs-fn=Addison&gsln=Armistead&ml_rpos=1&queryId=aed-35f7163a6675bf9887118e4a84059; Cullum, *Campaigns of the War of 1812-15 Against Great Britain, Sketched and Criticised, With Brief Biographies of the American Engineers*, 271. "Will of John Armistead of Caroline County," Prince William County, Va. Will Book H, 1792–1803, 478–480.

87   George S. Pappas, *To The Point: The United States Military Academy, 1802-1902* (Praeger, July 30, 1993), 17; Clyde H. Cocke, *Pass In Review, An Illustrated History of West Point Cadets, 1794-Present* (Osprey Publishing, March 20, 2012), 5–6, 161. The commander at the time was Henry Burbeck.

88   Joseph G. Swift, *The Memoirs of Joseph Gardner Swift* (Isha Books, January 1, 2013), 12.

89 Cocke, *Pass In Review*, 161; Wade, *Artillerists and Engineers*, 83; Cullum, *Biographical Register of the Graduates of the U.S. Military Academy at West Point, N.Y., 1802-1840*, 89–91.

90 Henry Dearborn to Thomas Jefferson, March 4, 1803, https://founders.archives.gov/?q=Project%3A%22Jefferson%20Papers%22&s=1211311113&r=25716.

91 Cullum, *Biographical Register of the Graduates of the U.S, Military Academy at West Point, N.Y. 1802-1840*, 91.

92 Wade, *Artillerists and Engineers*, 130.

93 Cullum, *Campaigns of the War of 1812-15 Against Great Britain*, 271.

94 Ibid., 271.

95 Stuart L. Butler, *Defending the Old Dominion: Virginia and its Militia in the War of 1812* (UPA, December 21, 2012), 180.

96 "Craney Island," http://www.virginiaplaces.org/transportation/craney.html.

97 Mark St. John Erickson, "War of 1812: An American surprise at Craney Island," June 22, 2013, http://war1812trails.com/State%20Reports%20Washington%20and%20VA.html; "Historic Fort Norfolk," https://www.historicforrest.com/Historic-FortNorfolk/FortNorfolkHistory/FortNorfolkHistory.html.

98 Gertrude Sprague Carraway, *The Stanly Family and the Historic John Wright Stanly House* (Tryon Palace Commission, January 1, 1969), 28; Garber, *The Armistead Family*, 66; Fauquier County, Va. Deed Book 23, 350; Motts, *Trust In God And Fear Nothing*, 10; Garber, *The Armistead Family*, 66. The names of the daughters were Lucinda, Mary, Elizabeth, Virginia, and Cornelia. The sons, in addition to Lewis, were Franck, Bowles, and Walker Keith Jr.

99 Cullum, *Biographical Register of the Officers and Graduates of the U.S. Military Academy at West Point, N.Y., 1802-1840*, 91. As Chief of Engineers, Walker also became Inspector of the Military Academy in 1818.

100 Ibid., 91. In general, a "brevet" was an advancement in rank without the accompanying increase in pay. It was bestowed either for battlefield valor or, in Walker's case, for ten years of "faithful service" in the same rank.

101   Garber, *The Armistead Family*, 63-66; Heitman, *Historical Regis-ter and Dictionary of the U.S. Army, Vol. 1*, 169; Sheads, *Guardian of the Star-Spangled Banner*, 3. George was born on April 10, 1780—a date agreed upon by his biographer, Scott Sheads, long-time historian at Fort McHenry, as well as all the published fam-ily genealogies. The only alternative date is April 10, 1779, which appears on his statue at Fort McHenry. The author, however, agrees with the published historians and accepts the 1780 date.

102   "George Baylor," https://www.mountvernon.org/library/digi-talhistory/digital-encyclopedia/article/george-baylor/.

103   Ibid.; Katheder, *The Baylors of Newmarket*, 75; "Baylor's Regi-ment: The Third Continental Light Dragoons," https://books.google.com/books/about/Baylor_s_Regiment.html?id=w_d5rgEACAAJ.

104   "Thomas Jefferson on Politics & Government—The Military & the Militia, part 47.2, Against Standing Armies," https://famguardian.org/Subjects/Politics/ThomasJefferson/jeff1480.htm.

105   Henry Dearborn to George Armistead, March 20, 1810, Fort McHenry Library, Armistead file; Heitman, *Historical Register and Dictionary of the U.S. Army, Vol. 1*, 169.

106   Sheads, *Guardian of the Star-Spangled Banner*, 49. Armistead arrived at Fort Niagara in September 1801 and was named assistant military agent in May 1802.

107   "History of Old Fort Niagara," https://www.oldfortniagara.org/history, 2, 7, 9–10, 15.

108   "The History of Fort George," 1, http://www.friendsoffort-george.ca/fort-george/history/index.html; Sheads, *Guardian of the Star-Spangled Banner*, 3.

109   George Armistead to Moses Porter, December 27, 1803, Fort McHenry Library, Armistead file.

110   Sheads, *Guardian of the Star-Spangled Banner*, 10, 78.

111   George Armistead to Mary B. (Armistead) Carter, March 13, 1807, Fort McHenry Library, Armistead file. Armistead overes-timated the length of the trip by about 2,000 miles, but citizens knew little about distances between regions in the early 1800s.

112   Harold W. Youmans, "Hear Ye! Hear Ye! All Rise For His Honor The Judge—George Armistead And Civil Process In

Arkansas, 1807-1808," Maryland Historical Society, 1–3, 10; Morris S. Arnold, *Unequal Laws Unto a Savage Race: European Legal Traditions in Arkansas, 1686-1836* (University of Arkansas Press, January 1, 1985), 5, 155.

113 Youmans, "Hear Ye! Hear Ye!" 4.
114 Ibid., 5, 7.
115 George Armistead to Mary B. (Armistead) Carter, March 13, 1807, Fort McHenry Library, Armistead file.
116 Youmans, "Hear Ye! Hear Ye!" 2.
117 Ibid., 1, 13. The New Madrid District encompassed both Fort Madison and Arkansas Post.
118 Ibid., 2, 10, 21; Arnold, *Unequal Laws Unto A Savage Race*, 155–156.
119 Youmans, "Hear Ye! Hear Ye!" 19, 25.
120 Sheads, *The Rockets' Red Glare*, 6–7; Vogel, *Through the Perilous Fight*, 212.
121 Harold I. Lessem and George C. Mackenzie, *Fort McHenry*, National Park Service Historic Handbook Series, 1-3; "The Star Fort," Fort McHenry National Monument and Historic Shrine, https://www.nps.gov/fomc/learn/historyculture/the-star-fort.htm; Sheads, The Rockets' Red Glare, 7; "Rebuilding The Dry Moat," http://fortmchenryguard.blogspot.com/2011/02/rebuilding-dry-moat.html.
122 Scott Sheads, *Fort McHenry*, 7–8.
123 Lessem and Mackenzie, *Fort McHenry*, 3; Sheads, *Guardian of the Star-Spangled Banner*, 4, 50.
124 Sheads, *The Rockets' Red Glare*, 8.
125 Lessem and Mackenzie, *Fort McHenry*, 3.
126 Sheads, *Guardian of the Star-Spangled Banner*, 4–5.
127 Ibid., 6; "Liberty Island Chronology," https://www.nps.gov/stli/learn/historyculture/liberty-island-a-chronology.htm; "History of Liberty Island (New York)," https://libertyisland.weebly.com/.
128 Wade, *Artillerists and Engineers*, 169.
129 Sheads, *Guardian of the Star-Spangled Banner*, 51; Garber, *The Armistead Family*, 63.
130 Letters Sent by the Office of the Adjutant General, February 8, 1813, Main Series, 1800–1899, Vols. 2–3, M 565, Roll 4, NA.

131 Heitman, *Historical Register and Dictionary of the U.S. Army, Vol. 1.*, 169; Ernest Cruikshank, *The Battle of Fort George*, 18. Cruikshank wrote that "a distance of only 1200 metres separated the two forts."

132 Thomas H. Cushing to George K. Armistead, February 8, 1813, *House Documents: Reports, Motions, Etc. Vol. 2, Nos. 49-97*, 93.

133 John Vincent to Sir George Prevost, May 28, 1813, from Ernest Cruikshank, *The Documentary History of the Campaign upon the Niagara Frontier in the Year 1813, January to June 1813, Vol. 1*, 250.

134 Cruikshank, *The Battle of Fort George*, 45-51.

135 Notes by Captain W.H. Merritt, *Documentary History of the Campaign upon the Niagara Frontier in the Year 1813*, 261.

136 William Holcroft to Francis de Rottenburg, August 15, 1813, *Documentary History of the Campaign upon the Niagara Frontier in the Year 1813*, 259.

137 Ibid., 260.

138 Henry Dearborn to Daniel Tompkins, May 27, 1813, *Documentary History of the Campaign upon the Niagara Frontier in the Year 1813*, 250.

139 Extract of a letter dated Fort George, Upper Canada, June 3, 1813, from *National Advocate (New York)*, June 23, 1813, *Documentary History of the Campaign upon the Niagara Frontier in the Year 1813*, 268.

140 Henry Dearborn to John Armstrong, June 8, 1813, Fort McHenry Library, Armistead file. Published in *Niles Weekly Register*, March 5, 1814.

141 John Armstrong to George Armistead, June 27, 1813, Letters Sent by the Office of the Adjutant General, Main Series, 1800-1899, Vols. 2-3, M 565, Roll 4, NA.

142 Vogel, *Through the Perilous Fight*, 22.

143 Ibid., 25–27.

144 Ibid., 29.

145 *Federal Gazette & Baltimore Daily Ad*vertiser, July 12, 1813.

146 Sheads, *The Rockets' Red Glare*, 17.

147 Ibid., 17–18.

148 Lord, *The Dawn's Early Light*, 274.

149 Mary Carole McCauley, "Rare Letter by Ft. McHenry's George Armistead to be auctioned," *Baltimore Sun*, September 8, 2014. Armistead's letter was dated May 3, 1811.

150 Taylor, Kendrick, and Brodie, *The Star-Spangled Banner: Making of an American Icon*, 64; Vogel, *Through the Perilous Fight*, 314; Author tour of the Star-Spangled Banner Flag House on East Pratt Street, Baltimore. Pickersgill's age is often misreported, but she was born on February 12, 1776 and was therefore 37 years old in the summer of 1813. There is often confusion, because the flag was made a year before the 1814 battle.

151 1810 Baltimore census; Sally Johnston and Pat Pilling, *Mary Young Pickersgill: Flag Maker of the Star-Spangled Banner*; Taylor, Kendrick, and Brodie, *The Star-Spangled Banner*, 64; https://amhistory.si.edu/starspangledbanner/making-the-flag. Most accounts list two of Mary's nieces, Eliza and Margaret. A third niece, Jane, is identified in a March 2014 news release from the Smithsonian, titled "History of the Star-Spangled Banner: Fact Sheet."

152 Vogel, *Through the Perilous Fight*, 313.

153 Caroline Pickersgill Purdy to Georgiana Armistead Appleton, September 9, 1876, Fort McHenry Library, Armistead file. Calhoun is identified on a copy of original receipt, located at the Star-Spangled Banner Flag House, Baltimore. It is also found in the Smithsonian Institutions accession file no. 58467.

154 Taylor, Kendrick, and Brodie, *The Star-Spangled Banner*, 63–67.

155 Ibid., 72–75.

156 Irvin Molotsky, *The Flag, The Poet and The Song: The Story of the Star-Spangled Banner* (Dutton Adult, June 1, 2001), 76–77; Taylor, Kendrick, and Brodie, *The Star-Spangled Banner*, 64–66; Vogel, *Through the Perilous Fight*, 314–315.

157 Johnston and Pilling, *Mary Young Pickersgill*, 25.

158 Taylor, Kendrick, and Brodie, *The Star-Spangled Banner*, 65.

159 Caroline Pickersgill Purdy to Georgiana Armistead Appleton, September 9, 1876, Fort McHenry Library, Armistead file. She refers to Armistead as "Col. Armistead." He was actually a major at the time of the battle but was promoted to lieutenant colonel for his performance at Fort McHenry.

160 Copy of original receipt located at the Star-Spangled Banner Flag House, Baltimore.

161 Vogel, *Through the Perilous Fight*, 315; Molotsky, *The Flag, The Poet and The Song*, 79; author tour of Fort McHenry. A display at the fort says the flagpole was made of Eastern White Pine.

162 Taylor, Kendrick, and Brodie, *The Star-Spangled Banner*, 67.

163 "Napoleon I," https://www.britannica.com/biography/Napoleon-I; "Battle of Leipzig," https://www.britannica.com/event/Battle-of-Leipzig; Vogel, *Through the Perilous Fight*, 6–7, 50.

164 Lord, *The Dawn's Early Light*, 33.

165 Vogel, *Through the Perilous Fight*, 6, 17–18.

166 Taylor, Kendrick, and Brodie, *The Star-Spangled Banner*, "President Madison's War Message to Congress," 14–15.

167 "James Madison," https://www.encyclopedia.com/people/history/us-history-biographies/james-madison; Vogel, *Through the Perilous Fight*, 7.

168 Taylor, Kendrick, and Brodie, *The Star-Spangled Banner*, 13. The "war hawks" were mostly western Congressmen who saw the opportunity for a land grab.

169 American Military History, "The War of 1812," Chapter 6, 125, https://history.army.mil/html/books/030/30-21/CMH_Pub_30-21.pdf.

170 "We have met the enemy and they are ours," Perry's Victory and International Peace Memorial, https://www.nps.gov/articles/met-the-enemy-4.htm.

171 Vogel, *Through the Perilous Fight*, 33.

172 Alexander Cochrane to George Cockburn, April 28, 1814, *The Naval War of 1812, A Documentary History, Vol. III*, 51-52 (hereafter referenced as *NW III*).

173 Vogel, *Through the Perilous Fight*, 43–44.

174 Alexander Cochrane to George Prevost, March 11, 1814, *NW III*, 38, 40.

175 Ibid., 40; "Colonial Marines," https://www.nps.gov/stsp/learn/historyculture/colonial-marines.htm. According to the National Park Service, "about 4,000 enslaved people gained their freedom by escaping to the British military. Many were given shelter at the British base on Tangier Island. There, about 200

of the men were trained and issued arms to fight side by side with British troop as a Colonial Corps of Marines."

176 Proclamation of Vice Admiral Sir Alexander F.I. Cochrane, R.N., April 2, 1814, *NW III*, 60; George Cockburn to Alexander Cochrane, May 9, 1814, *NW III*, 63. Overall, it is estimated that about 4,000 former slaves escaped to the British in 1814, although most did not enlist as soldiers. That was not a requirement for freedom. Some, however, assisted in other ways, including as guides and laborers.

177 Vogel, *Through the Perilous Fight*, 35–36.

178 George Cockburn to Alexander Cochrane, May 10, 1814, *NW III*, 65. According to the National Park Service, more than 4,000 former slaves gained their freedom through this initiative. About 2,600 settled in Nova Scotia and New Brunswick, and the rest found homes in Trinidad ("Enslaved African-Americans confront difficult choices," https://www.nps.gov/articles/slave-loyalism.htm).

179 Alexander Cochrane to George Cockburn, July 1, 1814, *NW III*, 130.

180 U.S. Bureau of the Census, Population of the 46 Urban Places: 1810, https://www2.census.gov/library/working-papers/1998/demographics/pop-twps0027/tab04.txt. Baltimore's population was listed as 46,555 in 1810, behind only New York (96,373) and Philadelphia (53,722). By contrast, the population of Washington, D.C. was 8,208.

181 Alexander Cochrane to Robert Saunders Dundas Melville, September 3, 1814, *NW III*, 270.

182 Vogel, *Through the Perilous Fight*, 19, 212.

183 Ibid., 212–213.

184 Ibid., 38–39.

185 "Baltimore During the War of 1812," https://www.battlefields.org/learn/articles/baltimore-during-war-1812.

186 Alexander Cochrane to George Cockburn, July 1, 1814, *NW III*, 130.

187 Alexander Cochrane to Earl Bathurst, July 14, 1814, *NW III*, 131.

188 Alexander Cochrane to Robert Saunders Dundas Melville, July 17, 1814, *NW III*, 132–134.

189 Alexander Cochrane to John W. Croker, July 23, 1814, *NW III*, 135.

190 Alexander Cochrane to Commanding Officers of the North American Station, July 18, 1814, *NW III*, 140.

191 Vogel, *Through the Perilous Fight*, 312–313; Sheads, *The Rockets' Red Glare*, 17.

192 Sheads, *The Rockets' Red Glare*, 37.

193 Ibid., 21, 38–39.

194 Samuel Smith to George Armistead, June 20, 1814, Fort McHenry Library, Armistead file.

195 Alexander Cochrane to Robert Saunders Dundas Melville, July 17, 1814, *NW III*, 132.

196 Lord, *The Dawn's Early Light*, 37, 47.

197 Vogel, *Through the Perilous Fight*, 63–64.

198 Ibid., 61.

199 Alexander Cochrane to John W. Croker, August 11, 1814, *NW III*, 189-190; Vogel, *Through the Perilous Fight,* 57.

200 Alexander Cochrane to John W. Croker, August 11, 1814, *NW III*, 190.

201 Vogel, *Through the Perilous Fight*, 59–60.

202 George Cockburn to Alexander Cochrane, July 17, 1814, *NW III*, 137–138.

203 George Cockburn to Alexander Cochrane, August 22, 1814, *NW III*, 195–196; Vogel, *Through the Perilous Fight*, 59–61, 75–76, 90–92, 105–108.

204 William Winder report, *American State Papers 1789-1838: Documents, Legislative and Executive, of the Congress of the United States, Military Affairs*, Vol. 1, 557 (There have been incorrect reports that Key, who had no military training, served as a lieutenant and commanded troops at Bladensburg; he was merely serving as a civilian aide to his neighbor, Brigadier General Walter Smith, who commanded the D.C.. militia. He is identified as "Mr. Key" in Winder's report, as opposed to having a military title); Vogel, *Through the Perilous Fight*, 69–71, 110–111, 116, 129, 132.

205 Vogel, *Through the Perilous Fight*, 145-150; Joseph W.A. Whitmore, *The Battle for Baltimore*, 1814, 232 (British order of battle); George Cockburn to Alexander Cochrane, August 27,

1814, *NW III*, 223; John McNish Weiss, *The Merikens: Free Black American Settlers in Trinidad* (McNish & Weiss, January 1, 1995), 1815–1816, 8.

206 "Summer 1814: American troops flee in humiliation, leaving Washington exposed," https://www.nps.gov/articles/bladens-burg-races.htm.

207 Ibid.; Vogel, *Through the Perilous Fight*, 145, 157.

208 George Cockburn to Alexander Cochrane, August 27, 1814, *NW III*, 221.

209 Vogel, *Through the Perilous Fight*, 161.

210 George Cockburn to Alexander Cochrane, August 27, 1814, *NW III*, 222.

211 Vogel, *Through the Perilous Fight*, 172.

212 George Prevost, "A Full Measure of Retaliation," January 12, 1814, from Hickey (ed.), *The War of 1812: Writings from America's Second War of Independence*, 381–382.

213 Mordecai Booth to Thomas Tingey, September 10, 1814, *NW III*, 213. Booth was a captain's clerk for the U.S. Navy, and his report covered events from August 22 through September 10.

214 Vogel, *Through the Perilous Fight*, 153–155, 178–180; George Robert Gleig, *A Narrative of the Campaigns of the British Army at Washington and New Orleans, Under Generals Ross, Pakenham, and Lambert, in the Years 1814 and 1815: With Some Account of the Countries Visited* (HardPress, October 1, 2018), 129–131.

215 Vogel, *Through the Perilous Fight*, 153–155, 178–180, 180.

216 G.R. Gleig, *A Narrative of the Campaigns of the British Army at Washington and New Orleans*, 129.

217 George Cockburn to Alexander Cochrane, August 27, 1814, *NW III*, 222.

218 Vogel, *Through the Perilous Fight*, 185.

219 Lord, *The Dawn's Early Light*, 227.

220 Vogel, *Through the Perilous Fight*, 212.

221 Sheads, *The Rockets' Red Glare*, 13; Sheads, *Guardian of the Star-Spangled Banner*, 8.

222 Sheads, *The Rockets' Red Glare*, 61–62.

223 William Winder to George Armistead, July 10, 1814, Fort McHenry Library, Armistead file. The original document is located in the William Winder Papers at the Maryland Historical Society.

224   Samuel Smith to George Armistead, July 11, 1814, Fort McHenry Library, Armistead file; Sheads, *Guardian of the Star-Spangled Banner*, 12.

225   Alexander Cochrane to Robert Saunders Dundas Melville, September 3, 1814, *NW III*, 269–270.

226   Alexander Cochrane to John W. Croker, September 17, 1814, *NW III*, 286.

227   Vogel. *Through the Perilous Fight*, 269.

228   Alexander Cochrane to John W. Croker, September 17, 1814, *NW III*, 286.

229   George Armistead to Louisa Armistead, September 10, 1814 (letter and envelope), Maryland Historical Society; "William Stewart," *Stewart Clan Magazine*, Vol. VII, No. 7, January 1929, 104. William's wife, Margaret Gettys Stewart, was identified as a relative of "the founder of Gettysburg," James Gettys. William Stewart, who owned one of the town's original lots on York Street, passed away in 1810. George Armistead refers only to "Mrs. Stewart" in his letter; https://www.mary-pennbb.com. Additionally, a modern-day bed & breakfast in the Gettysburg area (on the Pennsylvania-Maryland border) is located in a historic house owned in the late 18th century by a William Stewart, who also had "a grain storage business in Baltimore." The March 14, 1810 edition of the Gettysburg *Centinel* has a "Sale" notice for property on the state line that had "of late" belonged to William Stewart. Especially given the small population of the region, the circumstantial evidence is persuasive.

230   George Armistead to Louisa Armistead, September 10, 1814, Maryland Historical Society.

231   Ibid.

232   George Armistead to James Monroe, September 24, 1814, *NW III*, 302.

233   "Isaac Munroe to a Friend in Boston," September 17, 1814, *The War of 1812: Writings from America's Second War of Independence* (Donald Hickey, ed.), 542. According to Hickey, it is believed the letter was sent to David Everett, editor of the Boston *Yankee*. The paper published the letter on September 30.

234   Vogel, *Through the Perilous Fight*, 226–227, 271.

235   Ibid., 97, 221, 226–227; Lord, *The Dawn's Early Light*, 79, 186.

236 Gleig, *A Narrative of the Campaigns of the British Army at Washington and New Orleans*, 144.

237 Vogel, *Through the Perilous Fight*, 253; Sheads, *The Rockets' Red Glare*, 77–78; Lord, *The Dawn's Early Light*, 240. The request to Key on behalf of Beanes was made by Richard West, who was the brother-in-law of Key's wife, Polly.

238 Francis Scott Key to Anne Phebe Key, September 2, 1814, copy located at the Massachusetts Historical Society, Appleton Papers, Box 10, Folder 8c; Delaplaine, *Francis Scott Key: Life and Times*, 154.

239 Lord, *The Dawn's Early Light*, 240–241.

240 Vogel, *Through the Perilous Fight*, 255–257.

241 Ibid., 260. 271; Marc Leepson, *What So Proudly We Hailed*, 56; Lord, *The Dawn's Early Light*, 242–243.

242 Letter from Chief Justice Roger Taney, *Poems of the Late Francis Scott Key*, 20.

243 Vogel, *Through the Perilous Fight*, 272.

244 Letter from Chief Justice Roger Taney, *Poems of the Late Francis Scott Key*, 21.

245 Ibid., 21.

246 John S. Skinner, "Attack of the British on Baltimore," *Baltimore Patriot and Commercial Gazette*, May 29, 1849.

247 Alexander Cochrane to Robert Sanders Dundas Melville, September 3, 1814, *NW III*, 270.

248 Samuel Smith to James Monroe, U.S. Secretary of War, September 19, 1814, from Nathaniel Hickman, *The Citizen Soldiers at North Point and Fort McHenry*, Vol.1, 56; Vogel, *Through the Perilous Fight*, 283, 287–288. Published contemporary estimates of the distance between the British landing site at North Point and Baltimore ranged from ten to fifteen miles. Fort McHenry historian Scott Sheads says it was ten miles.

249 Ibid., 289.

250 John Stricker to Samuel Smith, September 15, 1814, from Hickman, *The Citizen Soldiers of North Point and Fort McHenry*, Vol. 1, 80–88; Vogel, *Through the Perilous Fight*, 279; "Hampstead Hill: The Bulwark of Baltimore's Defense," https://maryland1812.com.

251 Lord, *The Dawn's Early Light*, 261.

252 Sheads, *The Rockets' Red Glare*, 87.

253 Lord, *The Dawn's Early Light*, 262. Ross was disdainful of the American volunteers. Another of his oft-repeated quotes from this day was that he didn't care "if it rains militia" (261).

254 Vogel, *Through the Perilous Fight*, 294–296.

255 Ibid., 296–299; Lord, *The Dawn's Early Light*, 262. Local legend holds that one of two Baltimore teenagers, Henry McComas or Daniel Wells, fired the shot that brought down Ross. But both young men were also killed in that day's battle. The identity of the U.S. shooter who helped change the course of the war was never confirmed with certainty (Vogel, 342–343).

256 Vogel, *Through the Perilous Fight*, 300.

257 PBS, "The War of 1812," https://www.youtube.com/watch?v=Tq0LLB-X4is.

258 Alexander Cochrane to John Croker, September 17, 1814, *NW III*, 286. Cochrane reported that early on the morning of September 12, "the disembarkation of the Army" at North Point began, led by "the Second Battalion of Marines, the Marines of the squadron and the Colonial Black Marines. Rear Admiral Cockburn accompanied the General (Ross) to advise and arrange as might be necessary."

259 Lord, *The Dawn's Early Light*, 264–267; Vogel, *Through the Perilous Fight*, 271.

260 "Attack Upon Baltimore," *Niles Weekly Register*, September 24, 1814.

261 Vogel, *Through the Perilous Fight*, 303.

262 George Robert Gleig, *A Subaltern in America: Comprising the Narrative of the Campaigns of the British Army, at Baltimore, Washington, &c., &c., During the Late War* (HardPress, May 6, 2018), 133–134. Lieutenant Gleig kept a diary, and his book offers a vivid first-person account from the British perspective of the Bladensburg/Washington/Baltimore campaign.

263 Vogel, *Through the Perilous Fight*, 304.

264 "Attack Upon Baltimore," *Niles Weekly Register*, September 24, 1814.

265 Gleig, *A Subaltern in America*, 136.

266 Vogel, *Through the Perilous Fight*, 305.

267 "Isaac Munroe to a Friend in Boston," September 17, 1814, *The War of 1812: Writings from America's Second War of Independence* (Donald Hickey, ed.), 541.

268 George Armistead to Joseph Nicholson, September 10, 1814, Fort McHenry Library, Armistead file.
269 Vogel, *Through the Perilous Fight*, 315–316.
270 Lord, *The Dawn's Early Light*, 270.
271 Sheads, *The Rockets' Red Glare*, 90.
272 Lord, *The Dawn's Early Light*, 274.
273 Sheads, *The Rockets' Red Glare*, 93; Vogel, *Through the Perilous Fight*, 312.
274 George Armistead to James Monroe, September 24, 1814, *NW III*, 302; "Isaac Munroe to a Friend in Boston," September 17, 1814, *The War of 1812: Writings from America's Second War of Independence*, 542.
275 Lord, *The Dawn's Early Light*, 277.
276 Vogel, *Through the Perilous Fight*, 317.
277 "Isaac Munroe to a Friend in Boston," September 17, 1814, *The War of 1812: Writings from America's Second War of Independence*, 542.
278 Vogel, *Through the Perilous Fight*, 318.
279 "The Carcasses Red Glare," 2, https://www.nps.gov/fomc/learn/historyculture/the-carcasses-red-glare.htm.
280 Ralph Robinson, "The Use of Rockets by the British in the War of 1812," *Maryland Historical Magazine*, March 1945; Vogel, *Through the Perilous Flight*, 139-140.
281 PBS, "The War of 1812," https://www.youtube.com/watch?v=Tq0LLB-X4is.
282 George Armistead to James Monroe, September 24, 1814, *NW III*, 303.
283 Sheads, *The Rockets' Red Glare*, 109.
284 Vogel, *Through the Perilous Fight*, 319, 331.
285 "Attack Upon Baltimore," *Niles Weekly Register*, September 24, 1814.
286 Ibid.
287 Lord, *The Dawn's Early Light*, 197.
288 Vogel, *Through the Perilous Fight*, 283.
289 Alexander Cochrane to George Cockburn, September 13, 1814, *NW III*, 277. Cochrane preferred to write directly to Cockburn, a fellow naval officer, but his directions were also intended for Brooke, who commanded the combined forces on land.

290 "Attack Upon Baltimore," *Niles Weekly Register*, September 24, 1814.

291 Henry Newcomb to John Rodgers, September 18, 1814, *NW III*, 292. Lieutenant Newcomb commanded Fort Covington and described actions from each day (from September 10–14) in his letter; Vogel, *Through the Perilous Fight*, 323.

292 Sheads, *Fort McHenry*, 36.

293 Sheads, *The Rockets' Red Glare*, 99.

294 George Armistead to James Monroe, September 24, 1814, *NW III*, 303.

295 Sheads, *The Rockets' Red Glare*, 93.

296 "Isaac Munroe to a Friend in Boston," September 17, 1814, *The War of 1812: Writings from America's Second War of Independence*, 543.

297 Lord, *The Dawn's Early Light*, 254–255, 281.

298 PBS, "The War of 1812," https://www.youtube.com/watch?v=Tq0LLB-X4is.

299 Lord, *The Dawn's Early Light*, 281; Vogel, *Through the Perilous Fight*, 318.

300 Henry Newcomb to John Rodgers, September 18, 1814, *NW III*, 292.

301 "Isaac Munroe to a Friend in Boston," September 17, 1814, *The War of 1812: Writings from America's Second War of Independence*, 543; Vogel, *Through the Perilous Fight*, 324.

302 George Armistead to James Monroe, September 24, 1814, *NW III*, 303.

303 Vogel, *Through the Perilous Fight*, 324.

304 George Armistead to James Monroe, September 24, 1814, *NW III*, 303.

305 "Attack Upon Baltimore," *Niles Weekly Register*, September 24, 1814.

306 Lord, *The Dawn's Early Light*, 282.

307 George Armistead to James Monroe, September 24, 1814, *NW III*, 303.

308 Arthur Brooke to Alexander Cochrane, September 13, 1814, *NW III*, 277.

309 Vogel, *Through the Perilous Fight*, 322–323.

310 Arthur Brooke to Alexander Cochrane, September 13, 1814, *NW III*, 277.

311 Alexander Cochrane to George Cockburn, September 13, 1814, *NW III*, 277.

312 Vogel, *Through the Perilous Fight*, 326.

313 Ibid., 323, 326.

314 Ibid., 327.

315 Arthur Brooke to Alexander Cochrane, September 14, 1814, *NW III*, 279. The note was written at midnight.

316 Lord, *The Dawn's Early Light*, 286–287.

317 Henry Newcomb to John Rogers, September 18, 2014, *NW III*, 292.

318 Vogel, *Through the Perilous Fight*, 332.

319 Author conversation with Scott Sheads.

320 Letter from Chief Justice Roger Taney, *Poems of the Late Francis Scott Key*, 24.

321 Sheads, *The Rockets' Red Glare*, 99.

322 Alexander Cochrane to Charles Napier, September 13, 1814, *NW III*, 278.

323 Vogel, *Through the Perilous Fight*, 328.

324 Alexander Cochrane to Charles Napier, September 13, 1814, *NW III*, 278.

325 Vogel, *Through the Perilous Fight*, 329–330.

326 Sheads, *The Rockets' Red Glare*, 100.

327 George Armistead to James Monroe, September 24, 1814, *NW III*, 303.

328 "Attack Upon Baltimore," *Niles Weekly Register*, September 24, 1814.

329 George Armistead to James Monroe, September 24, 1814, *NW III*, 303.

330 Lord, *The Dawn's Early Light*, 291.

331 Ibid., 292; Letter from Chief Justice Roger Taney, *Poems of the Late Francis Scott Key*, 25.

332 George Armistead to James Monroe, September 24, 1814, *NW III*, 303; Vogel, *Through the Perilous Fight*, 338.

333 Letter from Chief Justice Roger Taney, *Poems of the Late Francis Scott Key*, 25.

334 Vogel, *Through the Perilous Fight*, 338.

335 Delaplaine, *Francis Scott Key: Life and Times*, 380.

336 Lord, *The Dawn's Early Light*, 292–293.

337 Vogel, *Through the Perilous Fight*, 339; Sheads, *The Rocket's Red Glare*, 104.

338 Barrett, "Naval Recollections of the Late American War," *The United Service Magazine*, Vol. 35, April 1841, 464.

339 Vogel, *Through the Perilous Fight*, 339.

340 Vogel, *Through the Perilous Fight*, 19-20, 411; Leepson, *What So Proudly We Hailed*, 25–27, 31–32; "Francis Scott Key," https://www.nps.gov/people/francis-scott-key.htm.

341 Delaplaine, *Francis Scott Key*, 100.

342 Vogel, *Through the Perilous Fight*, 12, 21.

343 Delaplaine, *Francis Scott Key*, 91–92; Leepson, *What So Proudly We Hailed*, 44, 49.

344 Vogel, *Through the Perilous Fight*, 273.

345 Letter from Chief Justice Roger Taney, *Poems of the Late Francis Scott Key*, 23–24.

346 Ibid., 24; Delaplaine, *Francis Scott Key*, 159.

347 Author conversation with Fort McHenry historian Scott Sheads, May 2022, on a visit to the site; Vogel, *Through the Perilous Fight*, 319; Leepson, *What So Proudly We Hailed*, 64; Lord, *The Dawn's Early Light*, 291. The Maryland Transportation Authority website notes that the Francis Scott Key Bridge crosses the Patapsco "within 100 yards of the site" where he witnessed the bombardment. Historian Walter Lord was among those who originally wrote that Key's ship was eight miles from Fort McHenry.

348 Letter from Chief Justice Roger Taney, *Poems of the Late Francis Scott Key*, 24.

349 Ibid., 26.

350 Delaplaine, *Francis Scott Key*, 379–380.

351 Vogel, *Through the Perilous Fight*, 348.

352 Anthem historian Mark Clague found that Key wrote three songs and ten hymns during his lifetime. Clague, "Separating fact from fiction about 'The Star-Spangled Banner,'" September 14, 2016, https://constitutioncenter.org/blog/separating-fact-from-fiction-about-the-star-spangled-banner.

353 Vogel, *Through the Perilous Fight*, 345–436; Harold Lessem and George Mackenzie, *Fort McHenry*, 23; Leepson, *What So Proudly We Hailed*, 66.

354 "To Anacreon in Heaven," Star-Spangled Music Foundation, *Poets & Patriots: A Tuneful History of "The Star-Spangled Banner,"* 2.

355 New York Historical Society Museum and Library, "Columbian Anacreontic Society Medal," https://emuseum.nyhistory.org/objects/5984/columbian-anacreontic-society-medal.

356 "Adams and Liberty," Star-Spangled Music Foundation, *Poets & Patriots: A Tuneful History of "The Star-Spangled Banner,"* 9–11.

357 Marc Ferris, *Star-Spangled Banner: The Unlikely Story of America's National Anthem* (Johns Hopkins University Press, September 13, 2014), 21.

358 Ibid., 22; Vogel, *Through the Perilous Fight*, 346-347; Taylor, Kendrick, and Brodie, *The Star-Spangled Banner*, 44.

359 "When the Warrior Returns," Star-Spangled Music Foundation, *Poets & Patriots: A Tuneful History of "The Star-Spangled Banner,"* 12–13.

360 Vogel, *Through the Perilous Fight*, 347.

361 Letter from Chief Justice Roger Taney, *Poems of the Late Francis Scott Key*, 26.

362 Vogel, *Through the Perilous Fight*, 348–350. Vogel's three-page, verse-by-verse examination of Key's lyrics is a remarkable foundation for research of the song's creation.

363 Original manuscript of the Star-Spangled Banner, found at both the Maryland Center for History and Culture, https://www.mdhistory.org/resources/the-star-spangled-banner/, and the Library of Congress, https://www.loc.gov/resource/hec.04309/. Key's original version was later edited slightly for punctuation.

364 "Attack Upon Baltimore," *Niles Weekly Register*, September 24, 1814; Letter from Chief Justice Roger Taney, *Poems of the Late Francis Scott Key*, 25.

365 Original manuscript of the Star-Spangled Banner, https://www.loc.gov/resource/hec.04309/. The four verses, with updated punctuation, are also available at the Star-Spangled Music Foundation, *Poets & Patriots: A Tuneful History of "The Star-Spangled Banner,"* 16.

366 Delaplaine, *Francis Scott Key*, 173.

367 Ferris, *Star-Spangled Banner*, 20.

368   Vogel, *Through the Perilous Fight*, 349.

369   Leepson, *What So Proudly We Hailed*, 72–73. For a different perspective on the third verse, please see: Ferris, "National anthem's third verse stirs passions, but the reading is erroneous," *Minneapolis Star-Tribune*, February 2, 2018. For a deeper look at Key and slavery, please also see: Vogel, *Through the Perilous Fight*, 13, 407–411; Leepson, *What So Proudly We Hailed*, 25–27, 77–83; and Delaplaine, *Francis Scott Key*, 191, 446–450.

370   John McNish Weiss, *The Merikens: Free Black American Settlers, in Trinidad 1815-16*, 8; "Battle of Baltimore," https://www.britannica.com/event/Battle-of-Baltimore-1814; "Fort McHenry," https://www.battlefields.org/learn/war-1812/battles/fort-mchenry. By contrast, the Americans suffered twenty-eight killed, 250 wounded and fifty captured. In the Fort McHenry naval battle, the U.S. suffered four killed and twenty-four wounded, while the British reported one casualty.

371   Vogel. *Through the Perilous Fight*, 2.

372   Ibid., 350; Ferris, *Star-Spangled Banner*, 20.

373   Taylor, Kendrick, and Brodie, *The Star-Spangled Banner*, 42.

374   Letter from Chief Justice Roger Taney, *Poems of the Late Francis Scott Key*, 27–28.

375   Ibid., 27–28; Vogel, *Through the Perilous Fight*, 351; Ferris, *Star-Spangled Banner*, 22–23.

376   "Francis Scott Key: 'Defence of Fort M'Henry,'" *The War of 1812; Writings from America's Second War of Independence*, 544–545.

377   Vogel, *Through the Perilous Fight*, 351.

378   Letter from Chief Justice Roger Taney, *Poems of the Late Francis Scott Key*, 28.

379   Marc Leepson, *Flag: An American Biography* (St. Martin's Griffin, May 30, 2006), 64.

380   P.W. Filby and Edward G. Howard, *Star-Spangled Books: Books, Sheet Music, Newspapers, Manuscripts and Persons Associated With the Star Spangled Banner* (Maryland Historical Society, January 1, 1972), 50, 113.

381   Leepson, *What So Proudly We Hailed*, 66.

382   Vogel, *Through the Perilous Fight*, 376–377; Filby and Howard, *Star-Spangled Books*, 61–62; "The First Public Performanc-

es of 'The Star-Spangled Banner,'" Cambridge University Press, May 1976, https://www.cambridge.org/core/journals/theatre-research-international/article/abs/first-public-performances-of-the-starspangled-banner/6A67E2AAF93F-847D3E3ED44D035349EE. Hardinge's first name was not recorded.

383 Leepson, *What So Proudly We Hailed*, 67; Taylor, Kendrick, and Brodie, *The Star-Spangled Banner*, 43, 46.
384 Taylor, Kendrick, and Brodie, *The Star-Spangled Banner*, 56. A bill passed both houses and was signed in to law by President Herbert Hoover on March 3, 1931.
385 Delaplaine, *Francis Scott Key*, 379.
386 Ibid., 381.
387 Sheads, *The Rockets' Red Glare*, 106. This quote was from General Sam Smith in a letter to the War Department.
388 Vogel, *Through the Perilous Fight*, 350.
389 Sheads, *The Rockets' Red Glare*, 109.
390 General Winder Division Orders, September 15, 1814, Fort McHenry Library, Armistead file.
391 Samuel Smith, General Orders, September 19, 1814, from Hickman, *The Citizen Soldiers of North Point and Fort McHenry*, Vol. 1, 92.
392 Original copy of Armistead commission, in possession of descendants.
393 *Federal Gazette and Baltimore Advertiser*, September 26, 1814, Fort McHenry Library, Armistead file.
394 James Wilkinson, *Memoirs of My Own Times*, Vol. 1, 795.
395 Sheads, *Guardian Of The Star-Spangled Banner*, 51.
396 George Armistead to Louisa Armstead, September 22, 1814, Fort McHenry Library, Armistead file.
397 George Armistead to James Monroe, September 24, 1814, *NW III*, 303-304.
398 George Armistead to Louisa Armistead, September 22, 1814, Fort McHenry Library, Armistead file.
399 John Rodgers to William Jones, September 14, 1814, *NW III*, 293.
400 Vogel, *Through the Perilous Fight*, 343.
401 David and Jeanne T. Heidler, "Things Fall Apart: The Road to 'Victory,'" https://www.nps.gov/articles/things-fall-apart.

htm; "Treaty of Ghent," https://www.history.com/topics/war-of-1812/treaty-of-ghent.

402 Sheads, *The Rockets' Red Glare*, 108.

403 Barrett, "Naval Recollections of the Late American War," *The United Service Magazine,* Vol. 35, April 1841, 464–465.

404 Alexander Cochrane to John W. Croker, September 17, 1814, *NW III*, 286–287.

405 Alexander Cochrane to Robert Melville, September 17, 1815, *NW III*, 289.

406 Vogel, *Through the Perilous Fight*, 353.

407 Walter R. Borneman, *1812: The War That Forged A Nation*, 262-264; Christopher Hughes diary, November 24, 1814, Fort McHenry Library, Armistead file (copied from Christopher Hughes Papers, Clements Library, University of Michigan); Peter Kumpa, "Christopher Hughes: career diplomat and fountain of royal gossip," (Baltimore) *Evening Sun*, February 13, 1989.

408 Borneman, 1812, *The War That Forged a Nation,"* 264.

409 Donald R. Hickey, "Turning the tide: the British Empire strikes back," https://www.nps.gov/articles/turning-the-tide.htm.

410 Donald R. Hickey, "Probing for Peace: Weighing the Burdens of War on Two Continents," https://www.nps.gov/articles/probing-for-peace.htm; "Summer 1814: Americans and British open peace negotiations at Ghent," https://www.nps.gov/articles/treaty-of-ghent-1.htm.

411 Walter R. Borneman, *1812: The War That Forged A Nation* (Harper Perennial, October 4, 2005), 266.

412 London *Times*, September 27 and 28, 1814, cited in Vogel, *Through the Perilous Fight*, 365.

413 Vogel, *Through the Perilous Fight*, 366.

414 Ibid., 367.

415 Ibid., 367, 375.

416 Borneman, *1812: The War That Forged A Nation*, 268. The speaker was Henry Goulburn, one of the British peace commissioners.

417 Ibid., 378.

418 Christopher Hughes diary, November 24, 1814, Fort McHenry Library, Armistead file.

419 "Treaty of Ghent," https://www.history.com/topics/war-of-1812/treaty-of-ghent; "Status Quo Ante Bellum," https://www.merriam-webster.com/dictionary/status%20quo%20ante; Borneman, *1812*, 269.

420 Borneman, *1812*, 269.

421 Vogel, *Through the Perilous Fight*, 381.

422 Ibid., 381; Kumpa, "Christopher Hughes: career diplomat and fountain of royal gossip," (Baltimore) *Evening Sun*, February 13, 1989.

423 Borneman, *1812*, 273, 283–284, 286, 291.

424 "General Order," *Baltimore American and Commercial Daily Advertiser*, February 6, 1815, Fort McHenry Library, Armistead file.

425 "The Senate Approves the Treaty of Ghent for Ratification," https://www.senate.gov/about/powers-procedures/treaties/senate-approves-treaty-of-ghent.htm; Kumpa, "Christopher Hughes," *Evening Sun*, February 13, 1989; Borneman, *1812*, 296; Vogel, *Through the Perilous Fight*, 383.

426 "Treaty of Peace and Amity between His Britannic Majesty and the United States of America, Concluded at Ghent, December 24, 1814," from Hickey (ed.), *The War of 1812, Writings from America's Second War of Independence*, 621–622.

427 "James Madison, Special Address to Congress, February 18, 1815," from Hickey (ed.), *The War of 1812, Writings from America's Second War of Independence*" 689–690.

428 Vogel, *Through the Perilous Fight*, 401.

429 George Armistead to Otto Williams, October 11, 1814, Fort McHenry Library, Armistead file.

430 Samuel Hollingsworth to George Armistead, August 26, 1815, Fort McHenry Library, Armistead file; *Niles Weekly Register*, Vol. 9, 3.

431 "Battle Monument Conservation," https://chap.baltimorecity.gov/monuments-and-conservation/battle-monument; "Battle Monument," https://explore.baltimoreheritage.org/items/show/2; "Maryland National Register Properties," https://mht.maryland.gov/nr/NRDetail.aspx?FROM=NRDBList.aspx-&NRID=174&COUNTY=&SEARCHTYPE=propertySe-arch&PROPNAME=Battle%20Monument&STREETNAM-

E=&CITYNAME=&KEYWORD=; Author visit to Battle Monument.

432 "Reward of Valor," U.S. House of Representatives, *Federal Gazette and Baltimore Daily Advertiser*, February 11, 1815, Fort McHenry Library, Armistead file.

433 *Maryland Gazette and Political Intelligencer*, Annapolis, Md., January 18, 1816, Fort McHenry Library, Armistead file.

434 "Honor to the Brave," *Baltimore American and Commercial Daily Advertiser*, May 14, 1816, Fort McHenry Library, Armistead file; Sheads, *Guardian of the Star-Spangled Banner*, 21.

435 "Honor to the Brave," *Baltimore American*, May 14, 1816, Fort McHenry Library, Armistead file.

436 Sheads, *Guardian of the Star-Spangled Banner*, 23, 52–53; George Armistead to Joseph Swift, December 31, 1817, Fort McHenry Library, Armistead file.

437 Taylor, Kendrick, and Brodie, *The Star-Spangled Banner*, 81.

438 Sheads, *Guardian of the Star-Spangled Banner*, 23.

439 Lonn Taylor, "Foreword" to Sheads, *Guardian of the Star-Spangled Banner*, viii.

440 Ibid.; "War of 1812 Pension and Bounty Land Warren Application Files," Louisa Armistead application, May 15, 1856, https://www.fold3.com/image/273461618.

441 "A HERO FALLEN," *Baltimore American and Commercial Daily Advertiser*, April 27, 1818, Fort McHenry Library, Armistead file.

442 "Lieut. Colonel Armistead," *Niles Weekly Register*, May 3, 1818, Fort McHenry Library, Armistead file.

443 "ON THE DEATH OF COL. ARMISTEAD," *New York Columbian*, reprinted in the *Baltimore American and Daily Advertiser*, May 14, 1818, Fort McHenry Library, Armistead file.

444 Author visit to Old St. Paul's Cemetery, Baltimore, courtesy of historian Scott Sheads. Key also was buried at Old St. Paul's upon his death in 1843, but his remains were later moved to a cemetery in Frederick, MD.

445 "Lt. Colonel George Armistead Monument, Federal Hill," https://maryland1812.wordpress.com; Sheads, *Guardian of the Star-Spangled Banner*, 23, 27; Taylor, Kendrick, and Brodie, *Star-Spangled Banner*, 29.

446 Fort McHenry Library, Armistead file, unidentified newspaper account from Annapolis, Md., January 12, 1839.

447 Sheads, *Guardian of the Star-Spangled Banner*, 36.

448 Sheads, "Lt. Colonel George Armistead Statue at Fort McHenry, Sept. 1914," (draft), Fort McHenry Library, Armistead file; Sheads, *Fort McHenry*, 76–78; "The Armistead Monument," Smithsonian Institution Research Information System; Author visit to Fort McHenry.

449 Sheads, "Lt. Colonel George Armistead Statue at Fort McHenry, Sept. 1914," (draft), Fort McHenry Library, Armistead file.

450 Sheads, *Guardian of the Star-Spangled Banner*, 34, 37, 39.

451 Taylor, Kendrick, and Brodie, *The Star-Spangled Banner: The Making of an American Icon,* 93, 97, 103.

452 Taylor, *The Star-Spangled Banner: The Flag that Inspired the National Anthem*, 59; Sheads, *Guardian of the Star-Spangled Banner,* 34.

453 Scott Sheads notes, Fort McHenry Library, Armistead file, 34.

454 "Lafayette in Baltimore," *Baltimore American*, reprinted in the *Daily National Intelligencer* (Washington, D.C.), October 12, 1824.

455 Sheads, *Guardian of the Star-Spangled Banner*, 34–35; "A Farewell Tribute to The Star-Spangled Banner," a lecture given by Lonn Taylor at the Smithsonian, March 31, 1998, Fort McHenry Library, Armistead file. Georgiana Armistead Appleton is quoted as saying, "The occasion that most impressed me was when it was used to adorn the tent in which Lafayette was entertained at Fort McHenry in 1824."

456 Taylor, Kendrick, and Brodie, *The Star-Spangled Banner*, 83.

457 "Lafayette in Baltimore," *Baltimore American*, reprinted in the *Daily National Intelligencer* (Washington, D.C.), October 12, 1824.

458 Sheads, *Guardian of the Star-Spangled Banner*, 34; Molotsky, *The Flag, The Poet & The Song*, 141. Though held on September 12 to mark the start of the Battle of North Point, the anniversary event honored the entire three-day battle.

459 Vogel, *Through the Perilous Flight*, 413.

460 *Baltimore Patriot*, September 13, 1830, advertisement titled "Splendid Illumination," Fort McHenry Library, Armistead file.

461 Taylor, Kendrick, and Brodie, *The Star-Spangled Banner*, 85.

462 "The 25th Anniversary of the Battle of Baltimore," *Baltimore American & Commercial Daily Advertiser*, September 14, 1839, Fort McHenry Library, Armistead file; Sheads, *Guardian of the Star-Spangled Banner*, 36.

463 *Baltimore American & Commercial Advertiser*, September 14, 1839, Fort McHenry Library, Armistead file.

464 Taylor, Kendrick, and Brodie, *The Star-Spangled Banner*, 83–84; Garber, *The Armistead Family, 1635-1810*, 41. William Henry Harrison was the grandson of Elizabeth Armistead Churchill.

465 Sheads, *Guardian of the Star-Spangled Banner*, 37; Taylor, Kendrick, and Brodie, *The Star-Spangled Banner*, 86.

466 Ferris, *Star-Spangled Banner*, 24.

467 Ibid., 23–24, 28.

468 Ibid., 5.

469 Taylor, Kendrick, and Brodie, *The Star-Spangled Banner*, 47–48.

470 "William Henry Harrison" and "Battle of the Thames," www.brittanica.com.

471 "Harrison and Liberty," Star-Spangled Music Foundation, *Poets & Patriots: A Tuneful History of "The Star-Spangled Banner,"* 20–21.

472 "Temperance movement," https://www.britannica.com/topic/temperance-movement; "Temperance Movements," https://www.encyclopedia.com/social-sciences-and-law/sociology-and-social-reform/social-reform/temperance-movements.

473 Ferris, *Star-Spangled Banner*, 31; Taylor, Kendrick, and Brodie, *The Star-Spangled Banner*, 52.

474 "Oh! Who Has Not Seen," Star-Spangled Music Foundation, *Poets & Patriots: A Tuneful History of "The Star-Spangled Banner,"* 21–22.

475 "Oh, Say Do You Hear," Star-Spangled Music Foundation, *Poets & Patriots: A Tuneful History of "The Star-Spangled Banner,"* 22–23.

476 Ferris, *Star-Spangled Banner*, 32.

477 "Lincoln and Liberty: About the Song," https://balladofamerica.org/lincoln-and-liberty/.

478 Molotsky, *The Flag, The Poet & The Song*, 141; Taylor, *The Star-Spangled Banner*, 53. The red chevron is not visible to vis-

itors at the Smithsonian, because it is located on the back side of the flag.

479 Interview with Margaret Armistead Appleton, *New York Herald*, 1895, Fort McHenry Library, Armistead file. Her married name was Margaret Appleton Baker.

480 Suzanne Thomassen-Krauss, "Discoveries Made while Preserving the Star-Spangled Banner," Proceedings of the 24th International Congress of Vexillology, Washington D.C., August 1–5, 2011, 965.

481 "Smithsonian's Star-Spangled Banner To Undergo Three-Year Conservation," https://americanhistory.si.edu/press/releases/smithsonians-star-spangled-banner-undergo-three-year-conservation; Leepson, *Flag: An American Biography*, 73.

482 Author interview with Marilyn Zoidis.

483 Taylor, Kendrick, and Brodie, *The Star-Spangled Banner*, 90.

484 Interview with Margaret Armistead Appleton, *New York Herald*, 1895, Fort McHenry Library, Armistead file.

485 Georgiana Appleton to George Preble, June 17, 1873, Fort McHenry Library, Armistead file (from the Preble papers). One suggestion is that the missing star was given to Lafayette in 1824, but there is no evidence to back it up. A theory that it was donated for Lincoln's burial seems preposterous, since the Appletons and most Armistead descendants were Confederate sympathizers.

486 Charles L. Bonney to Georgiana Armistead Appleton, October 26, 1845, Massachusetts Historical Society, Appleton Papers, Box 10, Folder 9c.

487 Stephen Salisbury to Georgiana Armistead Appleton, January 1, 1874 and January 30, 1874, Massachusetts Historical Society, Box 10, Folder 8a.

488 "Louisa Armistead Last Will and Testament," Fort McHenry Library, Armistead file. The flag was actually listed fourth among the items Georgiana received: "I give and bequeath to my daughter, Georgiana L.F. Armistead, the mahogany Wardrobe which stood in my chamber, and one embossed silver tea pot and one red Sugar dish, and also 'the Star-Spangled Banner' which floated over Fort McHenry during the bombardment in 1814."

489 Georgiana Armistead to George Preble, July 5, 1873, Fort McHenry Library, Armistead file.

490 "Louisa Armistead Last Will and Testament" and "Fort McHenry: An Incident in its History," May 15, 1875, Fort McHenry Library, Armistead file.

491 Sheads notes, Fort McHenry Library, Armistead file, 36. Christopher's residence was at 103 West Monument Street, which later became the site of the Maryland Historical Society (currently known as the Maryland Center for History and Culture).

492 Georgiana Armistead Appleton to Nathan Appleton Sr., April 15, 1861, Massachusetts Historical Society, Appleton Papers, Box 9, Folder 1b.

493 Georgiana Armistead to George Preble, July 5, 1873, Fort McHenry Library, Armistead file. Georgiana Armistead was born at the family home near Fort McHenry, but not at the fort itself. There is no record that the flag was raised in honor of her birth.

494 "Narrative of Benson J. Lossing for his magazine, *The American Historical Record*, January 1873," Fort McHenry library, Armistead file.

495 Mendus I. Cohen to George Preble, August 24, 1873, Fort McHenry Library, Armistead file. It should be noted that Cohen, the last surviving member of the "Sea Fencibles," wrote his account fifty-nine years after the battle. "I have a full recollection of the damage to the flag by the enemy. I have the recollection that one whole bomb shell passed through it and some three or four pieces passed through it." He never made a distinction between the storm flag and the larger garrison flag.

496 Georgiana Armistead Appleton to Armistead Appleton, November 4, 1861, Fort McHenry Library, Armistead file, Scott Sheads notes.

497 Agnes Gordon Armistead diary, Scott Sheads notes, 37, Fort McHenry Library, Armistead file.

498 William Darlington to Benson J. Lossing, October 5, 1861, Fort McHenry Library, Armistead file. Darlington, a U.S. Congressman, wrote that "Mrs. B. is a very pleasant, intelligent, Lady-sterling Patriotic Unionist, in these degenerate times, although her Virginia connections are...Secessionists." Georgi-

ana's sons, George and Eben, registered for the Union Army in 1863 but never served.

499 "Important Arrests," *Baltimore American and Commercial Advertiser*, September 9, 1861, 1; Sheads, *Guardian of The Star-Spangled Banner*, 38.

500 "Important Arrests," *Baltimore American and Commercial Advertiser*, September 9, 1861, 1.

501 Sheads, *Guardian of The Star-Spangled Banner*, 38.

502 Eben Appleton to George Armistead Appleton, October 3, 1861, and George Armistead Appleton to Mr. Coxe (pastor), November 27, 1861, Massachusetts Historical Society, Appleton Papers, Box 9, Folder 2.

503 *OR*, Series 2, Vol. 1, "Union Policy of Repression in Maryland: Summary of Important Events," 563; Abraham Lincoln to Winfield Scott, April 27, 1861, 567.

504 *OR*, Series 2, Vol. 1, Simon Cameron to Nathaniel Banks, September 11, 1861, 678–679.

505 *OR*, Series 2, Vol. 1, "Union Policy of Repression in Maryland: Summary of Important Events," September 12, 1861, 563; McClellan, *Own Story*, 165.

506 Scharf, *History of Maryland*, Vol. 3, 441–442; Harry A. Ezratty, *Baltimore in the Civil War*, 18–19.

507 John A. Dix to Montgomery Blair, August 31, 1862, *OR*, Series 2, Vol. 1, 591 (Blair's note to McClellan is a P.S. to the same letter).

508 *OR*, Series 2 Vol, 1, "Case of Howard and Glenn of the Baltimore Exchange Newspaper," 779.

509 "Arrests Extraordinary," *The Daily Exchange*, September 14, 1861, 1.

510 Frank Key Howard, *Fourteen Months in American Bastiles*, 9–11.

511 Ezratty, *Baltimore in the Civil War*, 30; Scott Sumpter Sheads and Daniel Carroll Toomey, *Baltimore During the Civil War*, 3.

512 Ezratty, *Baltimore in the Civil War*, 28; Sheads and Toomey, *Baltimore During the Civil War*, 153–154.

513 *OR*, Series 1, Vol. 2, Chapter IX, 139–140. In a letter from Major General Nathaniel Banks to Lieutenant General Winfield Scott, Banks reported that "This morning at 4 o'clock, the members of the board of police were arrested by my order and…are now securely held in custody…at Fort McHenry." Among those arrested were "Charles Howard, president of the

board." Charles Howard was married to Key's daughter, Elizabeth Phoebe Key.

514 "Removal Of The Political Prisoners To Boston Harbor," *Civilian & Telegraph* (Cumberland, Md.), November 7, 1861, 2.

515 Frank Key Howard, *Fourteen Months in American Bastiles* (Wentworth Press, August 26, 2016), 29–32.

516 *The Times* (Port Tobacco, Md.), November 28, 1861, 2. In an untitled news roundup, the paper reported that "The following named prisoners, belonging to Maryland, have been released from Fort Warren." Among the 16 names listed was "George A. Appleton."

517 Georgiana Armistead Appleton to George Armistead Appleton, December 30, 1861, Massachusetts Historical Society, Appleton Papers, Box 9, Folder 3b; Fort McHenry Library, Armistead file, Scott Sheads notes, 37–38.

518 John A. Dix to Robert C. Winthrop, January 23, 1862, *OR,* Series 2, Vol. 1, 617.

519 John A. Dix to Edwin M. Stanton, February 20, 1862, *OR*, Series 2, Volume 1, 738–739. The same letter stated that Frank Key Howard and several others should not be discharged from custody.

520 Howard, *Fourteen Months in American Bastiles*, 89.

521 Ibid., 89.

522 McHenry Howard, *Recollections of a Maryland Confederate Soldier and Staff Officer Under Johnston* (Wentworth Press, August 28, 2016), 28. The other Howard brothers in the Confederate Army were Charles Jr., James, Edward, and John. But Frank Key Howard never served.

523 Civil War Draft Records: Exemptions and Enrollments, 1, NA; Daniel W. Hamilton, "Enrollment Act (1863), 1, https://www.encyclopedia.com/history/encyclopedias-almanacs-transcripts-and-maps/enrollment-act-1863-conscription-act.

524 Civil War Draft Registration Records, 1863–1865, Baltimore City, Maryland, April 8-20, 1863, 5, NA (also found in Eben Appleton records at ancestry.com); Maryland Battery A Junior Light Artillery, https://civilwarintheeast.com/us-regiments-batteries/maryland/maryland-junior-battery-a/.

525 Ferris, *Star-Spangled Banner*, 39.

526   Ibid., 41.
527   Ibid., 41; George Henry Preble, *History of the Flag of the United States of America* (Sagwan Press, August 23, 2015), 518.
528   Preble, *History of the Flag of the United States of America*, 459.
529   Ibid., 394.
530   Ibid., 458–463
531   Ferris, *Star-Spangled Banner*, 5.
532   Star Spangled Music Foundation, *Poets & Patriots: A Tuneful History of "The Star-Spangled Banner,"* 2.
533   Ibid., "Complete Lyrics," transcribed by Mark Clague, Ph. D., American Music Institute, University of Michigan, Disc Two, Track 13, 24.
534   Ibid., "Banner Torn," 13; Disc Two, Track 11, 24.
535   Ibid., "Complete Lyrics," Disc Two, Track 11, 24.
536   Ferris, *Star-Spangled Banner*, 42.
537   Star Spangled Music Foundation, *Poets & Patriots*, 2; "Complete Lyrics," Disc Two, Track 14, 25.
538   Ibid.
539   Preble, *History of. the Flag of the United States of America*, 475–476.
540   Ferris, *Star-Spangled Banner*, 45–46.
541   Howard, *Recollections of a Maryland Confederate Soldier and Staff Officer Under Johnston*, 406.
542   Ibid., 6–7, 10; Military Service Records for McHenry Howard, National Archives.
543   Howard, *Recollections of a Maryland Confederate Soldiers and Staff Officer*, 3.
544   Virginia Armistead Garber, *The Armistead Family, 1635-1910*, 66, 240–241; George Washington Cullum, *Biographical Register of Officers and Graduates of the U.S. Military Academy at West Point, N.Y., 1802-1840, Vol. 1*, 91; Tom McMillan, *Armistead and Hancock: Behind the Gettysburg Legend of Two Friends at the Turning Point of the Civil War* (Stackpole Books, July 15, 2021), 15–17.
545   List of Orders Relating to Cadet Lewis A. Armistead, Extracted from "Post Orders/No. 6, 1832-1837, U.S. Military Academy," USMA Library.
546   Wayne Motts, *Trust In God And Fear Nothing*, 12-13; Krick, "Armistead and Garnett," *The Third Day at Gettysburg & Beyond*, 99–100.

547 Edward Stanly to Charles M. Conrad, March 11, 1852, U.S. Military Academy Application Papers, NA. Congressman Stanly wrote to the Secretary of War to endorse Lewis's younger brother, Franck, as a candidate for West Point. Had Lewis graduated, Franck would not have been eligible to attend the academy. Stanly wrote to clarify that Lewis had not graduated and, in fact, left school "when very young, on account of some boyish frolick." Franck was accepted as a cadet and went on to graduate.

548 List of Orders Relating to Cadet Lewis A. Armistead, Extracted from "Post Orders/No. 6 1832–1837", U.S. Military Academy, USMA Library.

549 McMillan, *Armistead and Hancock*, 27–29.

550 Cadmus Wilcox, *History of the Mexican War*, 385, 462.

551 McMillan, *Armistead and Hancock*, 58, 61–62.

552 Ibid., 65, 68, 75.

553 Lewis A. Armistead to W.W. Bliss, August 1, 1852, Letters Received by the Office of the Adjutant General Main Series, 1822–1860, National Archives.

554 Returns from U.S Military Posts, 1806-1916, for Lewis A. Armistead, Fort Mojave, AZ, September 1859, NA.

555 McMillan, *Armistead and Hancock*, 93–94.

556 James B. Avirett, *The Memoirs of General Turner Ashby and His Compeers (1867)* (Kessinger Publishing, LLC, September 10, 2010), 51, 58–64, 69–70.

557 Almira Hancock, *Reminiscences of Winfield Scott Hancock* (Wentworth Press, August 27, 2016), 66.

558 Compiled Service Records for W. Keith Armistead, Lewis A. Armistead to Samuel Cooper, December 2, 1861, Letters Received by the Adjutant and Inspector General's Office, NA.

559 Hancock, *Reminiscences of Winfield Scott Hancock*, 69–70.

560 McMillan, *Armistead and Hancock*, 107, 109, 113.

561 Lewis A. Armistead to J.B. Floyd, July 25, 1860, U.S. Military Academy Cadet Records and Applications, 1805–1908, for W. Keith Armistead, https://www.fold3.com/image/505285124.

562 Compiled Service Records for W. Keith Armistead, Letters Received by the Adjutant and Inspector General's Office, from

R. E. Lee, April 2, 1862, NA. Lee mentioned in his recommendation letter that W. Keith had been "at school in the North."

563   Ibid., Lewis A. Armistead to Samuel Cooper, December 2, 1861, Letters Received by the Adjutant and Inspector General's Office, NA. It includes the following notation: "Application for the appointment of cadet for his son, W. Keith Armistead."

564   Ibid., W. Keith Armistead to R.E. Lee, March 31, 1862.

565   Ibid., Letter from Robert E. Lee, April 2, 1862. The letter was originally filed under "Rebel Archives, Records Division, War Department."

566   Ibid., "Register of Appointments, Confederate States Army." Keith was appointed as his father's aide-de-camp on April 30, 1863 and began his duties two weeks later—less than two months before the Battle of Gettysburg.

567   Compiled Service Records for Lewis A. Armistead, NA.

568   *The War of the Rebellion: Official Records of the Union and Confederate Armies* (hereafter known as *OR*), Series 1, Vol. 11, Part 2, 945

569   *OR*, Series 1, Vol. 11, Part 2, 673.

570   James A. Hessler and Wayne E. Motts, *Pickett's Charge at Gettysburg: A Guide to the Most Famous Attack in American History* (Savas Beatie, June 19, 2015), 216–217.

571   "Letter of Daniel G, Brinton," March 22, 1869, in John Bachelder, *The Bachelder Papers*, Vol. 1, 358–359; Hessler and Motts, *Pickett's Charge*, 293, note 98.

572   C. Hughes Armistead to J.W.C. O'Neal, October 3, 1863, GNMP, Armistead file, "Copy of correspondence of C.H. Armistead with J.W. C. O'Neal, referring to removing the remains of General Lewis Armistead, who was killed at Gettysburg." Hughes made it clear he was skeptical of the need to embalm the remains: "I would have greatly preferred his having done nothing to them, and his embalming process I think is a pretense."

573   C. Hughes Armistead to J.W.C. O'Neal, October 15, 1863, GNMP, Armistead file.

574   C. Hughes Armistead to J.W.C. O'Neal, October 27, 1863, GNMP, Armistead file.

575   Sheads, *Guardian of The Star-Spangled Banner*, 24-29; Frederick N. Rasmussen, "Armistead's journey to Baltimore," *Baltimore*

Sun, July 4, 2013; Motts, *Trust In God And Fear Nothing*, 48; Harrison and Busey, *Nothing But Glory*, 115; Krick, "Armistead and Garnett," *The Third Day at Gettysburg & Beyond*, 123. The Hughes family connection stems from George Armistead's marriage to Louisa Hughes in Baltimore in 1810. They named their only son after Louisa's brother, Christopher Hughes Jr., who helped negotiate the end of the War of 1812.

576   John Mitchell Vanderslice, *Gettysburg*, 232.

577   John W. Frazier to Charles T. Loehr, May 11, 1887, reprinted in John Tregaskis, *Souvenir of the Re-Union of the Blue and the Gray on the Battlefield of Gettysburg*, chapter 20, 5.

578   John W. Frazier to Charles T. Loehr, May 23, 1887, reprinted in Tregaskis, *Souvenir of the Re-Union of the Blue and the Gray*, chapter 20, 6.

579   Tregaskis, *Souvenir of the Re-Union of the Blue and the Gray*, chapter 20, 10.

580   John E. Reilly, *A Brief History of the 69th Regiment Pennsylvania Veteran Volunteers* (Franklin Classics, October 14, 2018), 60–61.

581   "Minute Book of the Gettysburg Battlefield Memorial Association, 1874-1895," Gettysburg National Military Park, Armistead file; Vanderslice, *Gettysburg*, 234; David G. Martin, *Confederate Monuments at Gettysburg: The Gettysburg Battle Monuments, Volume 1* (Longstreet House, January 1, 1986), 148–149.

582   McMillan, *Armistead and Hancock*, 195.

583   Address of Comrade Joseph McCarroll, reprinted in Tregaskis, *Reunion of the Blue and the Gray, Philadelphia brigade and Pickett's Division, July 2,3, 4, 1887 and September 15, 16, 17, 1906*, 14.

584   The sword is displayed today at the American Civil War Museum in Richmond—see Glenn David Brashear, "A Review of Richmond's New American Civil War Museum," https://networks.h-net.org, August 5, 2019.

585   George Armistead (grandson) to John W. Frazier, May 9, 1907, published in "Linked in Patriotism," *Baltimore Sun*, May 21, 1907.

586   In addition to the "Armistead Fell Here" monument at the Angle, there are two markers to Armistead at the George Spangler farm: an Armistead brigade tablet on Seminary Ridge, and

the "Friend to Friend Masonic Memorial" at the entrance to the Gettysburg National Cemetery annex, showing Armistead being assisted by Union Captain Henry Bingham, a fellow Mason.

587   Scene from the movie "Gettysburg," released 1993. The British officer was Arthur Fremantle, who wrote extensively about his experience observing the Confederate army but did not speak with Armistead before Pickett's Charge. It is one of many fictionalized episodes in the movie, which was based on a novel—but nonetheless informed viewers of the family connection between Lewis and his uncle at Fort McHenry (never mentioned George by name).

588   "The George Henry Preble Collection at the Navy Department Library," compiled by George W. Emery, https://www. history.navy.mil/research/library/research-guides/george-henry-preble-collection-finding-aid.html; "Abraham Lincoln: Message to the Senate Nominating George Henry Preble to be a Commander in the Navy," Feb. 12, 1863, https://www. presidency.ucsb.edu/documents/message-the-senate-nominating-george-henry-preble-be-commander-the-navy. Preble was briefly dismissed from duty in 1862 by Secretary of the Navy Gideon Welles. One of many things in his favor was the knowledge that his uncle, Commodore Edward Preble, was a Revolutionary War veteran and commanded the U.S. fleet at Tripoli in the First Barbary War.

589   George Henry Preble, *Our Flag: Origin and Progress of the Flag of the United States of America, With an Introductory Account of the Symbols, Standards, Banners and Flags of Ancient and Modern Nations* (Andesite Press, August 11, 2015), ii, 11.

590   Ibid. 181, 209–210, 221–223. The flag was enlarged to fifteen stars and stripes because of the addition of Vermont and Kentucky as states in the early 1790s.

591   Ibid., 496–497.

592   Georgiana Appleton to George Preble, February 18, 1873, Fort McHenry library, Armistead file.

593   Ibid.

594   George Preble to Georgiana Appleton, February 26, 1873, Massachusetts Historical Society, Appleton Papers, Box 10,

Folder 6a; "Our Oldest Naval Flag: Government Gets Possession of Colors from the Bon Homme Richard," *New York Times*, December 9, 1898, 3. This was the battle when John Paul Jones proclaimed, "I have not yet begun to fight."

595 George Preble to Georgiana Appleton, February 26, 1873, Massachusetts Historical Society, Appleton Papers, Box 10, Folder 6a.

596 Ibid.; "Bonhomme Richard-Serapis Encounter," https://www.encyclopedia.com/history/dictionaries-thesauruses-pictures-and-press-releases/bonhomme-richard-serapis-encounter; "The Bonhomme Richard Flag Hoax," http://www.seacoastnh.com/Maritime-History/John-Paul-Jones/The-Bonhomme-Richard-Flag-Hoax/. Jones and the Americans won the sea battle, but the Bon Homme Richard sank—and its flag went with it.

597 George Preble to Georgiana Appleton, March 13 1873, Massachusetts Historical Society, Box 10, Folder 6b.

598 Charles Norton to Georgiana Appleton, March 27, 1873, Massachusetts Historical Society, Box 10, Folder 6b.

599 George Preble to Georgiana Appleton, May 15, 1873, Massachusetts Historical Society, Box 10, Folder 6c.

600 Georgiana Appleton to George Preble, May 27, 1873, Fort McHenry library, Armistead file (from the George Henry Preble Papers at the American Antiquarian Society in Worcester, MA).

601 George Preble to Georgiana Appleton, June 12, 1873, Massachusetts Historical Society, Box 10, Folder 6d.

602 Ibid.

603 Georgiana Appleton to George Preble, June 17, 1873, Fort McHenry library, Armistead file.

604 George Preble to Georgiana Appleton, June 30, 1873, Massachusetts Historical Society, Box 10, Folder 6d.

605 George Preble to Georgiana Appleton, June 22, 1873, Massachusetts Historical Society, Box 10, Folder 6d.

606 George Henry Preble, *Three Historic Flags and Three September Victories: A Paper Read Before the New-England Historic, Genealogical Society, July 9, 1873* (Wentworth Press, August 29, 2016), 3, 21–22.

607 Preble, *History of the Flag of the United States of America*, 733.

608 "Our Country's Flag: History of the Glorious Star-Spangled Banner," *Los Angeles Times*, April 30, 1889. The *Times* carried

a reminiscence of the event that first appeared in the *New York World*, provided by Georgiana's daughter, Margaret Armistead Appleton Baker.

609 Proclamation for Capt. George Henry Preble, New England Historical Genealogical Society, July 9, 1983; Massachusetts Historical Society, Box 10, Folder 6d; George Preble to Georgiana Appleton, August 21, 1873; "Receipt, New England Historical Genealogical Society, for a fragment of the flag of Fort McHenry," August 28, 1873, Box 10, Folder 7; Taylor, Kendrick, and Brodie, *The Star-Spangled Banner*, 94.

610 Preble, *History of the Flag of the United States of America*, 732.

611 George Preble to Georgiana Appleton, August 21, 1873, Massachusetts Historical Society, Box 10, Folder 7.

612 Alice C. Etting to Georgiana Appleton, December 29, 1873, Massachusetts Historical Society, Box 10, Folder 7. Alice's full name was Alice Taney Campbell Etting.

613 Stephen Salisbury to Georgiana Appleton, January 1, 1874; James Lick to Georgiana Appleton, January 4, 1874; Alice C. Etting to Georgiana Appleton, January 18, 1874 (among others), Massachusetts Historical Society, Box 10, Folder 8a.

614 Georgiana Appleton to Alice C. Etting, January 18, 1874, Massachusetts Historical Society, Box 10, Folder 8a.

615 George Preble to William Stuart Appleton, April 20, 1874, Massachusetts Historical Society, Box 10, Folder 8a.

616 George Preble to Georgiana Appleton, October 6, 1875, Massachusetts Historical Society, Box 10, Folder 9c. Earlier he had written, "I regret to hear of Mrs. A's health."

617 George Preble to Georgiana Appleton, November 10, 1874 and December 12, 1873, Massachusetts Historical Society, Box 10, Folder 9d.

618 Susan Warfield to Georgiana Appleton, January 3, 1876, Massachusetts Historical Society, Box 10, Folder 10a.

619 Taylor, Kendrick, and Brodie, *The Star-Spangled Banner*, 97.

620 Georgiana Appleton to George Preble, September 9, 1876, Fort McHenry library, Armistead file.

621 Nathan Appleton to Georgiana Appleton, November 2, 1875; Taylor, Hendrick, and Brodie, *The Star-Spangled Banner*, 97.

622 Nathan Appleton, *The Star Spangled Banner, An Address Deliv-*

ered by Nathan Appleton, at the Old South Meeting House, Boston, Massachusetts, On June 14, 1877, 4, 30, 31, 33.

623 "The Stars and Stripes: Centennial Anniversary of the American Flag," *Boston Daily Advertiser*, June 15, 1877.

624 Taylor, *The Star-Spangled Banner*, 60.

625 Eben Appleton to George Preble, March 15, 1879, Fort McHenry library, Armistead file; Last will and testament for Georgiana L.A. Appleton, signed in April 1872, courtesy of Christopher and Karen Morton family files: "To my son, Ebenezer Appleton, the flag now in my possession known as the Star-Spangled Banner."

626 Eben Appleton to George Preble, March 15, 1879, Fort McHenry library, Armistead file. The Armistead monument was later moved to is present location on Federal Hill.

627 Taylor, Kendrick, and Brodie, *The Star-Spangled Banner*, 98–99; "The Star-Spangled Banner Baltimore Battle of 1889," draft by Scott Sheads, Fort McHenry Library, Armistead file, 4–5. (Although the title of Sheads's draft is about a later controversy, he recounted details of the 1880 event).

628 "The Old Flag," *Baltimore American*, reprinted in the *St. Louis Globe-Democrat*, October 16, 1880.

629 Ibid.

630 "A Historic Flag," *Baltimore Sun*, reprinted in the *Idaho Avalanche*, October 24, 1885.

631 Taylor, Kendrick, and Brodie, *The Star-Spangled Banner*, 98–99; Sheads, *Guardian of the Star-Spangled Banner*, 39.

632 Sheads notes, Fort McHenry Library, Armistead file, 40–41. The flag fragments were presented to the Maryland Historical Society upon Carter's death and now are preserved at the Smithsonian.

633 Taylor, Hendrick, and Brodie, *The Star-Spangled Banner*, 101.

634 Sheads, "The Star-Spangled Banner, Baltimore, Battle of 1889," 1, 5, Fort McHenry library, Armistead file.

635 "Now Bring on the Flag: A Letter to Mr. Appleton from the War Department," *Baltimore American*, August 29, 1889, 5.

636 Ibid., Robert MacFeely to Eben Appleton, August 28, 1889.

637 Ibid.

638 "Mr. Appleton's Lame Excuse," *Baltimore American*, August 29, 1889, 6.

639 "Up With the Flags! It Worried Mr. Appleton. Mr. Stevens' Parting Shot Received—The Flag Still Three," *Baltimore American*, September 3, 1889, 5.

640 "He Won't Give Up The Flag," *Baltimore American*, August 30, 1889, quoted in Sheads, "The Star-Spangled Banner, Baltimore, Battle of 1889," 7, Fort McHenry library, Armistead file.

641 "Who Owns The Flag?" *New York Times*, August 28, 1889; "The Fort McHenry Flag: It's Condition Making Tender Handling Very Necessary," *New York Times*, August 29, 1889.

642 "Chicago Gets The Flag: The 'Star-Spangled Banner' of Key's Song Goes Not to a Sheep Show, but to Chicago in 1892," *Daily Inter Ocean*, Chicago, IL, September 2, 1889, 5, reprinted from the *Baltimore American*. If the headline seems confusing, it is because Eben said in the story that he would be willing to lend the flag to the upcoming world's fair in Chicago. Alas, that never happened, either.

643 "In Place of The Old Flag: Now the City Has a New One Made by Fair Hands—Let It Wave," *Baltimore American*, September 8, 1889, 5.

644 "Chicago Gets The Flag," *Daily Inter Ocean*, Chicago, IL, September 2, 1889, 5, reprinted from the *Baltimore American*.

645 Garber, *The Armistead Family*, 63; "A Guide to the Baylor Family Papers—Biographical Information," https://ead.lib.virginia.edu/vivaxtf/view?docId=uva-sc/viu00032.xml (all of the Baylor papers are housed at the University of Virginia); "The Naming of Baylor," https://www.baylor.edu/about/index.php?id=89305.

646 "A Guide to the Baylor Family Papers—Biographical Information," https://ead.lib.virginia.edu/vivaxtf/view?docId=uva-sc/viu00032.xml; "James Bowen Baylor" at www.findagrave.com.

647 Taylor, Kendrick, and Brodie, *The Star-Spangled Banner*, 5, 103–104.

648 James B. Baylor to Charles Walcott, May 29, 1907, Star-Spangled Banner Accession File 54876, Smithsonian Institution, National Museum of American History.

649 Charles Walcott to James B. Baylor, June 4, 1907, Accession File 54876.

650 Eben Appleton to James B. Baylor, May 24, 1907, Accession File 54876.

651 Eben Appleton to Charles Walcott, June 11, 1907; Charles Walcott to Eben Appleton, June 19, 1907; Eben Appleton to Charles Walcott, June 25, 1907, Accession File 54876.

652 Eben Appleton to Richard Rathbun, July 5, 1907, Accession File, 54876.

653 Richard Rathbun, "Registrar's File," July 6, 1907, Accession File 54876.

654 "Richard Rathbun Launched Wright Brothers' Research," Smithsonian Institution Archives, https://siarchives.si.edu/collections/siris_sic_3900/.

655 Richard Rathbun to Eben Appleton, July 11, 1907, Accession File 54876.

656 Ibid.; Eben Appleton to Richard Rathbun, Western Union Telegram, July 12, 1907 ("let newspapers have picture of flag as you suggest"); Eben Appleton to Richard Rathbun, July 12, 1907; Richard Rathbun to Eben Appleton, July 15, 1907, Accession File 54876.

657 Richard Rathbun to Eben Appleton, July 15, 1907, Accession File 54876.

658 Eben Appleton to Charles Walcott, December 12 1912, Accession File 54876.

659 Charles Walcott to Eben Appleton, December 14, 1912, Accession File 54876.

660 George Armistead (grandson) to Georgiana Appleton, September 6, 1872, Massachusetts Historical Society, Box 10, Folder 8c.

661 Eben Appleton to Charles Walcott, December 12, 1912, Accession File 54876.

662 Charles Walcott to Eben Appleton, December 14, 1912, Accession File 54876.

663 Richard Rathbun to George Stevens, February 7, 1913; George Stevens to Richard Rathbun, February 10, 1913, Accession File 54876.

664 Charles Walcott to Arthur B. Bibbins, December 29, 1913, Accession File, 54876.

665 Eben Appleton to Charles Walcott, January 5, 1814, Accession File 54876.

666 Arthur Bibbins to Charles Walcott, January 26, 1914, Accession File 54876; Taylor, Kendrick, and Brodie, *The Star-Spangled Banner*, 109.

667 Eben Appleton to Charles Walcott, January 10, 1914, Accession File 54876.

668 Eben Appleton to Charles Walcott, August 31, 1914, Accession File 54876.

669 Richard Rathbun to George Stevens, February 7, 1913, Accession File 58476.

670 Taylor, Kendrick, and Brodie, *The Star-Spangled Banner*, 109.

671 Theodore Belote report (letter to "Professor Holmes"), February 3, 1914, Accession File 58476.

672 Contract—United States of America and Amelia Fowler, for the repair of Star Spangled Banner, from the office of Samuel Davis, 73 Tremont St., Boston, MA; Samuel Davis to Richard Rathbun, March 30, 1914, and various other letters between January 26 and May 28, 1914, Accession File 58476.

673 Robert M. Poole, "Star-Spangled Banner Back on Display: After a decade's conservation, the flag that inspired the National Anthem returns to its place of honor on the National Mall," *Smithsonian Magazine*, November 2008, https://www.smithsonianmag.com/history/star-spangled-banner-back-on-display-83229098/; Cate Lineberry, "The Story Behind the Star Spangled Banner: How the flag that flew proudly over Fort McHenry inspired an anthem and made its way to the Smithsonian," March 1, 2007, https://www.smithsonianmag.com/history/the-story-behind-the-star-spangled-banner-149220970/; "The Star-Spangled Banner," pamphlet issued in 1980 by the Smithsonian's Museum of History and Technology, 11.

674 "The Star-Spangled Banner by Mrs. Amelia Fowler," April 7, 1916, from the Amelia Fowler Papers at the Massachusetts State Archives, Box 1, Folder 18 (a copy of which is included in the Smithsonian's Accession File 58476).

675 Letter to Arthur P. Sewell (flag house), February 6, 1940, Accession File 58476; photo in Smithsonian archives (where one can count eight visible stripes); Taylor, Kendrick, and Brodie, *The Star-Spangled Banner*, 74–75.

676 Taylor, Kendrick, and Brodie, *The Star-Spangled Banner*, 110–111, 114.

677 Oscar George Theodore Sonneck, *Report on "The Star-Spangled Banner," "Hail Columbia," "America," "Yankee Doodle,"* 28.

678 Ferris, *Star-Spangled Banner*, 2, 42–44; George J. Svejda, *History of the Star-Spangled Banner from 1814 to the Present*, 201–204.

679 Richard Grant White, *National Hymns: How They Are Written and How They Are Not Written; A Lyric and National Study for the Times* (Scholarly Publishing Office, University of Michigan Library, March 31, 2006), 17–22.

680 Ibid., 67–68, 95, 96, 102.

681 Ibid., 75, 114.

682 "The Opinion of John Philip Sousa Concerning 'The Star-Spangled Banner' as the National Anthem of the United States," found in Edward S. Delaplaine, *John Philip Sousa*, 79.

683 Vogel, *Through the Perilous Fight*, 420.

684 Ibid., 418.

685 Taylor, Kendrick, and Brodie, *The Star-Spangled Banner*, 52.

686 Ferris, *Star-Spangled Banner*, 136-137; https://www.findagrave.com/memorial/136192159/george-armistead-leakin; "Rev. Dr. Leakin Dead: Oldest Protestant Episcopal Clergryman in State Passes Away," *Baltimore Sun*, June 11, 1912. The obituary says Leakin was "named after Col. George Armistead, commander of Fort McHenry in 1814."

687 Ferris, *Star-Spangled Banner*, 64–65; "Col. George Armistead's Grand March," https://www.loc.gov/item/sm1882.15328.

688 General Order No. 347, "Adoption of the 'Star-Spangled Banner' by the Navy Department for Morning Colors," General Orders and Circulars, No. 4, Navy Department, July 26, 1889.

689 Taylor, Kendrick, and Brodie, *The Star-Spangled Banner*, 52–53.

690 "The National Hymn: Address by Miss Janet E. Hosmer Richards," *The American Monthly Magazine*, Vol. 7, published by the National Society of the D.A.R., June–December 1895, 540.

691 Ibid., 539–540.

692 Svejda, *History of the Star-Spangled Banner*, 223–224; Ferris, *Star-Spangled Banner*, 137.

693 Taylor, *The Star-Spangled Banner*, 33.

694 Sonneck, *The Star-Spangled Banner*, 8 (following his original report on four songs in 1909, Sonneck followed up with a focus on Key's song in 1914); Ferris, *Star-Spangled Banner*, 140–141.

695 Svejda, *History of the Star-Spangled Banner*, 322–323.

696 Ferris, *Star-Spangled Banner*, 143.

697 Taylor, Kendrick, and Brodie, *The Star-Spangled Banner*, 56; Vogel, *Through the Perilous Fight*, 419; Ferris, *Star-Spangled Banner*, 146–147.

698 Kitty Cheatham, *Words and Music of "The Star-Spangled Banner" Oppose the Spirit of Democracy Which the Declaration of Independence Embodies* (Palala Press, April 27, 2016), 3, 8, 14.

699 Text of Angela E. Stetson ad, re-printed in "News Letter of the Friends of Irish Freedom, National Bureau of Information," Vol. 3, No. 1, July 2, 1921.

700 "Star-Spangled Banner is Difficult for the Novice," *Detroit Free Press*, reprinted in the *Daily Ardmoreite*, Ardmore, OK, June 26, 1917, 9.

701 "National Songs," *Imperial Valley Press*, El Centro, CA, February 24, 1917, 6.

702 Lynn Sherr, *America the Beautiful: The Stirring True Story Behind Our Nation's Favorite Song* (PublicAffairs, October 1, 2001), 13, 20, 23, 29, 32.

703 Ibid., 15, 56; Melinda M. Ponder, *Katherine Lee Bates: From Sea to Shining Sea* (Windy City Publishers, July 14, 2017), 122, 135–136, 141.

704 Sherr, *America the Beautiful*, 37, 75.

705 Ponder, *Katherine Lee Bates*, 142.

706 Sherr, *America the Beautiful*, 56–57.

707 Ibid., 57, 75.

708 "The Listener," *Boston Evening Transcript*, November 19, 1904.

709 Sherr, *American the Beautiful*, 58–61. The composer of *Materna* was Samuel A. Ward. The clergyman who first made the pairing of the poem and music was Dr. Charles A. Barbour.

710 Ferris, *Star-Spangled Banner*, 155.

711 Ibid., 157.

712 Sherr, *America the Beautiful*, 93.

713 Svejda, *History of the Star-Spangled Banner*, 322–327.

714 J. Charles Linthicum to Mrs. Reuben Ross Holloway, March 30, 1918, cited in Svejda, *History of the Star-Spangled Banner*, 328.

715 Ferris, *Star-Spangled Banner*, 157.

716 Svejda, *History of the Star-Spangled Banner*, 328–338.

717 Ferris, *Star-Spangled Banner*, 146.

718 Ibid., 146, 157.

719 Svejda, *History of the Star-Spangled Banner*, 336.

720 Ferris, *Star-Spangled Banner*, 158.

721 U.S. Congress, *"Legislation to Make 'The Star-Spangled Banner' the National Anthem,"* Hearings before the Committee on the Judiciary, House of Representatives, Seventy-First Congress, Second Session on H.R. 14, title page, table of contents.

722 Ibid., "Statement of Hon. J. Charles Linthicum," "Statement of Mrs. N.L. Dashiell on Behalf of Mrs. Reuben Ross Holloway," 2–4; James Breig, "How Elsie Reilley Saved the Anthem," https://www.gettysburgflag.com/blog/elsie-reilley-saved-anthem-star-spangled-banner/.

723 Ibid., "Statement of Capt. Walter I. Joyce, Chairman, Americanization Committee, Veterans of Foreign Wars of the United States," 4–15.

724 Ibid., "Statement of Capt. Walter I. Joyce," 6.

725 Ibid., "Statement of Miss Kitty Cheatham, 118 Fifty-Seventh Street, New York City," 32–38.

726 Ferris, *Star-Spangled Banner*, 160; Svejda, *History of the Star-Spangled Banner*, 338–339.

727 U.S. Congress, *"An Act to make the Star-Spangled Banner the national anthem of the United States of America,"* Seventy-First Congress, Second Session, H.R. 14, in the Senate of the United States.

728 Theodore Beloite to Alexander Wetmore, March 7, 1931, Accession File 54876; "Alexander Wetmore, 1886–1978," https://siarchives.si.edu/history/alexander-wetmore. The letter was written four days after the bill was passed by Congress and signed by President Hoover.

729 William Sumner Appleton to Charles Walcott, March 23, 1925, Accession File 54876. Appleton quoted the request from a letter by Colonel James A. Morse of the 71st Regiment Armory in New York City.

730 Charles Walcott to James A. Morse, May 18, 1925, Accession File 54876.

731 John Marshall Butler to Leonard Carmichael, November 13, 1957; J. Glenn Beall to Leonard Carmichael, December 16, 1957; Helena Weiss to Remington Kellogg, December 18, 1957, Accession File 54876.

732 Eben Appleton to Charles Walcott, August 31, 1914, Accession File 54876.

733 Remington Kellogg to John Rodgers, December 20, 1957; Leonard Carmichael to J. Glenn Beall, January 2, 1958, Accession File 54876.

734 Martin Well, "John M. Butler, Senator from Md. in 1950s, Dies," *Washington Post*, March 17, 1978.

735 John Marshall Butler to Leonard Carmichael, February 24, 1958, Accession File 54876.

736 Leonard Carmichael to John Marshall Butler, February 27, 1958, Accession File 54876.

737 "Why the Star-Spangled Banner Should be Retained by the U.S. National Museum," Background document, May 1958, Accession File 54876

738 "Resolution Adopted by the Executive Committee of the Board of Regents in Reference to Senator Butler's Request for the Transfer of the Star-Spangled Banner to Fort McHenry," June 1958, Accession File 54876.

739 "In the Event of War," April 30, 2007, https://www.smithsonianmag.com/history/in-the-event-of-war-153775882/; "WWII: The Smithsonian on the Home Front," https://siarchives.si.edu/history/featured-topics/wartime/wwii-smithsonian-home-front.

740 Taylor, Kendrick, and Brodie, *The Star-Spangled Banner*, 112.

741 Ibid., 114–115.

742 "Report on the Star-Spangled Banner Conservation Project," Smithsonian Institution, January 26–November 6, 1981, 6, Accession File 54876.

743 Ibid., 115, 127–128; "Transforming the Museum: Part Two," National Museum of American History, http://americanhistory.si.edu/press/fact-sheets/transforming-museum-part-two.

744 "Making a Modern Museum: Part One," NMAH, https://americanhistory.si.edu; "Transforming the Museum: Part Two,"

NMAH, http://americanhistory.si.edu/press/fact-sheets/trans-forming-museum-part-two; Taylor, Kendrick, and Brodie, *The Star-Spangled Banner*, 127-129.

745 "Nixon Inaugural Ball, NMHT," January 20, 1969, https://siarchives.si.edu/collections/siris_sic_5629, photo collections, Star-Spangled Banner.

746 "Project to Preserve Star-Spangled Banner Begins at National Museum of American History," Smithsonian Institution News Release, June 14, 1982, Accession File 54876.

747 Peggy Thompson, "The Dust-Strangled Banner," *Washington Post*, June 18, 1982.

748 Carl Hartman, "O Say, Can That Banner Be Saved?" *Washington Post*, July 4, 1997.

749 "Quick Facts About The Star-Spangled Banner Flag," https://www.si.edu/spotlight/flag-day/banner-facts; Taylor, Kendrick, and Brodie, *The Star-Spangled Banner*, 136; "Report on the Star-Spangled Banner Conservation Project," January 26–November 6, 1981, 13, Accession File 54876.

750 Taylor, Kendrick, and Brodie, *The Star-Spangled Banner*, 136.

751 "Text of President Clinton's 1998 State Of The Union Address," *Washington Post*, January 27, 1998, courtesy of *Congressional Record*; "Save America's Treasures," www.nps.gov.

752 "Jacqueline Trescott, 13 Million Lauren Gift Will Fund Flag Project," *Washington Post*, July 13, 1998, D1; Trescott, "New Glory at the Smithsonian: Designer Lauded for Gift to Restore the Star-Spangled Banner," *Washington Post*, July 14, 1998, D1. The reports said that $10 million would go to restoration of the flag and $3 million toward "education and outreach projects."

753 Taylor, Kendrick, and Brodie, *The Star-Spangled Banner*, 139, 157–159 (Lauren wrote the foreword for their book); "Smithsonian Announces Preliminary Findings of Star-Spangled Banner Preservation," https://americanhistory.si.edu/press/releases/smithsonian-announces-preliminary-findings-star-spangled-banner-preservation.

754 "President William Jefferson Clinton's State Of The Union Address," January 19, 1999, clintonwhitehouse4.archives.gov.

755 "Smithsonian's Star-Spangled Banner to Undergo Three-Year Conservation," https://americanhistory.si.edu/press/releases/

smithsonians-star-spangled-banner-undergo-three-year-con-
servation, February 21, 1999. The conservation program ended
up taking seven years and was not completed until 2006.

756 Author interview with Marilyn Zoidis.

757 Lineberry, "The Story Behind the Star Spangled Banner:
How the flag that flew proudly over Fort McHenry inspired
an anthem and made its way to the Smithsonian," March 1,
2007, https://www.smithsonianmag.com/history/the-story-
behind-the-star-spangled-banner-149220970/; "Smithsonian's
Star-Spangled Banner to Undergo Three-Year Conservation," https://americanhistory.si.edu/press/releases/smithso-
nians-star-spangled-banner-undergo-three-year-conservation,
February 21, 1999. As chief conservator, Thomassen-Kraus was
interviewed multiple times by the Smithsonian's website and
magazine.

758 Georgiana Armistead Appleton to George Preble, June 17,
1873, Fort McHenry library, Armistead file.

759 Taylor, Kendrick, and Brodie, *The Star-Spangled Banner*, 140–
142.

760 Author interview with Marilyn Zoidis.

761 Emily Karcher Schmitt, "The keeping of the Star-Spangled
Banner: A story of emblematic resilience," Smithsonian Insider,
https://www.si.edu/stories/keeping-star-spangled-banner-sto-
ry-emblematic-resilience, July 4, 2017.

762 Taylor, Kendrick, and Brodie, *The Star-Spangled Banner*, 147–148.

763 "American History TV—American Artifacts: The Star-Spangled Banner," https://www.c-span.org/video/?319838-1/
star-spangled-banner," May 15, 2014. The C-Span video,
prepared for the two-hundred-year anniversary of the Battle of
Baltimore, featured an extensive joint interview with Thomassen-Krauss and Jones.

764 Schmitt, "The keeping of the Star-Spangled Banner: A story
of emblematic resilience," Smithsonian Insider, https://www.
si.edu/stories/keeping-star-spangled-banner-story-emblemat-
ic-resilience.

765 "Smithsonian Announces Preliminary Findings of Star-Spangled Banner Preservation," https://americanhistory.si.edu/
press/releases/smithsonian-announces-preliminary-find-

ings-star-spangled-banner-preservation. Archival records had recorded eleven patches to the flag. Researchers actually found twenty-seven areas that were patched.

766 Schmitt, "The keeping of the Star-Spangled Banner: A story of emblematic resilience," Smithsonian Insider, https://www.si.edu/stories/keeping-star-spangled-banner-story-emblematic-resilience.

767 "American History TV—American Artifacts: The Star-Spangled Banner," https://www.c-span.org/video/?319838-1/star-spangled-banner," May 15, 2014.

768 Taylor, Kendrick, and Brodie, *The Star-Spangled Banner*, 149–155; "Smithsonian Completes Star-Spangled Banner Conservation Treatment," https://americanhistory.si.edu/press/releases/smithsonian-completes-star-spangled-banner-conservation-treatment, April 11, 2006.

769 "American History TV—American Artifacts: The Star-Spangled Banner," https://www.c-span.org/video/?319838-1/star-spangled-banner," May 15, 2014.

770 Taylor, Kendrick, and Brodie, *The Star-Spangled Banner*, 155–159.

771 Ibid, 159–161.

772 Author tour of the Star-Spangled Banner display at the National Museum of American History.

773 "Sneak Peek at the Star-Spangled Banner Gallery," https://www.youtube.com/watch?v=ghQI9u2XsRo, November 5, 2008. Jeffrey Brodie hosts the six-minute video tour.

774 Author tour; Taylor, Kendrick, and Brodie, *The Star-Spangled Banner*, 164.

775 "Sneak Peek at the Star-Spangled Banner Gallery," https://www.youtube.com/watch?v=ghQI9u2XsRo, November 5, 2008.

776 Author tour; "Original Star-Spangled Banner Debuts in New State-of-the-Art Gallery at the Heart of the National Museum of American History," https://americanhistory.si.edu/press/releases/original-star-spangled-banner-debuts-new-state-art-gallery-heart-national-museum, November 16, 2008.

777 Taylor, Kendrick, and Brodie, *The Star-Spangled Banner*, 166.

778 Author tour—slide display.

779 Schmitt, "The keeping of the Star-Spangled Banner: A story of emblematic resilience," Smithsonian Insider, https://www.

si.edu/stories/keeping-star-spangled-banner-story-emblematic-resilience.

780 Zack Johnk, *New York Times*, "National Anthem Protests by Black Athletes Have a Long History," https://www.nytimes.com/2017/09/25/sports/national-anthem-protests-black-athletes.html, September 25, 2017; Craig Calcaterra, "Jackie Robinson: 'I cannot stand and sing the anthem; I cannot salute the flag,'" https://mlb.nbcsports.com/2016/08/29/jackie-robinson-i-cannot-stand-and-sing-the-anthem-i-cannot-salute-the-flag/, August 29, 2016, cited from Jackie Robinson, *I Never Had It Made-An Autobiography of Jackie Robinson*; Jesse Washington, "Still No Anthem, Still No Regrets for Mahmoud Abdul-Rauf," https://andscape.com/features/abdul-rauf-doesnt-regret-sitting-out-national-anthem/, September 1, 2016; "8 Memorable Protests By American Athletes," https://www.history.com/news/notable-protests-american-athletes.

781 Steve Wyche, "Colin Kaepernick explains why he sat during national anthem," https://www.nfl.com/news/colin-kaepernick-explains-why-he-sat-during-national-anthem-0ap3000000691077, August 27, 2016.

782 Ibid.

783 Jason Johnson, "Star-Spangled Bigotry: The Hidden Racist History of the National Anthem," https://www.theroot.com/star-spangled-bigotry-the-hidden-racist-history-of-the-1790855893, July 4, 2016.

784 Charles Curtis, "A Reminder of What Colin Kaepernick Actually Said, and a Timeline of His Actions," https://ftw.usatoday.com/2020/06/colin-kaepernick-anthem-protest-timeline-message, June 4, 2020.

785 "Gwen Berry Talks Decision to Turn Back on American Flag," https://www.youtube.com/watch?v=rfoQY6xSw0s, video taken from BNC Live on bnc.tv; "Olympian Gwen Berry Says 'It's Obvious' Parts of National Anthem are Racist," https://www.newsweek.com/olympian-gwen-berry-says-its-obvious-parts-national-anthem-are-about-slavery-1605583, June 30, 2021; "Gwen Berry responds to critics of her flag protest: 'I never said I hated the country,'" https://www.usatoday.com/story/sports/olympics/2021/06/30/gwen-berry-critics-protest-i-never-said-hated-country/7811325002/, June 30, 2021.

786 Alexander Cochrane to John Croker, September 17, 1814, *NW III*, 286. Cochrane reported that early on the morning of September 12, "the disembarkation of the Army" at North Point began, led by "the Second Battalion of Marines, the Marines of the squadron and the Colonial Black Marines. Rear Admiral Cockburn accompanied the General (Ross) to advise and arrange as might be necessary." The main British land attack on the approach to Baltimore took place that afternoon.

787 Jessie Capisi and A.J. Willingham, "Behind the lyrics of 'The Star-Spangled Banner,'" https://www.cnn.com/interactive/2018/07/us/national-anthem-annotated/.

788 Filby and Howard, *Star-Spangled Books*, 37.

789 Author visit to Fort McHenry.

790 Weiss, *The Merikens*, 8; "Battle of Baltimore," https://www.britannica.com/event/Battle-of-Baltimore-1814; "Fort McHenry," https://www.battlefields.org/learn/war-1812/battles/fort-mchenry. By contrast, the Americans suffered 28 killed, 250 wounded, and 50 captured. In the Fort McHenry naval battle, the U.S. suffered 4 killed and 24 wounded, while the British reported one casualty.

791 Original manuscript of the Star-Spangled Banner, https://www.mdhistory.org/resources/the-star-spangled-banner/.

792 Mark Clague, "'Star-Spangled Banner' critics miss the point," August 31, 2016, https://www.cnn.com/2016/08/31/opinions/star-spangled-banner-criticisms-opinion-clague.

793 Sheads, *The Rockets' Red Glare*, 60. For more on the contributions of free Blacks and slaves to the defense of Baltimore, see "Fortifying Baltimore" at the National Park Service's Fort McHenry website, https://www.nps.gov/fomc/learn/historyculture/fortifying-baltimore.htm. It notes that by 1810, free Blacks actually outnumbered slaves in Baltimore.

794 Christopher T. George, "Mirage of Freedom: African Americans in the War of 1812," *Maryland Historical Magazine*, Vol. 91, No. 4, Winter 1996, 444.

795 Gerard T. Altoff, *Amongst My Best Men: African-Americans and the War of 1812* (The Perry Group, May 1, 1996), 128.

796 Marc Ferris, "National anthem's third verse stirs passions, but the reading is erroneous," February 2, 2018, Minneapolis *Star-Tribune*.

797   Clague, "'Star-Spangled Banner' critics miss the point," August 31, 2016, https://www.cnn.com/2016/08/31/opinions/star-spangled-banner-criticisms-opinion-clague.

798   Jefferson Morley, *Snow-Storm in August: The Struggle for American Freedom and Washington's Race Riot of 1835* (Anchor, April 9, 2013), 41.

799   Leepson, *What So Proudly We Hailed*, xiii.

800   U.S. Census Records for Georgetown, Washington, District of Columbia, 1820 and 1830, and Washington, Washington, District of Columbia, for "Francis S. Key," https://www.ancestry.com/discoveryui-content/view/662930:7734?tid=&pid=&queryId=4aed2297624d245cb14f2319c9d34335&_phsrc=k-dc382&_phstart=successSource.

801   Adams County Historical Society, "Clem Johnson Manumission Paper," October 3, 1831; Leepson, *What So Proudly We Hailed*, 130–131. Key also was licensed to practice law in Pennsylvania. He may have taken Johnson to Pennsylvania for this transaction because it was a free state, as opposed to Maryland, but no explanation was given.

802   Leepson, *What So Proudly We Hailed*, xiii, 182, 192; Morley, *Snow-Storm in August*, 40; Vogel, *Through the Perilous Fight*, 407–408; "Flag of Liberia," https://www.britannica.com/topic/flag-of-Liberia.

803   Morley, *Snow-Storm in August*, 40; Leepson, *What So Proudly We Hailed*, 103–105.

804   Vogel, *Through the Perilous Fight*, 408–410; Morley, *Snow-Storm in August*, 68, 136–139.

805   "The trial of Reuben Crandall, M.D.," https://www.loc.gov/item/18013203/; Leepson, *What So Proudly We Hailed*, xii, 169–172.

806   Morley, *Snow-Storm in August*, 104, 109, 127–129, 203, 219–220; Leepson, *What So Proudly We Hailed*, xii, 172–178.

807   Leepson, *What So Proudly We Hailed*, xii, 12–13; Vogel, *Through the Perilous Fight*, 409.

808   Mary Carole McCauley, "'Star-Spangled Banner' writer had complex record on race," *The Baltimore Sun*, https://www.baltimoresun.com/entertainment/arts/bs-ae-key-legacy-20140726-story.html, July 26, 2014.

809   Christopher Wilson, "Where's the Debate on Francis Scott Key's Slave-Holding Legacy?" *Smithsonian Magazine*, https://www.smithsonianmag.com/smithsonian-institution/wheres-de-bate-francis-scott-keys-slave-holding-legacy-180959550/, July 1, 2016. Wilson's piece pre-dated Jason's piece in *The Intercept* by three days that summer and came about six weeks before Kaepernick's first protest.

810   Justin Wm. Moyer, "Memorial to 'racist' Francis Scott Key, who wrote 'The Star-Spangled Banner,' vandalized in Maryland," *Washington Post*, https://www.washingtonpost.com/news/local/wp/2017/09/13/memorial-to-racist-francis-scott-key-who-wrote-the-star-spangled-banner-vandalized-in-maryland/, September 13, 2017. The vandalism apparently happened early in the morning of the 204th anniversary of the Battle at Fort McHenry.

811   Ella Torres, "Protestors bring down statue of Francis Scott Key," https://abcnews.go.com/US/protesters-bring-statue-francis-key-scott/story?id=71359718, June 20, 2020; Olga R. Rodriguez and Jeffrey Collins, "Statues of Ulysses S. Grant, Francis Scott Key toppled by protestors," *Associated Press* (published in *Pittsburgh Post-Gazette*), https://www.post-gazette.com/news/nation/2020/06/20/Statues-of-Ulysses-S-Grant-Francis-Scott-Key-toppled-by-protesters/stories/202006200045, June 20, 2020.

812   "Change America's National Anthem from 'The Star-Spangled Banner' to 'America the Beautiful,'" https://www.change.org/p/the-congressional-black-caucus-change-america-s-national-anthem-from-the-star-spangled-banner-to-america-the-beautiful-a-civil-rights-issue; Jody Rosen, *Los Angeles Times*, "Commentary: It's time to cancel 'The Star-Spangled Banner.' Here's what should replace it," https://www.yahoo.com/lifestyle/time-cancel-star-spangled-banner-171247658.html, July 14, 2020. Rosen proposed that "Lean on Me" by Bill Withers should become the national anthem.

813   "Bill would make the 'black national anthem' called 'Lift Every Voice and Sing,' the official national hymn," https://govtrackinsider.com/bill-would-make-the-black-national-anthem-called-lift-every-voice-and-sing-the-official-768ade53c168, Feb. 2, 2021; H.R. 301, "To amend title, 36, United States Code, to establish the composition known as 'Lift Every Voice and Sing'

as the national hymn of the United States," https://www.congress.gov/bill/117th-congress/house-bill/301.

814 Deborah Barfield Berry, "To help heal racial wounds, Black national anthem would become America's hymn under proposal," *USA Today*, https://www.yahoo.com/now/heal-racial-wounds-black-national-035933509.html, January 11, 2021.

815 "Lift Every Voice and Sing," https://www.pbs.org/articles/lift-every-voice-and-sing.

816 H.R. 301, "To amend title, 36, United States Code, to establish the composition known as 'Lift Every Voice and Sing' as the national hymn of the United States," https://www.congress.gov/bill/117th-congress/house-bill/301. The bill was introduced on January 13, 2021 and referred to the House Committee on the Judiciary on the same day. The Judiciary Committee referred it to the subcommittee on the Constitution, Civil Rights, and Civil Liberties on March 5, but no further action was taken during the session.

817 Wilson, "Where's the Debate on Francis Scott Key's Slave-Holding Legacy?" *Smithsonian Magazine*, https://www.smithsonianmag.com/smithsonian-institution/wheres-debate-francis-scott-keys-slave-holding-legacy-180959550/, July 1, 2016.

818 According to one estimate, the big garrison flag would cost $7,300 in today's dollars (inflation calculator at www.officialdata.org).

819 "Where to see famous American flags," https://nationalflagfoundation.org/where-to-see-famous-american-flags/. "Old Glory" is also at the National Museum of American History; the Iwo Jima flags are at the National Museum of the Marine Corps; the Ground Zero flag is at the National 9/11 Museum & Memorial; and a replica of the 1969 moon flag is at the National Air and Space Museum.

820 Georgiana Armistead Appleton to George Preble, June 17, 1873, Fort McHenry Library, Armistead file.

821 Georgiana took over ownership by the terms of her mother's will (see Chapter Eight for details).

822 "Marquis de Lafayette," https://www.britannica.com/biography/Marquis-de-Lafayette; "Marquis de Lafayette," https://www.mountvernon.org/library/digitalhistory/digital-encyclopedia/article/marquis-de-lafayette/.

823 "Lafayette in Baltimore," *Baltimore American*, October 12, 1824.

824 Sheads. *Fort McHenry*, 1–4.

825 Ibid., 5; James H. Clifford, "Fort McHenry, Maryland," *On Point*, Vol. 20, No. 2, Fall 2014, 44.

826 Clifford, "Fort McHenry, Maryland," *On Point*, Vol. 20, No. 2, 45.

827 "History of Fort McHenry," https://www.nps.gov/fomc/learn/historyculture/history-of-fort-mchenry.htm.

828 Sheads, *Fort McHenry*, 75–78.

829 Ibid., 79–80; Captain Maurice A. Hockman, "Construction Quartermaster Completion Report," 1919, Fort McHenry Library.

830 "Orpheus Statue," https://www.nps.gov/places/orpheus-statue.htm; Interpretive markers at Fort McHenry.

831 "Orpheus with the Awkward Foot," https://explore.baltimore-heritage.org/items/show/570.

832 Sheads, *Fort McHenry*, 88–91; "History of Fort McHenry: 20th Century," https://www.nps.gov/fomc/learn/historyculture/history-of-fort-mchenry.htm.

833 Interpretive panels and markers at Fort McHenry.

834 Sheads, *Fort McHenry*, 93.

835 Interpretive panels at Fort McHenry.

INDEX

A

H

I

J

K

L

Lafayette, Marquis de,
115–116, 164, 168,
237–239, 289, 291
Lauren, Ralph, 209, 231
Lazaretto Point, 53, 70–71
Leakin, George Armistead, 190
Lee, Light-Horse Harry, 23, 51
Lee, Robert E., 23, 141,
149–150, 155, 296
Leepson, Marc, 225–
227, 260, 319
Library of Congress, 58, 178,
188, 192, 203–204
"Lift Every Voice and
Sing", 228–229
Lincoln, Abraham, 121, 129–
130, 132, 134, 138, 158,
179, 205, 225, 237, 291
Linthicum, J. Charles,
192, 198–201
Lord Bathurst, 52, 102
Lord Liverpool, 102
Lossing, Benson J., 126

M

Madison, Dolley, 16, 58
Madison, James, 14, 20,
42, 48–49, 43, 58, 65,
67, 95, 96, 100, 105,
107, 231, 233, 238
Monroe, James, 19, 95, 226, 238,
260–261, 276–281, 285

Morley, Jefferson, 225, 227
Munroe, Isaac, 72, 74,
76, 82, 260, 276
"My Country 'Tis of Thee",
188, 192, 194
MacFeely, Robert, 174
McFeely, George, 33
McHenry, James, 39, 240

N

Napier, Charles, 79–80
National Museum of
American History, 7,
13, 206–207, 209, 211,
213, 228, 232, 234
New England Historical
Genealogical Society, 163
New York Times, 160,
176, 193, 219
Newcomb, Henry, 80, 279
Newmarket Plantation, 23,
25, 28, 35, 112,
Nicholson, Joseph, 43, 70,
73, 75, 92, 94–97
Niles Weekly Register,
69, 73, 110, 249
North Point, 16, 67–71,
106, 116–117, 128,
132–133, 220
Norton, Charles B., 161

O

"Oh, Say Do You Hear?", 120

ACKNOWLEDGMENTS

All standards for research on the Armistead family and the Star-Spangled Banner are still being set by Scott S. Sheads, the legendary historian and long-time park ranger at Fort McHenry National Monument and Shrine. Fortunately for the rest of us who follow his lead, Scott is exceedingly gracious with his time and always willing to share his knowledge. He accompanied me to the Fort McHenry library on multiple occasions; promptly responded to emailed questions, often with original documents to provide clarity; served as a sounding board for ideas and theories, no matter how obscure; and twice took me to George Armistead's gravesite at a private cemetery in Baltimore (Scott, of course, has a key to the gate). He is eager to assist anyone interested in researching the story of the Star-Spangled Banner. Thank you, Scott, and I hope this book does you proud.

Jennifer Jones, chair and curator of the Smithsonian Institution's Armed Forces Division, and one of the guardians of the Star-Spangled Banner exhibition at the National Museum History, was extraordinarily helpful in providing access to archives, documents, and photos. Jennifer also served as the key liaison when members of the modern-day Armistead family offered to donate some of George Armistead's personal items to the Smithsonian. Marilyn Zoidis, one of the conservators who worked on the flag project, and Dr. Brent Glass, director of the NMAH during the historic restoration, were kind enough to share their insight and memories. I also had the pleasure of speaking with Lonn Taylor, primary author of the Smithsonian's own book on the flag, before his passing several years ago.

I consider myself very fortunate to have met several direct descendants of the hero of Fort McHenry—led by second-great grandson Harry Armistead and third-great grandson George Lewis Armistead, both of Philadelphia. Harry and his wife, Liz, opened their home to me for a memorable visit and even shared three of the lieutenant colonel's *original* U.S. Army commissions. Over the years I have maintained correspondence with both Harry and their son, George (and can tell you that it is a bit surreal, when researching a story such as this, to look at your phone and see the name "George Armistead"). Another direct descendant, Christopher Hughes Morton, and his wife, Karen, provided access to key photos and intriguing background regarding Georgiana Armistead Appleton and Eben Appleton, who donated the flag to the Smithsonian in 1907. Chris and Karen have done amazing and extensive research on Armistead/Appleton family ancestry.

The Massachusetts Historical Society (MHS) in Boston is a marvelous research site that contains the rich and detailed Appleton Family Papers, including many handwritten letters to and from Georgiana. MHS Library director Elaine Heavey and her staff were most helpful in arranging access, even during the height of the COVID-19 pandemic. The original connection was made because Elaine wrote a story about Georgiana and the flag for the society's website and blog.

The staff at Fort McHenry National Monument and Shrine, led by superintendent David Moore, was unfailingly accommodating (and the on-site library at the fort is a gem)! Thanks also to Tina Cappetta, who was superintendent at Fort McHenry when I began my work there in 2017.

I owe a debt of gratitude to the American Antiquarian Society in Worcester, Massachusetts, home of the George Preble Papers, and, in particular, to Brianne Barrett, the society's library and program assistant, for making available the original photo of the flag that Preble took in 1873.

A list of authors and historians whose work provided a research road map to the flag and battle would take up too many pages, but I especially want to tip my hat to (in alphabetical order) Mark Clague, Marc Ferris, Marc Leepson, the late Walter Lord, and Steve Vogel.

It has been a great pleasure to once again work on a book with editor Alex Novak of Knox Press. Alex and I collaborated for the first time on *Gettysburg Rebels* in 2017. Thanks also to the staff at Knox Press and Post Hill Press, including Heather King, Stephanie Gutmann, and Hannah Lamb.

My literary agent, Uwe Stender, of the Triada Literary Agency in Sewickley, Pennsylvania, skillfully guided me through the book proposal process with his usual blend of constructive advice and encouragement. *Our Flag Was Still There* is our fourth book together.

Dru Neil of the Neil Strategy Group in Gettysburg, Pennsylvania, provided valuable promotional and PR services, in addition to reviewing part of the manuscript. I often laugh that I met Dru when she was one of my interns with the Pittsburgh Penguins in the 1990s.

And none of this—none at all—could have happened without the love, support, and research assistance of my wife and dearest friend, Colleen. She accompanied me on numerous trips to discover new information about George Armistead and the Armistead family, including a previous book on George's nephew, Lewis Armistead, who led a brigade in Pickett's Charge at Gettysburg. More than one hundred folders jammed with Armistead family materials are stacked neatly (sometimes) in a closet of our home office. Indeed, there are times we have felt like "honorary" Armisteads.

Thanks to all.

ABOUT THE AUTHOR

A lifelong student of history, Tom McMillan has served on the board of trustees of Pittsburgh's Heinz History Center, the board of directors of the Friends of Flight 93 National Memorial, and the marketing committee of the Gettysburg Foundation. He has written three previous books, including *Flight 93: The Story, The Aftermath, and the Legacy of American Courage on 9/11*. McMillan recently retired after a forty-three-year career in sports communications, which included twenty-five years as VP/Communications for the NHL's Pittsburgh Penguins. He has a journalism degree from Point Park University and resides with his family in Pittsburgh.